DVOŘÁK

DVOŘÁK

John Clapham

W · W · NORTON & CO · INC
NEW YORK · LONDON

Contents

To the memory of Otakar Šourek,
the founder of Dvořák research

Introduction

Periodically it becomes essential to re-examine the commonly held and often deeply entrenched views of the life and work of leading figures in the artistic world. Many of these views will be found to be valid, whereas some others will not. The unreliability of the latter may be due to misconceptions, to unwarranted assumptions, to ignorance of the facts as far as they are known, and may often result from too great a reliance being placed on factual information as it is presented by non-specialists in the currently available literature. At present, among the books on Dvořák available in English, there is not one that provides a reasonably full and accurate account of his life, not excluding one that incorporates a small number of corrections that I supplied to the author when my knowledge of this composer remained minimal. Without easy access to reliable information, mistaken ideas are bound to be transferred from one book to another, thus giving the errors wider currency.

Anyone who attempts to make a serious study of Dvořák, owes an immense debt of gratitude to that dedicated, indefatigable and ever enthusiastic amateur, Otakar Šourek. Single-handed he made available for the most part in the Czech language a great wealth of basic information on this highly important composer of the latter part of the nineteenth century. The most recent editions of his monumental *Life and Work of Antonín Dvořák* appeared more than twenty years ago, and so include none of the most recent discoveries. Although he was extremely thorough in what he attempted, he was inclined to rely too much on the sources of information that lay most readily to hand, and in consequence overlooked some important foreign sources. He was also handicapped by ignorance of the English language, a factor which has particular significance, due to the very great success that Dvořák enjoyed in England and the United States. Consequently, although in many aspects Šourek's work has stood the test of time, it is clear that in a number of areas it must now be used with extreme caution. The more recent (1960) *Antonín Dvořák Thematic Catalogue, Bibliography and*

Survey of Life and Work by Jarmil Burghauser, published in three languages (Czech, German and English) and now unfortunately out of print, in many ways updates Šourek. By now, however, a few small cracks have appeared in it, caused mainly by a little legacy of mistakes stemming from Šourek. It is to be hoped that a second revised edition may be issued before long. It is hardly credible that an author should write a book on Dvořák or revise one already published without reference to this invaluable source, or even without being aware of its existence; and yet there are notorious cases of this in recent times.

The present volume is offered in the hope that it may help to fill a serious gap in the literature on Dvořák, and that it may prove to be not only a useful addition, but also perhaps an essential supplement to the writings of Šourek. It may be salutary that since Dvořák has already been viewed extensively by a fellow Czech from the city where the composer lived and worked, he should now be examined in some detail by a foreigner, in a more detached way, as he is seen outside his own land, with greater emphasis on how his music was received abroad.

The author gratefully acknowledges Jarmil Burghauser's invaluable assistance and cooperation which has enriched this volume in innumerable ways, and Dr Karel Mikysa's continuing interest and help of various kinds, including providing most of the photographs for this book. I also wish to express my thanks to the Ministry of Culture of the Czechoslovak Socialist Republic and to Professor Jiří Vysloužil, chairman of symposia at the Brno International Music Festival, and to the directors of Artia, for their generous help of various kinds; also to Dr Kamil Šlapák for his assistance, to Karen Mills for drawing the map of Czech villages, to Dr John Stephens for his valuable contribution on the composer's final illness, to Dr William Ober for the photograph of the Dvořáks' home in New York City, to Mr Jaroslav Kubec for the photograph of Dvořák's bust and Mr Pavel Fekete for the photograph of the statue at Karlovy Vary, and to Dr Lubomír Dorůžka for his innumerable services and unstinting help in many ways. I should also like to express my appreciation to the many librarians in a number of countries of Europe and in the United States, who cannot be named individually here, but who have so many times given me substantial assistance in my work.

JOHN CLAPHAM
Bristol, January 1979

1 Casting the Die

Over the years music has held an important place in the everyday life of the people of Bohemia, the most western of the Slavonic lands. Here the village schoolmaster was expected to teach singing and the violin to his pupils, and he probably played the organ for mass as well. Even quite small communities had their own bands for local wakes, fairs and other festive occasions. Consequently, if a Czech lad possessed a spark of musical talent it is reasonable to assume that he would have been given some encouragement and that to a limited extent his talent would have been fostered. But it was a chance of perhaps a million or more to one that a family which for generations had tilled the soil, and in this instance had turned in more recent times to inn-keeping and the butcher's trade, should have thrown up a musical genius destined to fame and honour throughout the western world. Nevertheless, despite his spectacular rise to eminence, Dvořák remained unspoiled, and to the end retained his peasant's love of simple pleasures.

The composer came of sturdy stock. His ancestors had large families and lived to a good age, and his grandfather, Jan Nepomuk Dvořák (1764–1842), is known to have been short, thick set and exceptionally strong. Since he was not the oldest child in the family, Jan Nepomuk left his birthplace Třeboradice and settled at Vodolka (later renamed Odolena Voda), where he rented an inn. After twenty-five years he moved to Nelahozeves (formerly Mühlhausen) and leased the butcher's shop from Prince Lobkowicz, whose sixteenth-century castle dominates this peaceful hamlet beside the river Vltava. František Dvořák (1814–94), the father of the composer, was Jan Nepomuk's tenth child.[1] When he

---

1 Two centuries ago there were numerous Dvořáks to be found between the rivers Vltava and Labe (Elbe) a little to the north of Prague, and in particular at Dolní Chabry, Klíčany, Roztoky, Vinoř and Vodolka. The name 'Dvořák' comes from the Czech word '*dvůr*' (meaning 'court' and 'yard'), hence the words '*dvorce*' (farmstead) and '*dvořan*' (courtier). The surname is therefore a Slavonic equivalent to the German 'Hoffmann'. J. M. Květ's *Mládí Antonína Dvořáka* (The Youth of A.D.) (Prague 1943) provides the fullest account available covering Dvořák's ancestry and his early years.

settled down to married life in 1840, František rented an inn at Nelahozeves and took over the lease of the butcher's shop.

In looking for artistic leanings in the composer's forebears, it is perhaps worth noting that his charming maternal grandmother, Anna
Dvořáková, née Bobková, was greatly admired for the embroidered
designs of her aprons and kerchiefs. All Jan Nepomuk's sons took an
interest in music. Jan Křtitel, who was considered to be a good violinist,
was eclipsed by his brother Josef, whose principal instruments were the
violin and the trumpet, but he played several others besides. František's
attainments were rather more modest; he was a zither player and composed a few simple polkas for this instrument, but he was also a fiddler
of sorts, for he gave his son Antonín his first violin lessons. It is only
possible to guess at the musical standards of the three brothers, but it is
known that inaccurate playing was an anathema to Josef, who promptly
ejected culprits of this sort when in charge of his own inn at Vepřek.
Anna Dvořáková, née Zdeňková (1820–82), the composer's mother, is
not known to have been musical. She was the daughter of the steward at
Uhy, whose ancestors for a span of a century had been peasants and
cottagers at Hospozín, near Velvary. František and Anna were doubtless
delighted when Antonín, their first child, was born on 8 September
1841, and it cannot have been long before they began to look on him as
the potential successor in the family line of business.

In the following year, late on the night of 5 July, the inn was visited
by two young lords. When they departed in an extremely tipsy condition they neglected to extinguish the light in the stable, and in
consequence fire broke out an hour or more after midnight and the inn
was razed to the ground. František rescued his ten-month-old son,
placing the cradle on a pile outside, and then dashed back into the
blazing building to see what else he could save. The loss of so important
a source of income was a severe blow to him, but he managed to take
on a second butcher's shop near Zlonice, thanks to help from his
brother Josef with the business at Nelahozeves. No time was lost over
rebuilding the inn, which was apparently reopened early in 1843.[2]

Antonín, or Toník (Tony) as he became known, seems to have
displayed a natural aptitude for fiddle playing when he was only five.
For his part, František felt a glow of pride to see how much the customers at the inn enjoyed the polkas and other tunes they heard whenever

2 František's second son, František Serafín, was born at Nelahozeves no. 12 (the inn) on 3 February
1843.

his small son brought out his fiddle to entertain them.[3] Toník probably started his schooling as soon as he reached the age of six. Josef Spitz, the schoolmaster, who was also the church organist and was affectionately known as 'dušinka' (the dear soul), helped the young boy considerably with his music, and almost certainly gave him his first piano lessons. Toník was already beginning to make himself useful in the Nelahozeves band, and before long began going to Veltrusy to play in sung high mass, and to his uncle Josef's village, Vepřek, for the special musical events that took place there. He had a severe attack of nerves when he was about to play a solo for the first time in Nelahozeves church, and was unable to keep his bow steady. According to the account he gave of this episode to V. J. Novotný many years later, he mastered the situation by addressing these words to himself: 'Boy, stand firm! This is no time or place to be afraid!'[4]

We can be quite certain that young Toník must have been greatly interested in an enterprising development that was likely to have a profound effect on the peaceful existence of the inhabitants of Nelahozeves. A railway was being constructed running from Prague to Kralupy nad Vltavou and passing through Nelahozeves itself, with the track flanked by the castle, the little church and the rest of the hamlet on one side, and the river Vltava on the other. Work was begun in 1845, and five years later, just twenty-five years after the Stockton and Darlington railway was opened, a military train passed along the line. To see a train for the first time in his life was an unforgettable experience for the nine-year-old boy. The climax came when a special festive train carrying the Archduke Albrecht and his retinue proceeded by stages from Prague to Kralupy to mark the official opening of the railway. There is obviously a strong link between these events and the keen interest that Dvořák showed in locomotives right up to the end of his life.

When Toník's six years at the village school drew to a close, he became apprenticed to his father in the butcher's trade. These were not particularly happy times, especially if he was entrusted with a heifer bought by his father at a neighbouring village, and the animal took

3 František gave up the inn in September 1847, so that it is certain that Antonín must have played to the guests when he was only five. The family moved from the inn to the butcher's shop, Nelahozeves no. 24.

4 *Hudební revue*, iv (1911), p. 445. In an interview with *The Sunday Times* (10 May 1885) Dvořák discussed the dancing that followed mass on Sundays and which often went on far into the night. The dancing was free, but from time to time a pair of dancers would be stopped and made to pay what they could spare. The kreutzers that Toník received when the takings were divided amongst the players were always passed on immediately to his father.

fright and dragged him in the mire, or if he tried to force a stubborn calf
to cross a bridge over a broad stream and they both landed up in the
water. We are assured that on occasions such as these the young lad
felt it was impossible for him to become a butcher, and music, which
meant everything to him, was hovering over him like a guardian
angel.[5] František rejected out of hand any suggestion that his son might
become a musician, and was determined to see him follow the traditional line of family business.

At the end of a year's apprenticeship František thought it wise to send
his son away to the small town of Zlonice, where the chances of
becoming thoroughly familiar with all aspects of the trade were very
much better than at Nelahozeves. In addition there would be an
opportunity for Toník to learn German, which would undoubtedly be
an asset when he became master of his trade. All was arranged, and so
the thirteen-year-old boy set off for the home of his uncle Antonín
Zdeněk, his mother's bachelor brother who was steward to Count
Kinský.[6] Toník was extremely happy at Zlonice. He was treated like a
son by his uncle, and took no time to discover that Zlonice had much
to offer him in music. He regarded his apprenticeship as an unfortunate
necessity and devoted all the time he could spare to music. He came
under the influence of Josef Toman, who was headmaster of the
secondary school, choirmaster of the church, and besides having a
good baritone voice played the violin, organ, trumpet and double bass.
Toník, however, was helped very much more by Antonín Liehmann,
the school's German master, who, although not professionally trained,
was an extremely keen amateur musician whose talents were primarily
of a practical kind. He was the organist of the church, he played the
violin, clarinet and French horn, had quite a good orchestra of his own
and composed sacred music[7] and numerous dances. Thanks to him
Toník was able to have lessons on the violin, viola, piano and organ
and in keyboard harmony, and after a time he was given the experience
of playing the organ at church services. Liehmann also taught him German, a subject that did not interest Toník greatly. When Count
Kinský needed a programme of music at Zlonice castle, a mixture

5 V. J. Novotný: 'S Dvořákem v Anglii', *Hudební revue*, iv (1911), p. 445. J. Lambl, in *Podřipský
kraj*, i (1934), no. 1, p. 25 and no. 2, p. 63; Květ, op. cit., p. 41.

6 There is no reliable evidence to support the assertion of B. Kalenský in *Antonín Dvořák Sborník*
(1911) that Dvořák departed for Zlonice in 1853, an error which has been given wide currency.

7 The violin solo played by Dvořák in Nelahozeves church, which has already been referred to,
occurred in a choral offertory by Liehmann. Dvořák knew Liehmann's brother Václav, a fine
tenor, for whom he had played when he visited Vepřek.

perhaps of chamber music and music for a small band, he invariably expected Liehmann to provide this. Consequently Toník, now one of Liehmann's players, was an active participant on these occasions. There may also have been some similar visits to Princess Wilhelmina's seat at Budenice.

In later life Dvořák had warm words of praise for Liehmann, from whom he learnt so much; yet this fiery-tempered man was not a good teacher. As one who experienced no difficulty in playing fluently from a figured bass, he assumed his pupils ought to be able to do much the same, and so, whenever the figures came in clusters, they found themselves being pummelled every time they made a mistake.[8] Years later, in his opera *The Jacobin*, Dvořák modelled the character Benda on his idealized impressions of the Zlonice schoolmaster.[9]

After weighing up the advantages of moving to a bigger place, František Dvořák negotiated in 1855 to rent a butcher's business and simultaneously take on The Big Inn at Zlonice. Fortunately, he was released from his Nelahozeves contract, which still had one year to run. He was undoubtedly well aware, too, that Toník was not putting his heart into his apprenticeship, and probably thought his son would benefit from closer parental supervision. In consequence, Toník's second year at Zlonice was entirely different from his first. His father made excessive demands on him and monopolized so much of his time that his musical activities had to be severely curtailed. No wonder the unfortunate boy's mother sometimes heard loud shrieks coming from the shop.[10]

Toník may have first tried his hand at composition sometime towards the end of his first year at Zlonice, but in any case the outcome was the *Forget-me-not Polka*, for which Liehmann wrote an introduction and the trio. Another polka, for strings, two clarinets, two horns, a cornet and a trombone, was quite possibly written shortly afterwards. Years later Dvořák related how he had proudly taken this with him when he visited Nelahozeves, but because he was not sure about the correct way to write for transposing instruments and had got the cornet in the wrong key, the piece failed to make the impression he had hoped for.[11]

---

8 J. Michl: 'Z Dvořákova vyprávění', *Hudební revue*, vii (1914), p. 401. In the interview with *The Sunday Times* (10 May 1885) he says: 'Liehmann was an excellent musician, but he left his pupils to find out a great deal for themselves.'

9 Liehmann's daughter, and in the opera Benda's daughter, both bear the same name: Terinka.

10 Květ, op. cit., p. 62.

11 *The Sunday Times*, loc. cit.

Towards the end of 1856 his two-year term of apprenticeship at Zlonice expired. On 2 November that year 'Antonius Dvořák of Nelahozeves' was awarded his journeyman's certificate—or so we are told. It is true that no good reason has been offered to explain why anyone might wish to fake such a document, yet it would be prudent to regard this one with grave suspicion. Jan Roubal, the principal signatory, is described in the text as Dvořák's 'Master', yet his name is unknown in the Zlonice records of that period. Similarly his co-signatory Jan Warský cannot be traced. In the 1850s the Zlonice journeymen's certificates were either in German or alternatively in both German and Czech, but this one is in the Czech language and not bilingual. The style of the printing appears to correspond with that of a slightly later period. Finally, in the town records of those who qualified as journeymen there is no mention of Dvořák's name.[12] This weight of evidence strongly suggests that Toník never completed his apprenticeship. According to the composer himself, it was Liehmann, with backing from Antonín Zdeněk, who succeeded in overcoming František Dvořák's stubborn determination that his son should follow the traditional family line of business, and persuaded him that, despite the risk and the uncertainties ahead, the only right course for so talented a youth was to train to become a musician. The matter was probably decided during the summer of 1856, and in any case before the time the apprenticeship would have ended, had it run its full course.

There was no need for the fifteen-year-old youth to start his professional training immediately; but since he had such a meagre grasp of German, the language used officially at the Prague Organ School, it was essential for him to remedy this weakness without delay. His father therefore arranged for him to go for a year to the secondary school at Česká Kamenice(Böhmhisch-Kamnitz),in the mountainous border region in the north of Bohemia where German was spoken. Toník stayed with Josef Ohm, a miller, in exchange for Ohm's son, who went to Zlonice. He got on extremely well with his schoolmates, taking a full part in their games and their long rambles to places of scenic beauty and historic interest. According to his constant companion, Franz Böhm, 'Friend Dvořák was lively, witty, decent and lovable. He was popular and was

12 Květ was a little uneasy when he failed to find any trace of Roubal and Warský at Zlonice, but he was inclined to regard the certificate as genuine. I am indebted to Jarmil Burghauser for providing me with the additional reasons for considering the document suspect. The certificate, which cannot now be found, appears in facsimile in Šourek: *Život a dílo Antonína Dvořáka*, i, 3rd edn; *Hořejš: Antonín Dvořák: the composer's life and work in pictures;* and Herzog: *Antonín Dvořák v obrazech.*

invited everywhere.'[13] He was placed in the school's third class. His German improved rapidly and with his above-average intelligence he was soon able to benefit fully from the teaching, and at the end of three terms he emerged with a 'Merit' classification.[14] He made further strides with his music thanks to Franz Hancke, who, unlike Liehmann, had had the advantage of studying for a short time at the Prague Organ School. But in after years it was always the enthusiastic amateur of Zlonice whom Dvořák recalled with unqualified gratitude and affection.

Ever since his move to Zlonice, František Dvořák had experienced difficulties of one kind or another. He did about as much trade in the shop as František Pachmann, the rival butcher, but with seven children to support he found the rent of 300 zloty burdensome. Business at the inn seems to have been reasonably satisfactory, and just as many dances were held there as at František Gruber's tavern nearby, but he found himself on bad terms with his landlord, František Novotný, due, it is thought, to the latter's envy. On top of all this he was having occasional trouble with the police.[15] He was obviously not in a position to finance Toník while he was a music student. Seeing that the future of his young protégé lay in jeopardy, Liehmann prevailed upon the youth's uncle Zdeněk, who had no dependants, to provide the necessary basic support.

Towards the end of September 1857 František Dvořák and his son set out on foot on the twenty-six-mile journey to Prague, trundling a small hand cart piled with Toník's belongings, including his fiddle. During his first year in the Bohemian capital he lodged with his cousin Marie Plívová and her tailor husband, Jan Plíva, and afterwards he moved to the home of another of his father's Prague relations, Toník's aunt Josefa, the wife of Václav Dušek, a railway employee. Apparently the possibility that the young musician should enter the Conservatory,

---

13 B. Kalenský: 'Antonín Dvořák, jeho mládí, příhody a vývoj k usamostatnění, *Antonín Dvořák sborník statí* . . . (Prague 1912), p. 20. The word *'slušný'* means 'proper, respectable, fair, reasonable and decent'.

14 His leaving certificate states that he was *sehr gut* in all subjects, i.e. religious instruction, reading, writing, arithmetic and essay writing. The certificate is dated 31 July 1857, and thus refutes Kalenský's belief that Dvořák was at Kamenice two years earlier. A facsimile appears in Květ, op cit.

15 According to František Fryč, a priest who lived nearby, Novotný, in his endeavour to get the inn back into his own hands, 'repeatedly led away Dvořák's customers to another inn, and on Sunday took them to a neighbouring village'. Perhaps this did happen occasionally, but an easier way to turn Dvořák out would have been to refuse to renew the lease. Nevertheless the lease is believed to have been renewed in 1857. Kalenský, op cit., p. 22, and Květ, op. cit., p. 70. In 1855 František Dvořák failed to keep his record of foreign visitors properly, his meat and scales were not clean, and he was caught selling drink after hours. In 1857 he was accused of allowing a harpist to play and beer to be drunk until 12.30 am, Květ, pp. 64–5 and p. 70.

which catered for orchestral players and singers and to a lesser extent for pianists, had been speedily rejected in favour of the Institute for the Cultivation of Church Music's organ school. This establishment was highly regarded for its sound teaching of composition and the organ along strictly traditional lines, and was able to count among its most successful pupils Josef Krejčí, František Skuherský, Karel Bendl and Karel Šebor, and after Dvořák's time Josef Bohuslav Foerster and Leoš Janáček,[16] musicians who by no means had an overriding bias towards sacred music.

When he was enrolled at the school, Toník knew very little music by any of the great masters, and it is almost inconceivable that he could have heard a performance given by a first-class musician. The principal of the organ school was seventy-one-year-old Karel F. Pitsch, a great admirer of Bach, Handel and Beethoven, who taught organ playing and counterpoint and was reputed to be a fine organist. His assistant professors were František Blažek, teacher of harmony and the author of some theoretical text books, Josef L. Zvonař, who specialized in liturgical music and was a distinguished author and editor of the period, and Josef Foerster, the father of the leading composer Josef Bohuslav Foerster, who shared the organ teaching with Pitsch and later became the organist of St Vitus Cathedral.

Toník felt ill at ease in his new surroundings. He was ragged by his fellow students when they discovered he was composing a kyrie,[17] and he resented the fact that those who were more proficient than he was in the German language were the ones who were invariably commended for their work. Such partial treatment obviously stemmed from the director himself. Due to his inhibitions about speaking German, the only official language at the organ school, Toník was often tongue-tied in class. In order to remedy his shortcomings he attended a continuation school during the first year of his studies, at the end of which the school assessed his German as *sehr gut*. The ageing Pitsch died in the summer of 1858, and so for his second year at the organ school his director was Josef Krejčí. Although Krejčí's background, unlike that of his predecessor, was Czech and not German, he was Draconian in his insistence on German being spoken. His tastes, although basically

16 Krejčí rose to be principal of the organ school, and later director of the Conservatory. Skuherský composed a considerable amount of church music, some operas and other works, and he succeeded Krejčí at the organ school. Bendl was a distinguished conductor and a composer of operas. Šebor wrote five operas, some symphonies and choral works. Foerster was a highly esteemed composer of choral music and wrote several operas, the most successful of which is *Eva*.

17 According to J. Michl's 'Z Dvořákova vyprávění', in *Hudební revue*, vii (1914), the students jeered: 'Would you believe it! Did you know that Dvořák too composes?'

classical, extended as far as the works of Liszt. In consequence, a breath of fresh air started to penetrate the institution and disturb the dust and cobwebs that had been accumulating for so long.

Toník struck up a warm friendship with Karel Bendl, who was completing his third year of study, and this proved to be extremely beneficial for the young student who lacked a piano in his lodgings and had no money to spare to buy scores. Bendl possessed a large selection of scores of standard works, which he allowed Toník to borrow, and he also allowed him to use his piano regularly.

There is no reason to doubt that Toník's musical horizons expanded immeasurably from the time he arrived in Prague. By joining Antonín Apt's St Cecilia Society Orchestra as a viola player, probably as early as November 1857, he had a chance of playing several contemporary works, and made direct contact for the first time with the work of a composer whom Apt greatly admired, but who was frowned upon at the organ school—Richard Wagner. During that season the society performed his *Das Liebesmahl der Apostel* and the finale of the third act of *Rienzi*. The young student was influenced by Apt's enthusiasm, and the beginning of his unbounded admiration for Wagner's music dates from that time. Since it soon became known that he was a very competent viola player, it is extremely probable that he was called upon regularly as an extra whenever the orchestra of the Estates Theatre was augmented, as it invariably was whenever *Tannhäuser* and *Lohengrin* were being performed, and also for some of the Meyerbeer operas. Toník was extremely poor, and had no money to spare for opera tickets, so it was impossible for him to get to know the basic works in the repertory. He may have been able to see a performance of *Der Freischütz*, although this is not certain because in one account that he gave he said he saw the opera from the gallery, and in another version he declared that he waited outside the theatre while a friend went to try to raise ten kreutzers for a ticket and failed to return.[18]

When an ad hoc orchestra was needed, for a Jednota hudební umělců (Union of Musical Artists) concert or a Žofín Academy programme, it is highly probable that he may have been asked to play, but there is no record of him having taken part in any particular concert. It is known that he could sometimes attend a rehearsal of the Prague Conservatory orchestra, which required no stiffening with outside players. This gave him the chance of hearing Beethoven's Choral

18 Interviews with *Pall Mall Gazette* (13 October 1886) and *The Sunday Times* (10 May 1885).

Symphony on 9 July 1858, conducted by Spohr during the Conservatory's golden jubilee celebrations. It made such a profound impression on the young student that he described it several years later as 'the first real orchestral performance I ever heard'.[19] He contrived to hear some good concerts by slipping into the orchestra and concealing himself behind the drums.[20]

During his second year as a student Tomík might have been at the Conservatory when the distinguished Czech virtuoso, Alexander Dreyschock, rehearsed Beethoven's *Emperor* concerto. No doubt he would have been even keener to hear Hans von Bülow's concert on 12 March 1859 when the programme included the Prelude to *Tristan and Isolde*, *Mazeppa* by Liszt, and the latter's transcription of Schubert's *Wanderer Fantasia*. Perhaps this was one of the 'good concerts' he managed to attend without buying a ticket. Early in that season the St Cecilia Society performed Schumann's *Der Rose Pilgerfahrt* and his Overture, Scherzo and Finale, and in April they combined with Jednota hudební umělců to perform Handel's *Samson*, with František Škroup conducting. This was probably the season when Adolf Čech joined the St Cecilia orchestra, and shared a desk with the young man, whose music he was so frequently to perform for the first time in later years. Čech remembered Tomík as having 'a dishevelled head like that of a genius, covered with an abundant thatch of black hair'. While Tomík played he was continually criticizing the playing of Čech and other members of the orchestra, and even his own. He found fault with Apt's conducting, and sometimes he stopped playing altogether and began humming some sort of a tune. Čech found all this very disconcerting.[21]

Tomík and the other thirteen students who qualified to take the advanced second-year course at the organ school were expected to become proficient in the disciplines traditionally associated with church organists, that is, organ playing, improvisation and various compositional techniques, including canon and fugue. Since so few were admitted to the course, it may be presumed that standards were reasonably good. However, it was hardly ideal for anyone aspiring to compose symphonies, chamber music and operas. At the practical examination in June he played a Prelude and Fugue in A minor by

19 *The Sunday Times*, loc. cit.

20 Idem. Květ, in *Mládí Antonína Dvořáka*, failed to appreciate how few of the numerous concerts and operas in Prague Dvořák would have been able to attend. I am grateful to Jarmil Burghauser for much valuable information on this subject.

21 Čech: *Z mých divadelních pamětí* (1903), p. 89.

J. S. Bach[22] and his own Praeludium in D major and Fugue in G major. In addition he and Sigmund Glanz, the other contender for the main graduation prize, played Schallenberg's four-hand arrangement of Bach's great G minor Fugue. He and Glanz were commended equally for all their work but, ironically, it was Glanz, who vanished into obscurity after leaving the School, who was awarded the prize. The final decision hinged on the examiners' general impression of the two candidates. Glanz, the son of a northern Bohemian band-master, was said to possess 'outstanding talent and a maturity of mind leading to excellent application', a remark that seems to imply that he was particularly good at playing from a figured bass. Dvořák, on the other hand, was described as 'excellent, but inclined to show a more practical talent. Practical knowledge and accomplishment appear to be his aim; in Theory he achieves less.' Curiously enough, what he learned about musical theory (the basic technique of composition) at the organ school must have played an initial and very essential part towards equipping him to become one of the most outstanding and individual composers of his generation.

22 We may presume that this was BWV 551 rather than BWV 543 ('The Great'), for Dvořák was never regarded as an outstanding organist.

2 The Long Road to Success

Of one thing Dvořák was absolutely clear when he finished his studies at the organ school: it was imperative that he should remain in Prague, the musical heart of Bohemia. He was not primarily interested in securing an organ post in the city because he was confident he could make a modest living as an orchestral player, a life that appealed to him strongly and one which would allow him to supplement his earnings, either as an organist or by teaching. Just at that time the band-leader and composer Karel Komzák, a man who trained his small team efficiently and had an eye for promising instrumentalists, was in need of a viola player. Dvořák very willingly accepted the vacancy, and for several years remained a regular member of the band. They played at various Prague restaurants, were in great demand for balls, and were engaged periodically for the classical concerts at the Žofín Hall. Dvořák failed to secure the organ post at St Henry's church, but from time to time was able to keep his hand in by deputizing for Komzák at the organ of the lunatic asylum.

Apparently Dvořák composed a few dances at this time, including a Polka and Galop for Komzák's band, which are now lost. However, it is not possible to be certain about the authenticity of the slightly earlier Polka in E major, dated 27 February 1860. Its peculiar inscription in a mixture of German and ungrammatical Czech has no parallel in the composer's autographs, and he is not known to have used the German form 'Anton' of his first name after finishing his studies.[1] Ephemeral *dances d'occasion* such as these pieces give no hint that the composer was on the point of launching out into what still remained for him an uncharted region, one that demanded sustained thought and concentration; yet it was inevitable that he would feel

---

1 The inscription reads: 'Polka Pianoforte von Anton Dvořák, v Zlonicích dne 27 února 1860 o jarmark' (. . . at Zlonice on 27 February during the fair). In the 1860s Dvořák signed his MSS 'Antonín Leop. Dvořák' or alternatively 'Antonín Dvořák'. It is not certain that the Polka is written in Dvořák's handwriting, and if he composed it it might be a copy. I am indebted to Jarmil Burghauser for drawing my attention to these inconsistencies.

the urge to compose chamber music, and soon rather than later. By doing so he provided tangible evidence of the high regard he had for the Viennese classical masters and displayed a viola player's delight in the sonorities that are only possible with a small ensemble of strings. He completed his three-movement String Quintet in A minor, op. 1, on 6 June 1861, and in March of the following year he wrote the String Quartet in A major, op. 2, preferring this time to adhere to the traditional four-movement plan. Rather significantly he called this 'Quartet number one', implying that others would probably follow. The Quartet is dedicated to Josef Krejčí, director of the Conservatory, 'with the deepest respect'. The première of the Quintet did not take place until 1921, but the Quartet fared rather better. Dvořák retained an affection for this early work and took the trouble to revise it in 1887. It was then played on 6 January 1888 by Ondříček, Pelikán, Mareš and Alois Neruda.

When Dvořák began to earn a meagre living as a musician, the atmosphere in Bohemia was brighter than it had been at any time since the flower of Czech chivalry was crushed by the Hapsburgs at the beginning of the Thirty Years' War. The tide turned in 1859, when following Franz Joseph's defeat at Magenta and his failure to retrieve the position at Solferino, the emperor was no longer able to continue resisting with his former intransigence the demands of his Hungarian, Czech and Croatian subjects for a greater measure of liberty. Making the most of a rare opportunity, the conservative *staročeši* (Old Czech Party) assisted by the radical *mladočeši* (Young Czech Party) decided that a Provisional Theatre must be established for the performance of plays and operas in the Czech language and in Czech translations. Smetana, to his intense disappointment, failed to secure the conductorship, which went instead to Jan Nepomuk Maýr, an operatic tenor who was director of a school for singing. Komzák's band formed the nucleus of the orchestra, which at full strength consisted of thirty-four players, but for a while Dvořák was the only viola player. There was tremendous rejoicing accompanied by a strong glow of national pride when the theatre was first opened on 18 November 1862 with performances of Vojáček's *Festival Overture* and Vítězslav Hálek's drama *King Vakušín*. At this time very few Czech operas existed, and it was clear that none of these was sufficiently worthy of selection for the important operatic inauguration on 20 November. In consequence Cherubini's *The Water Carrier* was given on that occasion.

In contrast with the time when, as an impecunious student, it was out of the question for Dvořák to go to the opera whenever he felt

inclined to, he at last had a splendid chance of becoming familiar with
the whole of the current repertory. At first Maýr placed particular
emphasis on Italian operas, but during his third and fourth seasons there
were rather more performances of operas by German and Austrian
composers—but no Wagner; his romantic operas could be seen at the
German Theatre. French operas held a steady third place, but towards
the end of Maýr's directorship, when Smetana's *Brandenburgers in
Bohemia* and *The Bartered Bride* were first staged (1866), operas by
native composers were rapidly catching up.[2] Dvořák must undoubtedly have played for every work that was mounted during this period.

Apart from his theatre duties and Komzák band engagements,[3]
Dvořák participated in a few other musical events. It is probable that
he played in the first performances of the symphonic poems *Richard III*
and *Wallenstein's Camp* at Smetana's disastrous concert on 5 January
1862, when an untimely blizzard kept most of the audience away; and
it is virtually certain that he took part in the première of Smetana's
third symphonic poem from his Swedish period, *Haakon Jarl*, on 24
February 1864, the work which Jan Neruda, the poet and journalist,
facetiously referred to as the composer's 'cobbler's music'.[4] He most
certainly played in Berlioz's *Romeo and Juliet*, which Smetana conducted at the Umělecká beseda concert on 23 April that year, during the
Shakespeare Centenary celebrations. But undoubtedly the most
significant event of all took place a year earlier, on 8 February 1863.
On that occasion Richard Wagner appeared in person to conduct an
entire programme of his own music, including several extracts from
some of his most recent works, hitherto unknown in the Bohemian
capital. The concert consisted of: *A Faust Overture;* Entry of the
Mastersingers, and Pogner's Address; Prelude to *The Mastersingers of
Nuremburg;* Prelude to *Tristan and Isolde;* Siegmund's Love Song (*Die
Walküre*); Overture to *Tannhäuser*. For the young Dvořák this was an
intoxicating experience.

2 During Maýr's term of office (1862–6) fifty-four different operas were performed. The composers represented and the number of their works mounted was as follows: *Italian:* Bellini (3),
Donizetti (8), Rossini (3), Verdi (3); *German and Austrian:* Dörstling (1), Flotow (2), Gluck (2),
Kreutzer (1), Lortzing (2), Mozart (3), Nicolai (1), Weber (1); *French:* Adam (1), Auber (6),
Boieldieu (2), Cherubini (1), Halévy (2), Hérold (1), Méhul (1), Meyerbeer (3), *Czech:* Skuherský
(1), Smetana (2), Šebor (1), Škroup (1); *Russian:* Glinka (1); *Irish:* Balfe (1). Smetana's operas were
not conducted by Maýr, but by the composer himself . . . An article in *Politik* (18 February 1874)
signed 'V. V.' (V. Linhardt) gives a slightly inaccurate list of Maýr's repertory. Josef Bartoš's
Prozatímní divadlo a jeho opera (The Provisional Theatre and its opera) (Prague 1938), upon
which Šourek relied, is not entirely trustworthy.

3 Komzák took his players to the International Trade Fair at Hamburg in 1863. The band ceased
to exist in 1865 when the players were completely integrated with the theatre orchestra.

4 The pronunciation of the words '*švedská*' (Swedish) and '*švecká*' (cobbler's) is almost identical.

When composing, Dvořák needed to try out what he had written at the piano, but since the Dušeks did not possess one, and it was not convenient to have to call on his trumpeter friend Kváča for this purpose, he decided to change his lodgings. He joined up with his colleague Moric Anger, and Karel Čech, Adolf's brother, who at that time was a medical student, but later became a leading bass singer. They shared their flat with three others, one of whom acted as a guide to foreigners by day and often returned home late at night in such a tipsy state that he disturbed the slumbers of the other five and belied his name Anděl (i.e. angel). These lodgings were not ideal, but Dvořák was able to use Anger's 'spinet' (which might very well have been a square piano) and was so encouraged by this that in 1865 he poured out one big composition after another.

Whatever he may have composed between the spring of 1862 and that prolific year failed to satisfy him, and he made sure that it did not survive. Now there was a chance of making a fresh start, and so, aiming high, he settled down on 14 February 1865 to write a symphony, and in no more than five and half weeks the score was complete. As he wrote it his thoughts turned back towards his second home, Zlonice, to its church, which had been a focus for a large part of his musical activity there, and to Liehmann from whom he had learnt so much. So he gave this C minor Symphony a title, (*The Bells of Zlonice*) *Zlonické zvony*. He next wrote a Cello Concerto in A major for his friend Ludevít Peer, finishing it in short score on 30 June, in which form it has remained, without any attempt on Dvořák's part to orchestrate it.[5] He composed his third work, a cycle of eighteen songs entitled *Cypresses* based on poems by G. Pfleger-Moravský, over a period of two and half weeks during July—for an important reason. He had fallen deeply in love with a charming 16-year-old pupil of his, Josefa Čermáková, the daughter of a goldsmith, and he was intensely disappointed when she repeatedly failed to respond to his advances. After an interval of four days he began working on another symphony, op. 4 in B flat major. This occupied him from 1 August to 9 October, almost twice as much time as the first, perhaps partly because he felt the need this time to take greater care. Two baritone songs completed this unprecedented spate of creative energy.

Dvořák submitted *The Bells of Zlonice* for a prize competition in

---

5 Günther Raphael's edition of the concerto (1929) is so unlike Dvořák's original, that it must be regarded as a travesty of Dvořák's intentions. Raphael even reshapes Dvořák's themes. *Vide* my article 'Dvořák's First Cello Concerto', *Music & Letters*, xxxvii (1956), pp. 350–5.

Germany, but was unsuccessful. When the score was not returned to him he dismissed the work from his mind, realizing no doubt that it had been a useful experience composing it, but he was capable of writing something a good deal better. The work was lost, until it turned up unexpectedly in 1923.[6]

Important changes took place at the Provisional Theatre in the autumn of 1866. J. N. Maýr lost his position as conductor, and Smetana was appointed principal conductor with Adolf Čech as his assistant. In the next five seasons, while Dvořák remained a regular member of the orchestra, a number of interesting new works were added to the repertory, several of which Dvořák must have been glad to get to know. Smetana personally introduced *William Tell*, *Jessonda* (Spohr), *Die Entführung aus dem Serail*, *Fidelio*, *Faust*, *Roméo et Juliette* (Gounod), *Halka* (Moniuszko) and his own *Dalibor*; Čech took charge of *La Traviata*, *Nabucco*, *Un Ballo in Maschera*, *Don Pasquale* and *La Cenerentola;* and Glinka came to Prague in order to present his *Ruslan and Lyudmila*. During this period no fewer than twelve works by Czech composers were given first performances, which gave Dvořák much food for thought.[7]

For rather more than three years Dvořák seems to have composed very little, and except for some orchestral Intermezzi, written early in 1867, he did not allow anything from this time to survive. Apparently he composed a Clarinet Quintet in B flat minor, and possibly two Overtures (in E minor and F minor?),[8] but it seems unlikely there could have been anything really big. The position in 1869–70 was quite different, even though he was dissatisfied with his achievement. Apart from the three String Quartets which belong to this period, he also ventured to compose a three-act opera, although he was extremely careful to conceal this fact from his most intimate friends. It is a little curious that he should have picked on a German libretto.

6 In the possession of Dr Rudolf Dvořák, who was not related to the composer. The Symphony was performed for the first time at Brno on 4 October 1836.

7 The Czech operas were as follows: 1866–7: *The Swedes in Prague* (J. N. Škroup); 1867–8: *Drahomíra* (Šebor), *In the Well* (Blodek), *Lejla* (Bendl), *Lora* (Skuherský) and *Dalibor;* 1868–9: *The Hussite Bride* (Šebor) and *The Captured Maid* (Vojáček); 1869–70: *Blanka* (Šebor); 1870–1: *Břetislav* (Bendl), *Mikuláš* (Rozkošný) and *Marie Potocká* (Měchura). The composers usually conducted their own works, but Smetana directed *Lejla* and *Marie Potocká*. Among the French operas were three by Auber, three by Adam and one by Grisar. Brian Large's *Smetana* (1970) provides a list of 'new productions' of operas which Smetana conducted during his first six seasons, on p. 208. It should be noted that all except ten of these had already been presented at the Provisional Theatre during Maýr's tenure of office. I am indebted to Jarmil Burghauser for much information about the operatic repertory of this period.

8 He listed these among works he claimed later to have torn up and burnt, but his memory was rather unreliable.

Perhaps he was unable to find anything else suitable, and at least Karl Theodor Körner's 'Alfred der Grosse' possessed a subject with an appeal for freedom-loving Czechs, in much the same way that *Nabucco* had for Verdi's compatriots.[9] He wrote his *Alfred* on quasi-Wagnerian lines between 26 May and 19 October 1870, and having completed it he stowed it away out of sight, realizing it was a hopeless failure. Some ten years later he rescued the overture and revised it, but avoided revealing its origin by renaming it *Tragic Overture*. Despite his improvements it was neither performed nor published until after his death. Eventually the whole opera was staged at Olomouc on 10 December 1938.

About six months after finishing *Alfred*, and spurred on by his dissatisfaction with this first attempt, Dvořák set to work on a second opera, completing the sketch in June and the full score and overture by 20 December 1871. The subject was drawn from an old puppet play, and the libretto in the Czech language was written by Bernard Guldener, a notary who wrote his plays under the pseudonym B. J. Lobeský. He called it 'Feel at Home, Mr Matthew' ('Pane Matěj, jako doma'), but this was changed to *King and Charcoal Burner*. As in the case of *Alfred*, Dvořák conceived the new work in Wagnerian terms. He made no secret of what he was doing, and as a result Dr Ludevít Procházka, the lawyer-editor of the weekly musical paper *Hudební listy*, announced rather prematurely on 14 June that Dvořák had just completed an opera, following this up a fortnight later with favourable comments about the work.[10] Dvořák had probably already been thinking he ought to devote more time to composition. The timely encouragement from Procházka may well have strengthened his resolve to make this possible by resigning from the Provisional Theatre orchestra at the end of his ninth season, but he was well aware of the risks involved. He would be obliged to sacrifice a regular salary of 420 zlotys, and rely solely on casual fees from private teaching. He took the decisive step in July, and thus severed his connection with the orchestra.

At this critical point in Dvořák's career, the interest that Dr

9 Körner's libretto is in two acts, whereas Dvořák's opera has three. Flotow and J. P. S. Schmidt set Körner's libretto, but only the latter's was performed, at Königsberg in 1830. Reuling's and Raff's operas on the same subject use librettos by O. von Müller and G. Logan respectively.

10 Procházka, who was a staunch supporter of Smetana, was pleased to see that Dvořák showed himself to be in sympathy with the most progressive school of composition, i.e. that of Wagner and Liszt, and declared that his opera 'shows everywhere the purest artistic endeavour to shun banal expedients'.

Procházka showed in the struggling composer was particularly
valuable. Procházka and his wife, the coloratura soprano Marta
Reisingerová, were arranging at that time a series of informal, or
'free', musical evenings in their own and other people's drawing
rooms, and a few of Dvořák's compositions were given a hearing. His
song 'Vzpomínání' (Remembrance), one of the Krásnohorská set
which he wrote in November, was sung on 10 December 1871.
Another from the same set, 'Proto' (The Reason), together with his
setting of K. J. Erben's ballad 'Sirotek' (The Orphan), were heard on
10 April, and on 5 July the Adagio from one of the two Piano Trios,
written at that period but now lost, was played by Procházka and the
Hřímalý brothers, Vojtěch and Jaromír. In addition, thanks to Smetana including the overture to *King and Charcoal Burner* in his Philharmonic concert at the Žofín Hall on 14 April 1872, a much wider
audience had an opportunity of hearing something that was fully
representative of this still unrecognized thirty-year-old composer at
this particular stage of his development.[11]

These were small beginnings, but the tide was gradually rising in
Dvořák's favour. This became even clearer during the next season.
When the Piano Quintet in A major, op. 5, was presented at the
midday concert at the Konvikt Hall on 22 November 1872, Procházka
had taken care to see that a splendid team of players would do justice
to it, and these included the internationally famous pianist and violinist,
Karel ve Slavkovských and Vojtěch Hřímalý. The Quintet was
placed first in the programme and was the principal item.[12] It
was certainly fortunate for Dvořák that he was befriended by the
wealthy merchant Jan Neff and his wife, both of whom were keen
amateur singers, and that they engaged him to teach their two children.
Then in March 1873 his song 'Skřívánek' (The Lark), from his cycle of
Songs from the Queen's Court Manuscript, appeared as a supplement to
the musical weekly *Dalibor*, of which Procházka was the editor. Before
long Starý published the complete set of six songs, and also the composer's Potpourri on themes from *King and Charcoal Burner*. On top of
these encouraging developments, Dvořák had the satisfaction of

11 Rather surprisingly, in the programme the work was called 'Concert Overture'. The score also
gave the title as 'Koncertní Ouvertura', but subsequently the first of these words was deleted.

12 This Quintet, composed in August 1872, should not be confused with the Piano Quintet, op.
81, in the same key and dating from 1887. At the same concert Slavkovský played pieces by L.
Żeleński and Vojtěch Hlaváč, and there were two groups of songs, by Fibich and by Franz
and Wagner.

knowing that the Provisional Theatre had decided a year earlier that they would produce his opera.

The real turning point, however, came in March 1873. In the previous year between May and 3 June Dvořák had composed a cantata for mixed chorus and orchestra on Vítězslav Hálek's patriotic ode *The Heirs of the White Mountain*, an assertion of the undying love of the Czechs for their country, which had suffered so humiliating a defeat in 1620. This work of Dvořák's, frequently referred to as his Hymnus, was sung by the 300-strong Prague Hlahol Choral Society and conducted by Karel Bendl on 9 March. Its theme made a direct appeal to the hearts of the composer's countrymen, and the performance convinced those who were present that Dvořák had responded finely to the lofty tone of the text and that they were listening to the work of a man of great talent. The warmth of the response from both audience and critics showed it to have been an unqualified success.[13]

This cantata opens with a lament in E flat major, which expresses the despondency and intense sorrow of the Czechs in a wholly convincing manner. A dramatic change to C major heralds the second part, a fervent and inspiring call to the people to show their faith in the fatherland by dedicating themselves at whatever cost to the greater glory that lies ahead. At the climax the original key returns. This work, the second part of which was considerably improved in the revisions of 1880 and 1884. deserves to be heard more frequently today.

Early in the 1870s Dvořák felt the need to put to good use the best ideas from his missing symphony, *The Bells of Zlonice*, and so he incorporated them into several of his sketches for a series of piano pieces, the *Silhouettes*, which, however, did not reach their final form until much later. He soon decided it was high time he wrote another symphony, the outcome being the three-movement symphony in E flat major, op. 10—his third. Despite its indebtedness to Wagner, it shows him moving steadily in the direction of classical models, a tendency that is apparent in the other compositions of the period. This work, written in the summer months of 1873, was closely followed by a *Romeo and Juliet* Overture for full orchestra, and an Octet for piano, strings and wind, with the alternative title Serenade, but both these compositions were destroyed by the composer. The Symphony gives the clearest possible indication of the progress he was making. No

13 Procházka's glowing criticism in *Dalibor* (1873), pp. 88-9, is quoted by Šourek in *Život a dílo Antonína Dvořáka*, i, 3rd edn (1954), p. 146.

earlier work of his gave the slightest hint that he was capable of commencing anything with the broad sweep and assurance that we find
here.[14] It was unorthodox and certainly bold to select G flat major,
lying a minor third above the main key, for his second subject. This
may be viewed as yet another indication of his growing self-con-
fidence, besides being a striking example of a modulation which is very
characteristic of him. In the first two movements a cor anglais is
added to the normal orchestra, and in the Adagio molto additional
colouring is provided in the middle section and coda by a harp. The
two movements are linked thematically. Like numerous other themes
of Dvořák, the first bars of the Adagio molto have apparently been
influenced by a feature to be found in Czech folksong, repetition of
the initial notes of the song. The parallel can be seen in the following:

In the autumn of 1872 Procházka noticed that no steps had been
taken at the Provisional Theatre to mount *King and Charcoal Burner*
that season, and no explanation for the delay had been offered. He
knew that the timing of the production rested to a large extent with
Smetana, and, realizing that the chief conductor's reputation as a
champion of Czech operas apart from his own had become somewhat
tarnished, he hoped that in Dvořák's case there would be no undue
delay. In the circumstances he felt it was desirable to remind the
Theatre Association of their promise to Dvořák.[15] In the following

---

14 Dvořák appears to have incorrectly dated this work '1872'. It seems reasonable to assume that it
was composed in 1873 and completed on 4 July that year. The theory advanced by František
Bartoš (Introduction to the Critical Edition score, Prague 1963) that the work was fully sketched
in 1872 and orchestrated a year later, may be partly true, but it seems preferable in that case to
think that because of the obvious maturity of the symphony it would have been considerably
reshaped in the summer of 1873.

15 In October he complained in *Dalibor* about the production having been postponed. František
Pivoda pointed out in *Pokrok* (3 March 1870) that there were far more performances of operas by
Smetana than by other Czechs, that Bendl's *Lejla* had been given only two performances with
an eight-month interval between them, and claimed that Smetana was jealous over Šebor's
success with *Drahomíra*, a point which Smetana failed to refute convincingly, but he was no match
for Pivoda in argument.

year, the Association, having taken note of the success of the Hymnus, resolved to mount Smetana's *The Two Widows*, Fibich's *Bukovín* and also *King and Charcoal Burner* during the approaching season. Early in September the rehearsals began. The soloists quickly discovered that their vocal parts were ungrateful and awkward to sing, so that complaints became more and more frequent. In this highly charged atmosphere Dvořák asked to have the score returned to him, after which he was thought to have destroyed it. According to Smetana: 'It is a serious work, full of ideas and genius, but I don't believe it can be performed.' This appears to have been the general opinion, and there was nothing Dvořák could do but accept the verdict with reluctance. It seems improbable that he attempted to destroy the full score, for acts one and three were discovered in Nuremberg in 1916.[16]

Judging by what we know of Dvořák's volatile temperament, he must have been livid over the incompetence of the singers. And if there really was any justification for their complaints, why had they not been foreseen when his work was considered for performance in the first place? But he also possessed considerable resilience, and on recovering from the initial shock he began to realize what a mistake it had been to go to such extremes in attempting to follow the example of Wagner. He knew that his next opera would have to be quite different. Looking ahead a few months, we find that by April he was busily setting the *King and Charcoal Burner* libretto entirely afresh, in a totally different manner, and without utilizing anything from the ill-fated earlier version. This astonishing procedure must surely be unique in the history of music.

By 1873 eight years had passed since the unhappy time when Dvořák's proposals of marriage to his enchanting pupil Josefa Čermáková had been so firmly rejected. Her younger sister Anna was also one of the composer's pupils for several years. By now she was nineteen, and appearing as a contralto soloist at the Týn and St Adalbert (Sv Vojtěch) churches and elsewhere in the Old Town. Although she was not nearly so attractive as Josefa, Dvořák's admiration for her increased. The extremely warm reception given to the Hymnus, coupled with other indications suggesting that a bright future might lie ahead, despite his temporary lack of success with his opera and his still meagre earnings, are usually thought to have offered sufficient justification for him to consider marriage. This,

---

16 Following the discovery of an entire set of parts in the archives of the National Theatre, Ostrčil performed the opera in 1929.

however, overlooks the fact that Anna was already pregnant.[17] For this reason the wedding must have been arranged with some haste. It took place on 17 November 1873, and led to a long and happy married life.

Three months later Dvořák became the organist of St Adalbert's church, a less responsible post than that of choirmaster, which was held at that time by his former professor, Josef Foerster. Even though the salary was a mere pittance of ten and a half gulden a month, this was a welcome addition for the young couple. For the first six months they lived with Anna's parents, and then they moved to a flat of their own at Na rybníčku no. 10.

17 Anna's first child, Otakar, was born on 4 April 1874, less than five months after her wedding.

3 A Genius Emerges

It was extremely unpleasant for Dvořák to have his opera rejected while it was being actively prepared for production, but in this instance it proved to be both necessary and beneficial. A stage performance of *King and Charcoal Burner* would have been a disaster, for Dvořák was far too inexperienced to succeed in his over-ambitious attempt to write in a Wagnerian idiom, and it would have been more damaging to his prospects if his opera was a fiasco than for it to be withdrawn at an earlier stage. Dvořák felt the withdrawal to be a stinging rebuff, but it forced him to face up to the situation and clarify his ideas. We may well be right in thinking that the tragic tone of the Andante con moto in the F minor String Quartet, op. 9, written just at that time, was coloured by his feelings of intense frustration.[1] At the end of that year he tried to write another similar work, the String Quartet in A minor, op. 12, but he was so unsure of himself that he abandoned his plan to write it in one continuous movement; he divided it up to make it conform to a more classical design, and finally left it incomplete.[2] This, however, marked the turning point. He apparently made a New Year resolution to compose on orthodox lines and renounce all experimentation in 1874, for on 1 January he turned over a new leaf and began writing a four-movement symphony, No. 4 in D minor, op. 13. Twelve weeks later the new work was complete. The symphony pays homage to Wagner in one respect, for the theme of the Andante sostenuto could almost have come directly out of *Tannhäuser*.

It is possible that Dvořák may have ventured to compose this work in D minor because he was aware of what this key meant to Mozart, just as he had chosen to write his first symphony in the same key as Beethoven's Fifth. In general he appears to have been successful in

---

1 At a later date this movement became the Romance in F minor, op. 11, for violin and piano and also violin and orchestra.

2 When preparing this Quartet for publication, Burghauser was able to complete it without adding more than the barest minimum of material of his own.

satisfying his ambitions, even though it must be acknowledged that the finale scarcely measures up to the remainder of the work. In the heroic first movement he favoured a fair amount of structural freedom. He omitted the twenty-five-bar first subject from the recapitulation, postponed the return of the second subject by some sixty bars, continued to rivet our attention in the coda, and finally returned to the mood of the opening bars. In the Andante, a meditation on a single theme, rather than an example of variations, the Wagnerian implications are whittled away as Dvořák's own individuality emerges more and more strongly. The scherzo, in compound duple rather than in the customary triple time, is a worthy foil to the previous movement.

Just two days after Dvořák had put the final touches to the score of his new symphony, Smetana made a gesture of goodwill towards him. He conducted the combined orchestras of the Provisional and German Theatres in a performance of the earlier E flat Symphony at the Philharmonic concert on 29 March,[3] and then followed this up by presenting the scherzo of the new work at the Slavonic Concert of the Academic Reader's Society on 25 May. These encouraging events, together with the joyful news of the birth of the Dvořák's son Otakar on 4 April, would have done much to dispel any lingering traces of disappointment over his opera. In the middle of April, Dvořák turned again to the libretto of *King and Charcoal Burner*, determined to convert a failure into a success by resetting the entire text in a style not far removed from that of the comedies of Weber and Lortzing.[4] By 12 August he had completed the task, apart from the overture, which could wait. He then submitted the opera in its new form to the theatre management. While awaiting their verdict he composed the orchestral Rhapsody in A minor, and then, evidently intending to provide a replacement for his unfinished String Quartet in A minor, op. 12, he set to work on the op. 16 Quartet in the same key.

Dvořák was rewarded for his patience and perseverance with Guldener's far from perfect libretto. The theatre management accepted the new opera and rehearsals began in September. Adolf Čech, the assistant conductor, directed the première on 24 November, and three more performances were given. The composer must have been particulary pleased to see his opera rise like a phoenix from the ashes of the earlier version. For the revival in 1881 he wrote a new ballad for

---

3 František Bartoš, in his introduction to the Critical Edition score, has pointed out that Šourek was incorrect in giving the date as 30 March.

4 Unlike the earlier versions of Smetana's *The Bartered Bride* and *The Two Widows*, and Weber's and Lortzing's Singspiele, Dvořák's opera has no spoken dialogue.

The area north of Prague where Dvořák's ancestors lived

Dvořák's birthplace at Nelahozeves, with the composer (third from left)
standing in the foreground

Dvořák's father František and his aunt Josefina Dušková

King Matyáš, and for the new production of 1887 he remodelled the final act, using V. J. Novotný's revisions to the libretto. He evidently considered his opera to be a sufficiently worthy composition to merit the trouble he took to improve. it. He retained a particular affection for this work, due partly to the fact that it was the first of his operas to reach the stage.[5] Shortly after preparations for mounting *King and Charcoal Burner* had been put in hand, Dvořák was already thinking of writing another opera. Josef Štolba, a notary and the author of a successful farce, had given him a libretto for a one-act comedy some time before. Dvořák found it unsuitable during his period of preference for operas on Wagnerian lines, but now he found it attractive, and decided to set it. This new work, begun early in October or at the end of September and finished at 8.00 a.m. on Christmas Eve 1874, bears the title *Tvrdé palice*, the most suitable translation for which is *The Stubborn Lovers*.[6] Dvořák was not so fortunate this time, and had to wait seven years for the first performance.

During midsummer 1874, after hearing about the newly instituted Austrian State Stipendium that was being offered to young, poor and talented artists in the western half of the empire by the Ministry of Education, Dvořák decided he must compete. Having first armed himself with a certificate from the Prague Town Clerk's office, testifying that he was poor, he submitted a selection of his more recent compositions, some programmes and press notices, for consideration by the judges of the music section, Johann Herbeck, the director of the Court Opera, Eduard Hanslick, the critic, and Johannes Brahms. The result of the contest was announced sometime in February of the following year. The report of the minister, Karl Stremayer, has recently come to light and states:

Anton DWOŘÁK of Prague, 33 years old, music teacher, completely without means. He has submitted 15 compositions, among them symphonies and overtures for full orchestra which display an undoubted talent, but in a way which as yet remains formless and unbridled. This talent is shown in a much purer and more pleasing manner in Dvořák's pictures from the 'Dvůr Kralové Manuscript', which display genuine and original

---

5 In the interviews Dvořák gave to the *The Sunday Times* (10 May 1885) and *Pall Mall Gazette* (13 October 1886), this is the only opera he mentioned. Yet at that time *The Cunning Peasant* had been performed at Dresden and Hamburg, and *Dimitrij* had been quite successful in Prague. Unquestionably, *Dimitrij* was the best opera he had written up to that time.

6 It is clear from this that it is the young couple, not their parents, who are stubborn. Literally the title means 'The rigid pigheaded ones'.

gifts. The fact that Dvořák's choral and orchestral compositions have been performed frequently at big public concerts made a favourable impression. The applicant, who has never yet been able to acquire a piano of his own, deserves a grant to ease his straitened circumstances and free him from anxiety in his creative work.'[7]

This report shows that Dvořák submitted a much larger number of his compositions than has previously been realized. It is at least certain that his third and fourth Symphonies and the set of *Dvůr Kralové* songs were among them, but there was much else besides. There seems to be a strong possibility that he would have sent his Hymnus, and if he had already destroyed the *Romeo and Juliet* Overture he only had the overtures to *Alfred* and the first version of *King and Charcoal Burner* to turn to. It seems probable that he would have submitted the Piano Quintet in A, op. 5, and the F minor String Quartet, op. 9. He was awarded 400 gulden, but it is not known how he may have used this, except perhaps towards a short journey for the sake of study.

Dvořák's good fortune in winning this award led to a remarkable burst of creative energy. First he polished off the G major String Quintet (for string quartet and double bass), which was already half written, and then in rather less than five months he wrote the four *Moravian Duets* for soprano and tenor, op. 20, for his friends the Neffs, the Piano Trio in B flat, the delightful E major Serenade for Strings, the Piano Quartet in D major, and his finest symphony to date, No. 5 in F major. Surprisingly enough, this last work took only five and a half weeks to write, from 15 June to 23 July 1875.

It is as if a new world is revealed in this symphony. Dvořák's new-found mastery is first noticed in the magical opening for clarinets and a *pianissimo* background of horns and strings, quoted lower down, and subsequently seen in the remainder of the work. But nowhere is it more apparent than in the powerful finale. This remarkable movement commences in the mediant key, A minor, and avoids the principal key of F major for well over fifty bars. This ploy was by no means new, but no composer had previously attempted it on so extended a scale. The finale's development section is the most dynamic that

---

7 The director of the Österreichisches Staatsarchiv, Allgemeines Verwaltungsarchiv, has kindly drawn my attention to this document, and confirmed that both Herbeck and Brahms were members of the jury, despite what Hanslick says in his *Neue Freie Presse* feuilleton of 23 November 1879.

Dvořák had produced up to this time. After all the turbulence, peace
is finally established by means of an easily recognized reminder of the
harmonic framework alone of the first movement's main theme:

Next he boldly tackled his most ambitious project so far, a heroic
five-act grand opera *Vanda* on a libretto by V. B. Šumavský. The
subject is drawn from the ancient legend about a Polish princess who is
so distressed to see her country torn by warfare because of the enmity
of her rival suitors, Slavoj, a Pole, and Roderich, a German, that she
resolves to sacrifice herself to the gods in gratitude when the invading
army is crushed. The composition of this big work occupied him from
9 August to 22 December. When the opera was mounted with a strong
cast on 17 April 1876, the resources of the Provisional Theatre were
found to be totally inadequate for the witchcraft scene in the third act,
and so this was cut in the three remaining performances and a choral
recitative decribed the missing scene. The work was presented once in
1877 and revived briefly in 1880, but it was then shelved and not even
heard during the celebrations marking the composer's sixtieth birthday
when most of his operas were performed.

Prague publishers turned wary eyes in Dvořák's direction when he
won the State grant, but only Wetzler and Starý were prepared to take

the risk of publishing anything just then. Wetzler brought out his Potpourri for piano on the second version of *King and Charcoal Burner* in March, shortly followed by Starý's edition of the parts, but not the score, of the A minor String Quartet, op. 16. Nothing else appeared until Starý issued the as yet unwritten *Moravian Duets* for female voices. The A minor Quartet was the first chamber music work to be published in Prague.

The Piano Trio in G minor and E major String Quartet, written at the beginning of 1876, may quite possibly reflect the composer's despondent mood which followed a tragedy of the year before. Being a man whose love for his family was paramount, he was deeply upset at losing his first daughter. Josefa, born on 19 September, died only two days later. His Trio is in the same key as the Trio Smetana wrote as a memorial to his very gifted daughter, the same key that Mozart turned to for tragic arias. The Quartet, too, has a marked tendency to veer away from bright major keys towards those in the minor mode. There may have been other reasons why he should have sketched his *Stabat Mater* next. Having already written a patriotic cantata, his deep religious conviction would have led him to select a religious subject for his next big choral composition and he evidently felt it was now time he did so. We should not, however, link his decision to proceed in this way with the season of Lent.[8] After completing the sketch on 7 May, he laid this on one side and turned to works of a rather different kind.

He was very strongly attracted by folksongs and had already written songs on Serbian folk poetry and a few vocal duets on similar texts from Moravia. Rather later he wrote part-songs on Czech, Slovak and Lithuanian folk poetry, but now, as the summer was approaching, he turned again to František Sušil's large collection of Moravian folk-songs,[9] and chose a number of poems which would be suitable for accompanied duets for soprano and contralto. The fifteen *Moravian Duets* that he then wrote show him in a completely relaxed mood, and have a significant position in his output as a whole, because it was partly due to these unpretentious and spontaneously conceived compositions that Dvořák's genius became more widely recognized. During this same time he set a cycle of twelve *Evening Songs* on texts by the nature poet Vítězslav Hálek. Jan Neff was kind enough to pay Starý to publish the *Moravian Duets* (op. 29 and 32), and Dvořák dedicated them to Neff and his wife. Without breathing a word to

8 He commenced the sketch on 19 February 1876. Ash Wednesday fell on 1 March that year.
9 *Moravské národní písně* (Brno 1835; 3rd edn 1860).

the composer, Neff arranged for several copies to be splendidly bound, and then sent these to Brahms, Hanslick and others.[10]

At this time a tempting proposition presented itself. Eduard Rüffer, who had already provided librettos for Šebor and Rozkošný, offered Dvořák the text for a comic opera, 'Die Wunderblume', for fifty gulden. Naturally this would have to be translated into Czech, but with the German text ready to hand the composer visualized the possibility of performance abroad, just as Smetana had when he began setting *Dalibor*. Unluckily he could not afford the fee and the cost of the translation, and when he asked at the Provisional Theatre if he might have an advance against the royalties which would be due to him on future performances of *King and Charcoal Burner* and *Vanda*, they ruled this out altogether. So instead of composing an opera just then, he wrote the G minor Piano Concerto, op. 33, confidently hoping that the young Czech pianist Karel ze Slavkovských would take an interest in it. He finished the score on 14 September 1876, four days before his daughter Růžena (Rose) was born. Slavkovský presented the Concerto at a Slavonic Concert which Adolf Čech conducted on 24 March 1878. Towards the end of 1876 Dvořák wrote his first Dumka and the Theme and Variations for piano, and in January there followed the set of male voice part-songs which provided him with the theme on which he later based his *Symphonic Variations*.

After having won the Austrian State Stipendium at the first attempt with an impressive selection of works, Dvořák entered for the award annually. The compositions he was able to submit on the second occasion were less favourably received by the judges and he failed to gain the award. When he tried for the third time he would have been able to send his G minor Piano Trio, the String Quartet in E major and the fifth Symphony in F major. He was given the prize, which had been increased in value to 500 gulden. This success must have helped him to decide on resigning from his organ post on the completion of three years' service.

More than a year had passed since he wrote an opera, and he was becoming eager, perhaps a little too eager, to start on another. Though doubtless aware that it was no easy matter to acquire a good libretto, he was prepared to accept the first that caught his fancy, in this instance one by Josef Otakar Veselý, a medical student who had a flare for drama. Dvořák was quite prepared to overlook the extent of Veselý's borrowing from *The Marriage of Figaro*, which must have

10 M. Neffová: 'Dvořák, Brahms a Moravské dvojzpěvy', *Hudební listy*, 30 June 1904.

been obvious to all. However, he wisely changed the title from 'A Slap for the Prince' ('Políček knížeti') to *The Cunning Peasant* (*Šelma sedlák*),[11] and set to work with relish. By July 1877 the opera was complete, and it was mounted at the Provisional Theatre with Adolf Čech in charge on 27 January of the following year. There was every reason for Dvořák to be delighted at the way his opera was received. The overture and several of the arias were encored at the première, and before the year was out eight performances had been given. It was also particularly gratifying to have such a pleasant word of commendation from Jan Neruda, the poet and journalist who was one of Smetana's staunchest supporters. He described Dvořák as 'a strapping youth with sparkling eyes, a springy step and at all times a song on his lips', and he believed the new opera to be just as national and Czech as those of Smetana.[12]

After going for a walking tour in central and southern Bohemia with the twenty-three-year-old composer Leoš Janáček, and then paying a brief visit to Sychrov castle, where his friend Alois Göbl was tutor and secretary to Prince Kamil of Rohan, Dvořák responded to a request from Procházka for an orchestral composition. He wrote this between 6 August and 28 September 1877, and evidently enjoyed the task, judging by the inscription on the score, which reads: 'Symphonic Variations on an Original Theme from the partsong "Já som guslar" [I am a fiddler] for full orchestra assembled and entangled by Antonín Dvořák'. At this time performances of Dvořák's music were becoming a little more frequent.[13] On the face of it, Procházka's programme promised well. He had booked the Žofín Hall for 2 December and engaged the Provisional Theatre orchestra, but because the purpose of the concert was to raise money for the Smíchov church building fund it was given practically no Press coverage. Dvořák was so disappointed that he promptly shelved this fine work and gave it no further serious thought until nine years later when he was endeavouring to meet the great demand for his music by resurrecting and revising old works.

11 In order to secure a rich husband for his daughter, Martin uses his peasant cunning and displays roguishness, but he is no knave; consequently it is misleading to translate the Czech title literally as 'The Peasant Rogue'.

12 *Humoristické listy*, 16 February 1878. A shortened version of Neruda's feuilleton appears in Šourek: *Antonín Dvořák: Letters and Reminiscences*, pp. 44-5.

13 Earlier that year Slavkovský, Ondříček and Sládek had played the Piano Trio in B flat, the Prague Hlahol Choral Society had presented the Male Voice Part-Songs, and the Serenade for Strings, which was heard for the first time at the end of 1876, was repeated in Prague, and conducted by Janáček in Brno and by Dvořák at Lipník nad Bečvou in Moravia.

Dvořák had attempted writing variations in the Piano Quartet in D major, op. 23, and displayed greater perception and skill in his Theme and Variations for piano, op. 36, but neither of these can compare with the *Symphonic Variations*. The new theme suited him admirably, and with his lively musical imagination, his flair for orchestration, the resources of the full symphony orchestra to draw upon and the example of the great masters before him, he revelled in his task and created a masterpiece. There are twenty-seven variations and an extended finale. From Variation 18 onwards fresh moods and new tonalities are explored, and eventually the work is crowned with a joyful fugue.

For Dvořák and his wife this was a year which lingered in their memories for a long time. In an unguarded moment their daughter Růžena, who was still not quite eleven months old, got hold of a solution of phosphorus intended for making matches, drank it, and died on 13 August. Then, while the poor parents were still reeling under this cruel blow, their three-and-a-half-year-old son Otakar contracted smallpox, and died on 8 September, which was also the composer's thirty-sixth birthday. The Dvořáks were left childless. Just then the composer was in the middle of orchestrating the *Symphonic Variations;* but once he had got that out of the way he immediately sought solace from his Maker by returning to the neglected *Stabat Mater* sketch. During October and the first fortnight of November he scored this completely. It is certainly curious that he should have had to wait fully three years for his most famous choral work to be performed, and particularly so perhaps because after publication it played such an important role in consolidating his reputation abroad.[14]

Minor keys are dominant in the *Stabat Mater's* first four sections. In the remaining numbers, however, in which the petitioner seeks to share completely in the Mother's grief for her crucified Son so that, if granted divine grace, his soul may ultimately find peace in Paradise, major keys tend to prevail. At the beginning of the work our eyes seem to be drawn upwards towards the figure of Christ on the cross. Then there follow at intervals in this impressive opening number some poignant passages expressing pity and sorrow, conveyed by means of intertwining descending and ascending chromatic strands, as shown in the following extract:

14 Adolf Čech conducted the first performance on 23 December [!] 1880 in Prague. Simrock published the score in November 1881.

During the composer's lifetime the 'Inflammatus et accensus' (No. 9) was particularly admired for its telling vocal line superimposed upon a rhythmically patterned motif in the orchestra, and leading contraltos quite frequently sang it as an independent concert item.

While occupied with the orchestration of his sacred cantata, Dvořák was awaiting hopefully the outcome of his fourth application for the Ministry of Education's annual award. This time he had submitted the recently published *Moravian Duets* and most probably he also sent his Piano Concerto, the Theme and Variations for piano, and perhaps the *Evening Songs* as well. He was kept on tenter-hooks until the beginning of December, when he received a personal letter from Eduard Hanslick.[15] This was far from being just a brief announcement that Brahms, the minister (Karl Stremayer) and he were unanimous in agreeing that Dvořák fully deserved the grant of 600 gulden, for it also offered the friendly assistance of Brahms and Hanslick himself towards making his music known outside his native Bohemia. Both men had been deeply impressed by the *Moravian Duets*, and Brahms now wished to recommend these to Simrock, his publisher. Hanslick urged Dvořák to write to Brahms and suggested he might send him some of his other music. All this was magnificent news for one whose achievement so far was almost entirely local. It was a little unfortunate, however, that Hanslick should have ended his letter with the words '. . . it would be advantageous for your things to become known beyond your narrow Czech fatherland, which in any case does not do much for you', for although there was more than a modicum of truth in what Hanslick said,

15 Letter of 30 November 1877. This letter appears in full in my article, 'Dvořák's Relations with Brahms and Hanslick', *Musical Quarterly*, lvii (1971), p.242. For the original German text, see *Hudební věda*, x (1973), p. 214.

Dvořák was enough of a patriot to resent the implication that his fellow Czechs were on the whole inferior to the Germanic races.

It took Dvořák some time to realize what an incredible change in his fortunes would be brought about by this kind gesture of Brahms; but he rapidly became convinced about the famous composer's sincere interest in his music, and his very genuine wish that he might give him some practical assistance towards achieving much wider recognition than hitherto. He found this extremely flattering, and his humility is very apparent in his letters to the great man. Directly Dvořák heard that Simrock wished to publish his *Moravian Duets*, he wrote to Brahms asking to be allowed to dedicate to him his new String Quartet in D minor, op. 34.[16] Brahms's response was to say he considered himself honoured by the dedication. To the Czech composer's surprise and delight, Simrock next commissioned him to compose a set of Slavonic dances for piano duet with an orchestral arrangement, offering him a fee of 300 marks. He could hardly have picked on a type of work that would have appealed more strongly to Dvořák, or have improved on the timing of his request. Dvořák was keenly interested in the folk dances of his country, and just then national tendencies were beginning to appear in his music. Simrock's letter arrived as he was completing his first *Slavonic Rhapsody* in D major for orchestra, and so on 18 March 1878 he was free to start work on the first set of *Slavonic Dances*, op. 46.

In response to a plea from Dvořák about his String Quartets in E major and D minor, Brahms recommended both works to Simrock with the words: 'Dvořák possesses the best that a musician can have, and it is seen in these compositions.'[17] But Simrock was not prepared to proceed further until he knew how the duets and dances would fare. Work on the dances proceeded apace, both in their piano duet and orchestral versions, but between whiles Dvořák turned to other things, notably the *Bagatelles* for two violins, cello and harmonium, the String Sextet in A major, op. 48, and some songs entitled *Three New Greek Poems*. He and his wife Anna were overjoyed during this productive period when on 6 June their daughter Otilie (Otilka) was born. Before the year was out the *Moravian Duets* and both versions of the *Slavonic Dances* were published.

Dvořák made one final attempt to win the Austrian State Stipendium

16 Letter of 23 January 1878 from Dvořák to Brahms. Brahms's reply, dated 'March 1878', crossed Dvořák's next letter to him, and was probably written on 24 March.

17 Letter of 5 April 1878 from Brahms to Simrock.

that year, submitting his *Stabat Mater* and no doubt other recent compositions as well.[18] It is extremely doubtful if he could still claim to be young, which was a necessary qualification, for after all he would very soon be thirty-seven years old. He did not receive the award this time. Between 20 August and 18 September he was at work on a second *Slavonic Rhapsody* in G minor. Next he sketched the third *Rhapsody* in A flat major and then began on the orchestration.

Soon there was further evidence that fortune was at last beginning to shine on Dvořák. On 15 November the Berlin *Nationalzeitung* published a review of the *Slavonic Dances* and *Moravian Duets* by the distinguished German critic Louis Ehlert, a review that can fairly be described as a rave notice. He believed that the *Dances*, like the *Hungarian Dances* of Brahms, was 'a work which will make its way round the world', and added, 'a heavenly naturalness flows through this music'. He was greatly impressed by the delightful freshness of the vocal duets. He was not prepared to proclaim Dvořák as a genius until he had seen more of his music, but was entirely convinced that he possessed a genuine and pleasing talent.[19] The effect of this review was electrifying. There was a run on the German music shops for the dances and duets of this hitherto completely unknown composer. Adolf Čech had already conducted the first, third and fourth dances in Prague as far back as 16 May, but performances were now arranged abroad. Benjamin Bilse presented the fifth and sixth dances in Hamburg towards the end of January 1879 and some were played at one of Baron P. von Dervies's concerts at Nice a few days later. August Manns introduced nos 1, 2 and 3 at the Crystal Palace, Sydenham, on 15 February, and later that year they reached the United States.[20] The *Slavonic Dances* were bringing fame to Dvořák in two continents.

Encouraged by the first indications of success for his new client, Simrock quickly decided to buy the orchestral version and piano duet arrangement of the three *Slavonic Rhapsodies*, the Serenade in D minor

18 According to the composers's interview with *Pall Mall Gazette*, 'From Butcher to Baton' (13 October 1886), 'the "Stabat Mater" that I sent was not even noticed.' It would be interesting to know whether Dvořák thought of submitting his *Symphonic Variations*, or even his first *Slavonic Rhapsody*.

19 Ehlert's review was reproduced in the Prague German-language newspaper *Politik* on 17 November 1878, and given in a Czech translation in *Národní listy* on the same date. It appears in Šourek: *Antonín Dvořák: letters and reminiscences.*

20 This is an incomplete list of performances during 1879, due to the difficulty of tracing performances of small works. Halíř, the leader of Bilse's orchestra, told Dvořák in January that the dances would be played in Berlin. Listermann, conducting the Boston Philharmonic Orchestra, played nos 5 and 6 in Boston on 7 November and nos 7 and 8 on 2 December 1879. Manns gave nos 5–8 at the Crystal Palace on 27 March 1880, and a selection from the earlier dances at Edinburgh and Glasgow on 13 and 14 December 1880.

for wind instruments and the *Bagatelles* for the sum of 1,700 German marks, and in the spring of 1879 gave a further 4,000 marks for the Serbian and *Dvůr králové* songs, the remainder of the *Moravian Duets* (opp. 20 and 38), the *Mazurek* and Romance in F minor for violin and piano, *The Cunning Peasant* Overture, the String Sextet, and the most recent work, the String Quartet in E flat major, op. 51, completed on 28 March. During the same period Starý took two Minuets and the Scottish Dances for piano, four Part-Songs for mixed choir op. 29, and the *Festival March* for orchestra; and Bote & Bock of Berlin bought the Serenade in E major for strings, a Dumka, the two Furiants and the Theme and Variations, op. 36. for piano, and the G minor Piano Trio, op. 26, for the sum of 1,000 marks. With the exception of the *Bagatelles*, all these works were published during that year.[21]

This sudden release of so much music came in good time for the 1879–80 musical season, and interest was shown over a very wide area: Gottlöber led the way with a performance of the second *Slavonic Rhapsody* at Dresden on 3 September, and Wilhelm Taubert followed on by conducting the Royal Band in the world première of the third *Slavonic Rhapsody* in Berlin on the 24th. This work was more favoured than any other. Thanks to Ehlert it was played at Wiesbaden on 19 October, it was given at Karlsruhe on 8 November, Erkel presented it at Budapest four days later, and Richter directed it twice in Vienna, on 16 November and 29 March, and introduced it to London on 27 May. During the first half of 1880 Theodore Thomas performed it twice in Cincinnati (4 February and 21 May), and on 16 March at Brooklyn, New York. It was also given at Frankfurt by Carl Müller on 13 February, by Reiss at Kassel on 12 March, by A. P. Peck at Boston on 4 April, and it may have been the Rhapsody which J. Dupont conducted at Brussels on 22 February. Asger Hamerik must take the credit for giving the second performance of the first *Slavonic Rhapsody* at Baltimore on 21 February, and this work was also heard at Riga on 4 April directed by Julius Ruthardt.[22] Hanslick's criticism of the third *Rhapsody*

---

21 Simrock wanted to obtain first refusal on all of Dvořák's compositions. Bote & Bock also hoped to come to a similar arrangement, and as an enticement offered to publish one of the symphonies (letter from Bote & Bock to Dvořák of 3 February 1879). They were unwise to lay so much emphasis on the loss they expected to make on the symphony, unless, that is, they were not very keen to come to terms. Simrock's willingness to take so many works made a favourable impression; so Dvořák decided to come to an agreement with him, but stipulated that Simrock could only have a claim on his new compositions. This allowed him to offer older works to other publishers.

22 The first performances of the first and second *Rhapsodies* were conducted by the composer himself in Prague on 17 November 1878.

in *Neue Freie Presse* on 23 November attracted attention in New York, Boston and London.[23]

At this time the chief champions of Dvořák's chamber music were Joachim and the leader of the Florentine Quartet, Jean Becker. Joachim gave the first public performance of the Sextet in Berlin on 9 November 1879, he introduced it at the Monday Popular Concerts in London on 23 February and repeated it there by request a fortnight later. Heckmann had performed it at Cologne on 9 December, and on 27 February Řebíček played it at Wiesbaden. It was disappointing for Becker that the E flat String Quartet was not published soon enough for him to include it in the programmes of his Swiss tour in the autumn of 1879, for it was written in response to his request for a Slavonic work. Due to the delay Antonín Sobotka was able to give the first performance in Prague on 19 December. The first German performance took place at Hamburg under Bargheer's leadership on 7 January, and then the Florentine Quartet followed with performances at Halle (18 January), Hanover (3 February) and Hildesheim (4 February). Dvořák dedicated the Quartet to Becker. Other performances took place at Kassel on 19 March, led by Wipplinger, and at Stuttgart on 8 May, but London did not have a chance of hearing this work until the following season.[24]

It is obvious that the national traits in Dvořák's music contributed immeasurably towards the rapidly growing interest in his work abroad. To western ears it was 'bizarre and fantastic', but as George Freemantle observed after hearing the first *Slavonic Rhapsody*, 'these semi-barbaric themes possess a freshness and charm which do not always accompany more classic forms'.[25] Following Fibich's example, Dvořák' had substituted a polka for a scherzo in the D minor String Quartet, but it was in the Sextet for Strings and the E flat String Quartet that national features make a really significant impression in his chamber music for the first time. The Sextet's Poco allegretto is a dumka in polka rhythm. We must be on our guard, however, regarding the title 'Furiant' given to the scherzo, and similarly, as it happens, in the case of the equivalent movement in the much later Piano Quintet in A, op. 81, for neither of

23 Hanslick's feuilleton in an English translation appeared in *Musical Review*, i (New York, 11 December 1879), 141–3, *Dwight's Journal of Music*, xl (Boston, 3 January 1880), 2, and *The Musical Standard*, xviii (new series, London 1880), 58.

24 There were a number of other foreign performances of Dvořák's music during the 1879–80 season. The Serenade in D minor for wind was presented by Bernhard Scholz at Breslau on 18 November, it was played at Wiesbaden on 23 November and at Dresden on 26 January, and together with the G minor Trio was included in Procházka's Hamburg concert on 24 April. Hallé, Wilma Norman-Néruda and Franz Neruda played the Trio in London on 21 May.

25 *Manchester Guardian*, 20 November 1880.

these movements is at all typical of this highly characteristic dance. Good examples are to be found in the first and eighth *Slavonic Dances*, and again in the Vivace section of the E flat Quartet's second movement, which is a splendid example of a typical Dvořákian dumka. This beautifully written work has never lost favour with the public, and stands second to the American String Quartet in popularity.

Hanslick had been quite truthful when he told Dvořák that Bohemia was not being much help to him.[26] Prague, after all, was a provincial city of the empire, its music publishers were small concerns lacking international recognition and prestige, and success in a Prague concert hall was liable to assume a semi-local character, with the audience to a large extent made up of acquaintances and friends. To be judged by and compared with artists of international repute and to be acclaimed by complete strangers were far more valuable experiences and much more significant. It was a completely new sensation for Dvořák to find himself the centre of attention when Joachim gave a soirée on 29 July 1879 at his Berlin home, and performed the E flat String Quartet and the Sextet. When writing to Alois Göbl next day, the composer said: '. . . after being here [in Berlin] for only a few hours I had spent so many enjoyable moments among the foremost artists, that they will certainly remain in my memory for the rest of my life'.

He was filled with awe and was again carried away when he went to Vienna for the performance of his third *Slavonic Rhapsody* by the famous Vienna Philharmonic Orchestra under Hans Richter's direction. Writing to Göbl again he said his work 'was very much liked, and I was obliged to show myself to the audience. I was sitting next to Brahms by the organ in the orchestra, and Richter pulled me out. I had to come. I must tell you that I won the sympathy of the whole orchestra, and of all the [sixty] novelties they considered . . . they liked my Rhapsody best. Richter actually kissed me several times . . .'[27] The conductor invited all the Czech members of the orchestra to a banquet, held in Dvořák's honour on the following day, and the composer described this as 'a glorious evening'. In later years he never became wholly accustomed to being lionized, but his innate modesty ensured that it did not turn his simple peasant's head.

---

26 In his letter of 30 November 1877 he said: 'es wäre doch wünschenswerth dass Ihre Sachen über das engere czechische Vaterland, das ohnehin nichts für Sie thut, bekannt würden'.

27 In his letter of 23 November 1879, Dvořák does not refer to the audience's reaction. According to Dr L. Steiger, the critic of *Neue Zeitschrift für Musik*, who may well have had a prejudice against Czechs: 'The talented composer has stimulated great expectations, but they have not been realized by this Rhapsody. The response of the audience was cool, and the composer, although present, was not called for.' *NZfM*, lxxv (1879), p. 493.

4 Further Progress at Home and Abroad

While Dvořák was being fêted after the Vienna performance of his third *Slavonic Rhapsody*, Hans Richter asked him to write a symphony for the Vienna Philharmonic Society, a suggestion to which the composer very readily agreed. During this visit to the Austrian capital, and due very probably to the initiative of Brahms, Franz Jauner, the intendant of the Vienna Court Opera, asked to see Dvořák and showed some interest in the forthcoming Prague production of his opera *Vanda*. A month before this, Jauner's principal violinist, Joseph Hellmesberger, had played through the Czech composer's Sextet and E flat String Quartet to a group of friends, among whom was Brahms. The two works made an extremely favourable impression on those present, and Hellmesberger expressed his keenness to get to know the E major and D minor Quartets.[1] He gave a public performance of the Sextet in Vienna on 31 March 1881, and another at Graz at about the same time. During this period he invited Dvořák to compose a work for the Hellmesberger Quartet, the outcome of which was the String Quartet in C major, op. 61.

Very naturally Fritz Simrock was keen to spur Dvořák on to produce fresh works which he thought would appeal to the musical public as well as be lucrative to himself. In January 1879 we find him encouraging his client to compose a violin concerto, nine months later he asked him to write a [piano] trio, and in mid-February 1880 he very much hoped he could persuade him to write another set of Slavonic Dances[2]—and no wonder, for the first set had turned out to be a veritable goldmine. Dvořák was keen to compose the violin concerto, and was able to tell Simrock that Karel Halíř would be willing to perform it. When he offered his earlier Piano Quartet in D, op. 23, in place of a trio, his

---

1 Letter dated 'October 1879' from Brahms to Dvořák.
2 Letter of 16 February 1880 from Dvořák to Simrock. *Vide* Šourek's article in *Smetana*, xxxvii (1944), p. 121.

publisher showed no interest. He was not prepared to write any more Slavonic Dances just then, but raised Simrock's hopes when he said he might do so in the autumn. He continually postponed making a start on the Dances, despite his publisher's protests, and Simrock was obliged to wait more than six years wondering whether his client would keep to his word.

Dvořák's visit to Berlin to hear the Joachim Quartet play his String Quartet and Sextet came when he was already making good progress on his Violin Concerto.[3] Meeting the eminent violinist personally made him realize how valuable it would be to have his advice about the solo part. On finding that Joachim was prepared to help him, he sent him the score at the beginning of December, and at the same time dedicated the Concerto to him. Joachim was delighted, and told the composer he looked forward to examining the work *con amore*. The two men discussed the Concerto in great detail in Berlin on 2 April, and directly after returning to Prague Dvořák set about revising it thoroughly. Although he finished his task by 25 May, he still withheld the Concerto, and made some further amendments two years later. Neither Joachim, nor Robert Keller, Simrock's right-hand man, was very happy over the composer's wish to dispense with the customary recapitulation in the first movement, but Dvořák was quite adamant about this. Simrock published the Concerto as op. 53 in 1883, and František Ondříček, not Joachim, gave the first public performance in Prague on 14 October that year, and repeated it in Vienna with Richter conducting on 2 December.

Having composed a piano concerto on orthodox lines a few years before, Dvořák was determined to break fresh ground in his A minor Violin Concerto. There were strong precedents for dispensing with an initial orchestral tutti, but none, it would seem, for proceeding towards a slow movement without a quasi sonata-type first movement being permitted to run its course. Dvořák's movement, enriched by ideas that are ideally suited for a solo violin, is to a large extent rhapsodic and improvisatory, and so attempts to analyse it on the basis of sonata form are unhelpful. The justification for the composer's experiment lies in the beauty of what he wrote. The Adagio is the first of Dvořák's symphonic slow movements to follow Haydn's example by introducing a stormy episode in a minor key. The principal theme of the finale is in furiant rhythm, and a dumka is introduced later in this movement.

---

3 The Concerto was written between 5 July and the first half of September 1879. Dvořák visited Berlin on 29 July.

Simrock added some more of Dvořák's works to his list of publications in 1880. The composer had completed the first of these, the eight Waltzes for piano, op. 54, on 17 January, just four days after his daughter Anna was born. Next, using a German text, he had written the delightful *Gipsy Melodies*, op. 55, which include the universally known and greatly loved 'Songs my mother taught me'. The third of these works, the Violin Sonata in F major, op. 57, was composed soon afterwards, and was tried through and approved by Joachim on 31 March during Dvořák's visit to Berlin.[4]

It was quite clear that Simrock would not agree to take any and every work that Dvořák might offer him, and so, if a way could be found to give other publishers a better chance of securing some of his more attractive compositions, this might result in a wider dissemination of his music. In business matters Dvořák's wife Anna was shrewder than he, and so it may have been she who suggested that a little juggling with opus numbers could be beneficial. If new works were given early numbers, Simrock would be unaware that he was being deprived of exercising his first option when they were published by other firms. It was due to this that the piano *Silhouettes*, most of which were originally conceived at the beginning of the 1870s but were rewritten in 1879, were published by Hofmeister of Leipzig in 1880, and the *Czech Suite* in D major, written just after the E flat Quartet in April 1879, was issued by Schlesinger of Berlin in 1881 as op. 39, instead of with its proper number, op. 52.[5]

Towards the end of August, after relaxing with his friend Göbl at Sychrov, visiting Ehlert at Wiesbaden, and going on from there to Cologne, Dvořák eagerly set to work on the symphony he had promised to write for Hans Richter, his sixth in D major. He finished it on 15 October, and during the latter part of November he travelled to Vienna, so as to play it to Richter on the piano. The conductor was immensely pleased by it, and kissed the composer after every movement. He was most anxious to be allowed to give the première. He counted on being able to perform it at his fourth concert, on 26 December, and looked forward to including it in one of his next London concerts. Unfortunately it could not be played at such short notice, so it was scheduled for 6 March; but the date was postponed yet again. This time Richter explained how distracted he had been when two of his children

---

4 Dvořák asked for 2,000 marks for the Waltzes and Sonata, to which Simrock agreed. He received 800 marks for the song cycle.

5 Dvořák strongly objected when Simrock published several of his earlier works with high opus numbers in 1888. By deceiving the public in this way, Simrock expected to improve sales.

Nelahozeves castle

The Provisional Theatre, Prague

Dvořák's wife Anna

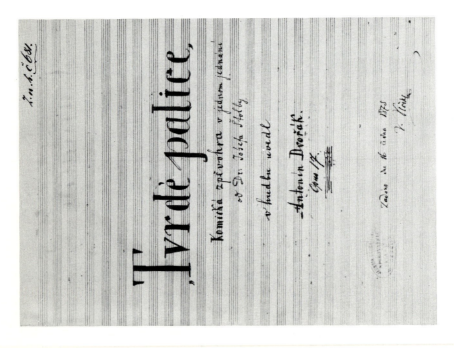

Title page of the manuscript score of the one-act opera
The Stubborn Lovers

and his own mother had contracted diphtheria, which made serious work impossible. Suspecting that the real cause of the delay was different from what he was being told, while still believing in Richter's good faith, Dvořák made this suggestion: 'I beg you to be so kind as to play [the Symphony] through at the earliest opportunity; then perhaps the gentlemen of the Philharmonic would be willing to perform it sooner.'[6] He was aware of strong anti-Czech feeling in Vienna. Later, after Richter had done as he asked and the orchestra had turned the symphony down, Dvořák found out that there were rooted objections to performing two works by a new Czech composer in successive seasons of the Philharmonic Society. Not wishing to waste any more time, Dvořák offered his Symphony to Adolf Čech, who performed it at the Slavonic Concert in Prague on 25 March 1881. In gratitude for his loyalty and continued support in frustrating circumstances, Richter was given the dedication.

The long and leisurely theme with which the Symphony commences is found before long to possess rather greater dramatic potential than might at first have been suspected. The Adagio remains entirely characteristic of Dvořák despite the initial debt it owes to the Adagio molto of Beethoven's Ninth Symphony. The finale has a splendid sense of movement and ends the work in a blaze of glory. But for racy vivacity, virility and originality the scherzo is outstanding. It is a furiant, that is a swaggerers' or obstinate fellows' dance, with a charmingly bucolic trio. The classic model for all true furiants is the folksong 'Sedlák, sedlák', well known to all Czechs, and the direct inspiration for a familiar example of this dance in *The Bartered Bride*. Dvořák's theme adopts the alternation of seemingly three 2/4 bars (or one 3/2 bar) with two bars of 3/4, as in the model:

Sedlák, sedlák

---

6 Undated letter from Dvořák to Richter, presumably written at the beginning of March. On 7 March 1881, Brahms reported to Simrock that Richter had given the Symphony the requested run-through.

and then shortly afterwards he enlivens matters by presenting the conflicting rhythms simultaneously.

Not long after Simrock published the D major Symphony, performances were taking place in half a dozen different countries, and generally the new work was so well received as to contribute greatly towards establishing Dvořák as one of the foremost composers of his generation. Paul Klengel appears to have led the way by presenting it at the eighth Euterpe concert at Leipzig on 14 February 1882. The brilliant, majestically flowing first movement was greatly admired by Moritz Vogel, who was also impressed by 'the fine manner with which the composer divides the orchestra into groups and then reunites them again, reminding us of that great strategist Beethoven'.[7] August Manns, ever on the alert for promising new works, performed it at the Crystal Palace on 22 April, and Richter, who had been unable to introduce it to London the previous year when it was still in manuscript, repeated it at St James's Hall on 15 May. Vienna heard the Symphony on 18 February 1883, but not at a Philharmonic Society concert; instead, it was directed by Gericke in a Gesellschaft der Musikfreunde programme.[8]

There was great excitement in the cultural circles of Bohemia in 1881, the year of the inauguration of the new National Theatre, an event which the crown prince had promised to grace with his presence. It was more than three years since Dvořák had written an opera, and with the promise of improved prospects he was impatient to start on another. Early in January he became extremely interested in a four-act libretto on the subject of the Russian pretender, Dimitrij (Boris Godunov's

7 *Leipziger Tageblatt*, 16 February 1883.

8 During the 1882–3 season the D major Symphony was also heard at Graz (26 November), Budapest (6 December, conducted by Erkel), New York (6 January, Theodore Thomas, Philharmonic Society), Frankfurt-am-Main (16 February, C. Müller), Cologne (20 February, Hiller), Breslau (13 March, B. Schulz) and Amsterdam (15 March, Cäcilia concert.)

successor to the imperial throne), which was handed to him by the conductor of the Provisional Theatre, J. N. Maýr.[9] When he told Maýr he was anxious to meet the gentleman who wrote it, he was surprised to hear that the librettist wore skirts. He learned that she was Marie Červinková-Riegrová, daughter of the statesman Dr Ladislav Rieger and granddaughter of the historian and patriot František Palacký. Foreseeing that there might be trouble in store if he accepted a libretto from such a source, Dvořák hesitated.

He had no wish to become involved in any unpleasantness with Smetana, whom he greatly admired as the father figure of Czech music, and whom he had staunchly supported when a powerful campaign was mounted in 1872 to oust him from his conducting post at the theatre. Smetana regarded Rieger as an arch-enemy and was well aware of Maýr's hostility to him. Dvořák wisely sought the advice of the editor and critic V. V. Zelený, who was a good friend and supporter of Smetana. Zelený, however, could see no strong objection to accepting this text; so when some modifications had been made to it in accordance with the composer's suggestions, Dvořák began sketching the new work on 8 May. For the convenience of Crown Prince Rudolf, the National Theatre's inauguration was advanced to 11 June, which meant there would have to be a second opening at the commencement of the autumn season. Smetana had the satisfaction of knowing that his great festival opera *Libuše*, completed in 1872 and still unperformed, would be given at the first of these, but he became extremely angry when the news reached him that *Libuše* would be replaced by *Dimitrij* at the autumn opening. Had the Theatre Association bothered to check, they would have realized that there was far too little time available for Dvořák to complete his grand opera. He did not finish the sketch until October, and making allowance for interruptions, the full score occupied him from 11 December to 16 August 1882, leaving the overture still unwritten. The nation was horrified to hear that their fine new theatre was burnt to the ground on 12 August 1881, so no second opening was possible in any case.

With the support of a strong cast of singers, Moric Anger conducted a very successful first performance of *Dimitrij* at the New Czech Theatre on 8 October 1882. Hanslick, noting the deafening applause that followed each act, realized that this was due to numerous German amateurs as well as to the great enthusiasm of Dvořák's compatriots.

9 Maýr resumed the conductorship following Smetana's enforced resignation, caused by the onset of his deafness.

But he was not happy about certain aspects of the action, which led to some modifications and adjustments being made soon afterwards. He was impressed, however, by Dvořák' s opera, and declared that it was 'rich in beautiful and original music, and the product of a genuine and eminent talent'.[10] Simrock was at the first night, and Bock attended the third performance.

Dvořák never took as naturally to opera as either Smetana or Janáček, but his works for the stage cannot be lightly dismissed. *Dimitrij* is a great advance on everything he had previously achieved in this important field. Hanslick, who was not known to be over-generous with praise, acknowledged that the work was 'rich in beautiful and original music', and that especially in the concerted pieces and big choruses strong effects were obtained. The four-act Meyerbeer-type libretto offered splendid opportunities for a composer as gifted as Dvořák, and as one of the greatest melodists of his century he took the fullest advantage of the lyrical possibilities. As an aid to the differentiation of the characters, like Smetana before him he created a strictly limited number of representative themes. Dimitrij has two, Xenia and Shuisky one each, and whereas Marina is frequently associated with mazurka rhythms, Ivan the Terrible's widow Marfa and the remaining dramatis personae are not identified in any such way. The powerful motif representing Dimitrij's tragic destiny and the one that reflects Xenia's sweetness and charm, which are heard at the beginning of the overture and may be regarded as the key to the whole work, are shown here:

10 *Neue Freie Presse*, 17 October 1882; English translation in *The Musical World*, ix (4 November 1882), pp. 683–4.

Hanslick was glad for Dvořák's sake that *Dimitrij* was so successful, for, as he remarked, 'he is as modest as he is talented.' Another aspect of the composer's character is revealed by a request which he made to Simrock: 'Many thanks for your kindness to my father, but please don't ever mention this in your letters to me'.[11] This suggests that he may not have wanted his wife to know he had asked his publisher to make regular payments out of his fees to his ageing and impoverished father. A little before this time, on 17 August 1881, he was overjoyed at the birth of his daughter Magda.

While Dvořák was immersed in the sketch for his opera, Hellmesberger reminded him that he had promised to write a Quartet, which the violinist wanted for the approaching season. Dvořák replied immediately, saying he was working on his opera in the mornings and the Quartet in the afternoons, and he was confident 'the dear Lord will whisper a few melodies to me.'[12] He was not satisfied with his first movement in F major, and so started again, this time in C major. A Press announcement early in November saying his new Quartet would be played on 15 December gave him a jolt, because he had not even reached the finale. However, by 10 November the String Quartet in C, op. 61, was finished. As it happens the Vienna performance could not take place, for just then concert arrangements were seriously upset by the fire at the Ringtheater. Dvořák dedicated the Quartet to Hellmesberger, but the first performance was given in Berlin on 2 November 1882 by the Joachim Quartet.[13] It was then heard on the 14th in Cologne, played by the Heckmann Quartet.

The C major Quartet may not have the 'exotic' colouring found in the Sexter or E flat String Quartet, but it is a typical Dvořákian composition and has a beautifully written first movement that is so full of interest that there is no apparent justification for the work's comparative neglect. As early as the third bar there is a hint of the broader than average tonal range that lies ahead. The second subject is seen to straddle two keys, E flat major and G major, and when this returns in the recapitulation, it is a pleasant surprise to find it does not approach the tonic key via A flat major, but makes straight for C major from where it moves off to E major. The scherzo has a thematic link with the first movement's main theme, and is coupled with a delightful Trio.

11 Letter of 1 November 1881 from Dvořák to Simrock.
12 Letter of 1 October 1881 from Dvořák to Hellmesberger.
13 Šourek was unaware of any performances earlier than Heckmann's at Bonn on 6 December. Hellmesberger is not known to have played this Quartet publicly.

Early in 1881 there were signs at the Vienna Court Opera of increasing interest in Dvořák's work. Jauner was extremely keen to stage *The Cunning Peasant*, and on 24 March he bought the exclusive performing rights for the Austrian capital.[14] Three months later he acquired similar rights for the one-act opera *The Stubborn Lovers*, and then began negotiating with Pollini for performances of both works at Hamburg, and encouraged Ernst von Schuch to mount *The Cunning Peasant* at Dresden. Because of these moves, Simrock decided to issue vocal scores of the two operas and the full score of *The Cunning Peasant*, the Vienna performance of which seemed assured. While the solo, choral and band parts were being copied in readiness for the Vienna performance, Jauner was trying to see if Dvořák could be enticed into composing a German opera especially for Vienna, but there was no positive response from the composer just then. Jauner's growing expectations for a successful launching of Dvořák's comic opera received a crippling blow when he discovered that Wilhelm Jahn, his successor as director of the Court Opera, had rejected this work because of its weak libretto. He found this quite incomprehensible.[15] He immediately offered to arrange a Hamburg performance and to contact Count Platen at Dresden, and in three weeks he obtained from Pollini an offer of 2,000 marks for the German and Austrian performing rights, which he assumed included royalties.[16] Meanwhile the Dresden Court Opera had reserved the right for the first German performance.

So on 24 October 1882 Dvořák was able to see his comic opera presented for the first time in the Saxon capital in the presence of the Queen. He was tremendously elated by the experience. Paul Bulss, as the prince, sang his aria superbly and was encored, and the composer received an ovation at the end of each act. Dvořák's one regret was that Simrock was not there to witness his triumph. The critic of the *Dresdner Nachrichten* found the opera just as delightful as Delibes' *Le roi l'a dit*, and would have liked to have heard the whole work repeated the same evening. The opera was less well supported after the first night, and was taken off after the fourth performance.

When the opera was mounted at Hamburg on 3 January 1883, the critics agreed that the libretto and translation were unsatisfactory, but

14 On signing the contract, Dvořák received 250 gulden, and after every twenty-five performances he would receive a further 250 gulden.

15 Letter of 13 February 1882 from Jauner to Dvořák. The unpublished letters from Jauner to Dvořák are in the possession of Dvořák's heirs.

16 Since Jauner already held the rights for Vienna the terms of the contract were changed; letter from Jauner of 5 March. Pollini sent the amended contract and 2,000 marks on 18 March.

they praised the music.[17] According to V. Hock the experience that is needed to achieve broad dramatic strokes was lacking, but 'enough remains that is beautiful, striking, even enchanting . . .'[18] Although the Hamburg audience was less responsive than that at Dresden, their appreciation led him to regard the opera as a success. Unfortunately the composer was not able to be there.

Between these two productions, Dvořák heard with pleasure that he had been made an honorary member of the Umělecká beseda, and then on 15 December he was saddened by the death of his mother, an event which cast a shadow over the Christmas festivities. In the first months of the new year he wrote the Piano Trio in F minor, op. 65, a work which reveals for the first time the self-criticism, the intensity and depth of feeling and the dramatic power of which he was capable. Recognition, he was fully aware, brought with it fresh responsibilities, and in particular an awareness of the need to aim considerably higher in all his creative work. This magnificent Trio is the only chamber music work by Dvořák to which the term epic is applicable. It starts with a *pianissimo* theme of tremendous intensity, as fine or even finer than any other of his main themes:

which when the piano joins in explodes in a *fortissimo*. This theme and an epigrammatic motif that comes after it form the basis of the action that follows, while a long expressive cello melody offers respite from the tension. Finally, an inflected version of the main theme brings the movement to a pathetic close. We may be certain that writing this Trio did more than a little to pave the way for the creation of the next epic work, the Symphony in D minor, op. 70. In a single instance the ultimate version of a theme from the Trio's Poco adagio was transformed to become the principal theme of the Symphony's finale (Allegro):

---

17 In his German translation Züngl had transferred the action from Bohemia to Upper Austria. But as Hock pointed out: 'The ever independent Austrian farmer does not fall on his knees before the lord of the manor and kiss the hem of his cloak.'

18 *Hamburger Nachrichten*, 4 January 1883.

During the spring and summer two more orchestral works were completed: the brilliant *Scherzo capriccioso*, which Adolf Čech presented to the Prague public on 16 May, and the *Hussite* Overture. This second work was intended as the Prelude to a patriotic trilogy dealing with the origins of the Hussite movement which the director of the National Theatre, F. A. Šubert, intended to write. He abandoned the trilogy after the first act. The Hussites were primarily regarded by Dvořák and his fellow countrymen as staunch fighters for the rights of the Czechs, and so there is nothing incongruous in the fact that Dvořák, a Catholic, should take as his two main themes the fifteenth-century melody 'St Wenceslas' and the celebrated Hussite chorale 'Ye who are God's Warriors'. On 7 March, before either of these two works was written, the composer's son Antonín was born.

Usually Dvořák's music needed the initial stimulus that publication in Berlin or Leipzig could give before adequate appreciation by the musical public was possible. This is certainly true of the *Stabat Mater*, completed late in 1877 and performed for the first time in Prague on 23 December 1880—a very curious season for such a work. No further performances took place until Janáček conducted it at Brno on 2 April 1882, some five months after it had been issued by Simrock. Ever since he had devoted the greater part of two feuilletons to Dvořák's music, Max Schütz, the Budapest critic, was making an effort to promote Dvořák's music.[19] Now came his big opportunity, and as a direct result the Musical Society of Budapest presented the *Stabat Mater* under the direction of Imre Bellovits three days after Janáček's performance. But it seems to have been Joseph Barnby's performance of this work at the Royal Albert Hall, London, on 10 March 1883 that sparked off a whole series of performances in England and the United States. American choral societies were a year ahead of similar organizations in Germany and Austria.[20]

19 In his articles 'Regentage in Ischl' which appeared in *Pester Lloyd* on 19 and 20 October 1880 he reviewed several of Dvořák's works. He said of the D minor Serenade: 'Only a master writes like this; only a poet by God's grace has such inspiration'. Among contemporary composers, he particularly admired Brahms, Dvořák and Robert Volkmann.

Barnby's successful concert was also influential in helping to bring about another important development, one that marks the beginning of a new stage in Dvořák's career as a composer. On 3 August 1883 Henry Hersee, the secretary of the Philharmonic Society of London, sent him the following invitation:

I have the pleasure to inform you that, at the last Meeting of the Directors of this Society, it was unanimously resolved that 'Herr Dvořák be invited to produce an orchestral selection (Suite or Overture) during the Society's Seventy-second Season (1884)'.

The Concerts of that Season will take place in February, March, April and May of next year. I shall therefore be glad to be favoured by you with an early reply stating whether you can accept this Invitation of the Directors and whether it would be agreeable to you to attend the Concert and conduct the performance of the work.

20 B. J. Lang introduced five numbers to Boston on 24 January 1884 and the whole work on 15 January 1885. Thomas conducted the *Stabat* in New York on 3 April and 13 November 1884, and Retter gave it at Pittsburgh on 21 June that year. It was performed in Vienna on 19 April 1885, and at Mannheim at about the same time.

5 The Visits to England

Obviously very keenly attracted by Dvořák's music, and noticing how rapidly it was finding favour in England, Oscar Beringer, the virtuoso pianist, decided to commission a piano concerto from the rising Czech composer. So, without being aware that Dvořák had already written one, he made his request a month before the Philharmonic Society issued their invitation.[1] By good fortune, Hainauer of Breslau had just published the G minor Concerto, in excellent time for the approaching concert season. Soon afterwards the two men met in Prague to discuss the matter, and Beringer offered to give his new friend hospitality when he came to London. With the pianist's concert at the Crystal Palace close at hand, Dvořák wrote to August Manns to thank him for the interest he had shown in his music, and at the same time told him that three of his compositions which had not so far been heard in England, the Violin Concerto, the *Nocturne* for strings and the *Scherzo capriccioso*, were either in print or being prepared for publication.[2] Beringer played the Piano Concerto at Manns's concert on 13 October 1883.[3]

Apart from the Philharmonic Society concert, Dvořák's impending visit to London led to other interesting possibilities. Alfred Littleton, writing on 21 November on behalf of his father's firm Novello, Ewer & Co, told Dvořák they were trying to see whether there was a chance of more of his music being performed and conducted by him during his stay. In particular they were hoping for a performance of his *Stabat Mater*. He also inquired if Dvořák would be prepared to compose a secular cantata for solo, chorus and orchestra for 'a big English festival' in 1885.[4] In reply Dvořák said it would only be possible for him to

1 Letter of 8 July 1883 from Beringer to Dvořák, in the possession of the composer's heirs.

2 Letter of 10 September 1883 from Dvořák to Manns; *vide* H. Saxe Wyndham: *August Manns and the Saturday Concerts* (London 1909).

3 Henry Hersee, critic of the *Observer* and Philharmonic Society secretary, was inclined to think this the best piano concerto to have appeared for a decade (*Observer*, 14 October 1883). A very detailed and unfavourable review by A. Naubert was published two years later in *Neue Zeitschrift für Musik*, lxxxi (1885), pp. 129–30 and 141–3.

4 Letter of 21 November 1883 in A. Littleton's handwriting to Dvořák, in the possession of Dvořák's heirs.

conduct the *Stabat* after the Philharmonic concert on 7 May was over. He was perfectly willing to compose the cantata, if Novello were prepared to acquire the rights for all countries for a fee of 5,000 German marks (£200).[5] Novello accepted these terms immediately. Dvořák had become keener to present his *Stabat Mater* when he discovered that the 525 marks (20 guineas) he was due to receive for conducting the *Hussite* Overture, the D major Symphony and second *Slavonic Rhapsody* at the Philharmonic concert would not cover his travelling expenses. However, the matter rested with the Society, for they had the first claim on him.[6] In order to make the second concert possible, the Society advanced the date of their concert to 20 March, and they were also willing for him to appear at the Royal Albert Hall a week earlier for the choral concert.

Dvořák's visit to London provided August Manns with a unique opportunity. Two days after the *Stabat Mater* performance Joachim would be playing a Mozart concerto at the Crystal Palace, and he was willing to play Dvořák's A minor Concerto as well, in which case Manns decided that it must be conducted by Dvořák himself. The composer gave Simrock the impression that everything was settled,[7] but he may have sensed there would be difficulties. The Philharmonic Society was allowing him to conduct a choral programme a few days before their own orchestral concert, because they had no choir and so were not in a position to perform the *Stabat Mater* themselves. They were entirely responsible for bringing him to London, and therefore could not possibly allow him to appear as composer-conductor on 15 March in a programme similar to their own on the 20th. They had no objection to Joachim playing Dvořák's concerto if Manns conducted.[8] In consequence of their ban, the concerto was dropped from the programme. This was the nearest that Joachim ever came to performing the work which he helped to create and which was dedicated to him. Manns made up for his disappointment by engaging Dvořák to conduct the *Nocturne* and *Scherzo capriccioso* on the 22nd.

The next request came from the Leeds Musical Festival. Their

5 Letter of 11 January 1884 from Dvořák to Novello (Dvořák Museum). Littleton in fact paid £250 for the cantata.

6 Undated letter from Dvořák to the Philharmonic Society (R.P. S. archives).

7 On 5 March 1884, the day he left Prague, Dvořák informed Simrock: '*Joachim* spielt Violinkonzert, und ich dirigiere im Krystallpalast.'

8 Hersee explained the Society's action in a letter dated 26 March 1884 to the *Musical World* (published 29 March). Manns informed Zavertal of the Society's 'prohibition' in his letter of 11 March; *vide* H. G. Farmer: *Cavaliere Zavertal and the Royal Artillery Band* (London 1951), p. 69.

committee wanted Dvořák to write a sacred choral work for their 1886 festival and to come to Leeds to conduct it. After consideration the composer expressed his willingness to write an oratorio, 'an important work', although he knew that Leeds was hoping for a shorter sacred cantata. His request for a fee of £100 satisfied them provided he promised them the first performance.[9] While he was in London, a demand came from yet another source. This caused him to return to England in September to conduct the *Stabat Mater* at the Three Choirs Festival, at 'Worcester' as he told his father.[10] By accepting all these offers, this first visit paved the way for three more in fairly rapid succession, and another visit was shortly to be added to the list. Dvořák realized that in the months ahead he would be completely occupied writing commissioned works for his English friends.

Much attention has been given to the belief that Littleton offered Dvořák £2,000 for his oratorio (*St Ludmila*). It is curious, however, that he should have been ready to pay ten times as much as the composer demanded in return for the publishing and performing rights in all countries for his cantata (*The Spectre's Bride*). The truth is that no sum of money was agreed to during Dvořák's visit, and the first mention of the need to settle terms does not occur in the correspondence until almost two years later. Dvořák hoped to receive £1,000, whereas Littleton had been expecting to pay £500. They finally compromised at £650, on 20 February 1886, with the proviso that if the composer proved to be right in thinking his work would be a great success, Littleton would give him an additional £350. In his letter to the publisher, Dvořák commented (in English): 'I believe your proposal is for you and me a very fine one'. After the initial enthusiastic welcome for *St Ludmila*, it was far from being a success.[11]

Final preparations were made for what was to be one of the most momentous and unforgettable events in the composer's life. He was leaping into the unknown, and was rather apprehensive about this. Since he did not understand English at that time, he would have to rely on German, which might not be understood. He was most insistent that

9 Letter of 25 March 1884 from Dvořák to F. R. Spark, and Spark's reply to this; *vide* F. R. Spark and J. Bennett: *History of the Leeds Musical Festival, 1858–1889*, 2nd edn (Leeds 1892).

10 Letter of 21 March 1884 from Dvořák to his father.

11 The matter is referred to and discussed in Alfred Littleton's letters to Dvořák of 29 January and 4 and 15 February 1886, which are in the custody of Dvořák's heirs. Dvořák's final acceptance appears in his letter in English of 20 February 1886, an autograph draft of which is in the Dvořák Museum, Prague. It is regrettable that Šourek overlooked these English letters of Littleton, and consequently lent the weight of his authority to the false statement concerning Dvořák's remuneration, which can only have been based on the flimsiest of evidence.

Zavertal should meet him at Dover, or even at Calais, and because he did not fancy journeying so far alone, he arranged for a pianist friend, Jindřich von Kaan, to accompany him. They broke their journey at Cologne and Brussels, were duly joined by Zavertal at Dover, and were met by Alfred Littleton and Beringer at Victoria station. On the following day, Sunday 9 March, Dvořák went to Woolwich to see Zavertal, with whom Kaan was staying, and on Monday he took the first choral rehearsal at the Albert Hall. He was astounded by the size of the hall and by the fact that he had more than 700 singers under his control, and was deeply moved when they greeted him enthusiastically. He accepted Alfred Littleton's invitation for the following evening, looking forward to having a pleasant time with his charming new friend, only to find he was the guest of honour at a banquet for 150 people, at which his music was played exclusively, and the proceedings went on until 2.30 a.m.

Madame Patey and Edward Lloyd sang splendidly when the *Stabat Mater* was performed on 13 March, but most of the laurels went to Dvořák. The audience's enthusiasm grew with each number, and at the end the composer was recalled many times. This wonderful reception convinced him that a new era was beginning to dawn for him, and he hoped that this would be beneficial to Czech art. On the previous day he had revisited Woolwich to attend the Royal Artillery symphony concert, at which Zavertal presented his Czech friend's *My Home* Overture, with the mistaken impression he was giving the first English performance.[12] Beringer invited the critics to meet Dvořák at a dinner party on the 14th, and during the course of the evening they listened to the F minor Trio.[13] Barnby, Prout of the *Athenaeum*, and C. A. Barry were among the guests, but the Czech composer's doughty champion, Joseph Bennett, the critic of the *Daily Telegraph*, and Francis Hueffer of *The Times* were apparently unable to be present.[14] When Hueffer, a keen Wagnerian, called on Dvořák shortly afterwards and the latter played him his *Hussite* Overture on the piano, it made a deep impression.

The Czech master scored another triumph at the Philharmonic Society concert on the 20th. The audience, shedding their customary

---

12 The Overture had been introduced by Manns at the Crystal Palace on 12 May 1883.

13 Fuller-Maitland had played the Trio at a charity concert at Kensington in January, Dawnreuther presented it on 27 February, and Hallé played it on 31 March at a Monday Pop.

14 The *Musical Standard* for 22 March 1884 lists some of the guests. J. Bennett wrote very appreciatively on Dvořák's music in the *Musical Times* in 1881, and contributed another article on the composer in April 1884.

restraint, were electrified by the D major Symphony's scherzo—a Czech furiant—and insisted on William J. Winch, the American tenor, repeating 'Songs my mother taught me' from the *Gipsy Melodies*. The one work that was new, the *Hussite* Overture, was very highly praised by the critics, and the *Pall Mall Gazette* commented: 'We have no desire to herald in a Dvořák mania, or to hear nothing but Dvořák till midsummer, and we are threatened by something like it. Still if each season we must have a musical lion, we might go further and fare worse.' At the Crystal Palace two days later Dvořák conducted the two novelties, the *Nocturne* for strings and the *Scherzo capriccioso*, and this time he accompanied Winch in his two songs from the *Gipsy Melodies*. On this occasion the hall was not quite full. The audience was carried away by the impetuosity and animation of the *Scherzo capriccioso*. Writing about this in the *Athenaeum*, Ebenezer Prout declared: 'The work has immense fire and spirit, and is most brilliantly scored for the orchestra. It made a great effect, as indeed it could not fail to do'. Two evenings later another banquet was given in honour of the distinguished Czech visitor, this time by the Philharmonic Society.

As his visit was drawing to a close, Francis Hueffer paid this tribute to Dvořák and made a prophecy:

> . . . those who have come in personal contact with the composer have been charmed by a singularly unassuming and simple nature, unspoilt by rapid success and bent upon its artistic aim alone. The general public has formed a most favourable idea of the rising star, and those who have studied the progressive development of the new composer's works have reason to expect that his consciousness of addressing no longer a local circle of admirers but the musical world generally, will enlarge his views and strengthen his purposes. It is probable, in short, that we have not yet heard the best of what Herr Dvořák has to say.[15]

In addition to commissions for big choral works for Birmingham and Leeds and the conducting engagement at the Three Choirs Festival, Dvořák was asked by the Philharmonic Society to compose a symphony for them, and he apparently agreed before he left London.[16] During

---

15 *The Times*, 24 March 1884.

16 A hitherto unknown letter in German, dated 7 July 1884, from Dvořák to A. Littleton, begins as follows: 'You know that I gave you my promise to write a new symphony for the Philharmonic Society. I want to keep my word!' It is clear from this that he had given his promise some time before, and it seems extremely probable that the request and his promise were made verbally towards the end of his stay in London.

midsummer a letter came from the Society to tell him he had been elected an honorary member, and no doubt reminding him of his promised symphony, the première of which they hoped he would conduct during their next season. A few months earlier at the Philharmonic Society banquet, Dvořák had attempted to make a little speech in English in reply to Sir Julius Benedict's toast. He now seized the opportunity of replying to the Society with a letter dated 3 July, written in the best English he could command:

I have received your letter and think you for it. The news of the rarely distinction give me very great honour and pleasure. I take my the liberty to beg you mine greatest thankfulness to express to the directory of the celebrated Philharmonic Society.

He followed this up four days later with a letter in German, repeating his promise and saying he would write the symphony directly the cantata for Birmingham was finished.

Dvořák took with him V. J. Novotný, the journalist and critic, on his second visit to England. They left Prague on 30 August and spent an entire day at Brussels where they made sure they did not miss any of the principal sights. Henry Littleton, the elderly proprietor of the Novello firm, met them at Dover and drove them in his carriage from there to Westwood House, his magnificent mansion at Sydenham, where they stayed for a few days. It was being rumoured that summer that during the coming season the Czech composer would be visiting the United States,[17] where he already had a considerable following. Hearing that his distinguished contemporary was about to arrive in London, Dudley Buck, the American composer, delayed his departure from there so that he could meet him. He offered him hospitality during his American trip. It is not known what approaches may have been made to tempt Dvořák to make the long journey, but Novotný reported that he was gradually becoming reconciled to the idea, provided he was made a reasonable offer.[18] After this we hear nothing more about any such proposal until preparations for the Columbian tercentenary were under way.

After a rehearsal with Emma Albani, Janet Patey, Edward Lloyd and

---

17 *Neue Zeitschrift für Musik*, lxxx (18 July 1884).

18 Report in *Dalibor*. Novotný wrote about Dvořák's second visit to England in the article, 'S Dvořákem v Anglii', *Hudební revue*, iv (1911), pp. 444–8.

Charles Santley, Dvořák's soloists in the *Stabat Mater*, he left for
Worcester, where he found his portrait was on sale in the shops and
admirers asked for his autograph as he walked around the streets.
Dvořák's compositions were planned to form the climax to the Three
Choirs Festival. The *Stabat Mater*, followed by *St Paul*, were sung
in the cathedral on the morning of 11 September, after which Lord
and Lady Compton gave a reception for 300 guests, but due to an
unfortunate oversight, the composer received no invitation. The D
major Symphony was the main item in the orchestral concert that
evening. The tumultuous welcome given to the composer as he
approached the rostrum continued for several minutes, holding up the
proceedings, and similar demonstrations occurred after each movement. Finally Dvořák was given a tremendous ovation. All this took
Novotný completely by surprise, and he was inclined to see it 'not as a
superficial kind of enthusiasm, but rather as an understanding and a
genuine appreciation such as has hitherto not generally been shown to
Dvořák at home'.

When nearing the end of work on *The Spectre's Bride*, Dvořák went
to Berlin to conduct an extra Philharmonic Society concert, designed to
consist solely of his own music. Joachim was expected to play the
Violin Concerto, but for some unexplained reason he did not do so.
At the concert on 21 November, only two of Dvořák's works were
played, the Piano Concerto, with Anna Grosser-Rilke as soloist, and
the *Hussite* Overture, which was preferred. Six days later Dvořák
completed his cantata.

While Dvořák retained vivid memories of basking in the sunlight
of his London audiences' wholehearted acclaim, a letter from Hanslick
arrived as a sharp reminder that he was faced with a perplexing
dilemma. Two years earlier the Vienna critic had recommended him to
make himself familiar with fine German poetry and set this to music.
His public expected big works from him, but it was unsatisfactory if
he set Czech texts for limited audiences, and the big German public
was fobbed off with bad translations.[19] In his letter of 3 May 1884
Hanslick told Dvořák that Baron Hoffmann, generalintendant of the
Court Opera in Vienna, hoped he would compose an opera for their
1885 or 1886 season; and he intended to commission an opera text on
the kind of subject that Dvořák favoured from the leading librettist,

---

19 Letter of 11 June 1882. This and the letter of 3 May 1884 appear in my article, 'Dvořák's
relations with Brahms and Hanslick', *Musical Quarterly*, lvii (1971), pp. 241ff. The German text
of the letters is given in *Hudební věda*, x (1973), on pp. 219–21.

Dvořák at the time of his first
visit to London (1884)

Joseph Joachim's London
quartet: Joachim, Ries, Straus
and Piatti

Seben Hundred and Second Popular Concert.
(February 16th, 1880.)

Hoch!

Dvořák's cottage at Vysoká and the summer house in which he frequently composed

Dvořák with his pigeons at Vysoká

Hugo Wittmann. There was a dearth of distinguished Germanic composers for the stage at that time, and Dvořák was consequently seen to stand head and shoulders above everyone.

This tempting proposition aroused his inherent ambition. He now knew what it was to win fame abroad, but whereas the English were free to rally to him in an unrestrained manner, the situation was rather different in Vienna, where political complications and prejudices existed. Basically his dilemma hinged on the question of loyalty. In his earlier letter Hanslick had thought it would be an advantage for his friend to live for one or two years in Vienna, and said this would not mean he would become a renegade. It was impossible for Dvořák to bring himself to take such a step, but to write a German opera for the Wiener Hofoper would be a less drastic move. If he did that, would he be acting disloyally to his own people? This was the crux of the matter.

Composing *The Spectre's Bride* does not seem to have caused the composer any serious trouble, for the circumstances were just right. He sketched it in just over seven weeks while he and his family were staying for the summer on the estate of his brother-in-law, Count Kaunitz, at Vysoká, which he loved, doing most of his work in the summer-house. He was able to write to Göbl: 'Thank God that this time my guardian angel has not deserted me, and since he is always so dear to me, how could it be otherwise. I believe (and you will see that I am not deceiving myself) that that work will excel in every respect those that precede it, not excepting the *Stabat*. But please don't mention this to anyone . . .' On the other hand, the F minor Trio (February-May [?] 1883) and the Symphony in D minor, op. 70 (December 1884-March 1885), written for London, caused him a great deal of trouble. Šourek has quite rightly linked these two works with the composer's spiritual crisis, and his struggle to resolve this to the satisfaction of his conscience. This must certainly have played a key role in helping Dvořák to create works possessing greater dramatic power, deeper emotional feeling and a breadth of vision unparalleled in anything else he had previously composed. It is also true that he knew how wrong it would be to rest on his laurels, continuing to write the type of nationalist music which thrilled his audiences, and how essential it was to strive to achieve the best of which he was capable.[20]

We can see how determined Dvořák was to compose a really outstanding symphony for his English friends from some passages in his

20 The sketches and early drafts of these works reveal how self-critical he was, and how much he rejected as unworthy.

letters. In February 1885 he wrote this to Simrock: '. . . I have been busy for a long, long time over my new symphony, but I want to justify Brahms's words when he said, "I imagine your symphony will be quite unlike this one (D major)." There shall be no grounds for thinking he was wrong.' On 13 December 1884 he had told Judge Rus: 'I am occupied at present with my new symphony (for London), and wherever I go I think of nothing but my work, which must be capable of stirring the world, and may God grant that it will!' This symphony took him twice as long to write as the previous one, so he was greatly relieved when he finished it on 17 March, only five weeks before the London première.[21] He usually wrote 'Bohu díky!' (Thanks be to God) at the end of his compositions, in much the same way that Haydn wrote 'Laus Deo', but during the crisis he was passing through he failed to do so. His return to this former custom on the completion of the D minor Symphony is assumed to be an indication that his dilemma was resolved once and for all—he had no intention of providing Vienna with a German opera.

Dvořák's music gives the impression of being extremely fluent and spontaneous and natural, which has led a number of distinguished musicians to assume that since composition was for him an instinctive process, there was no need for him to think as he wrote. If these men had attempted to find out how Dvořák set about composing, they would surely have been greatly astonished. If only they had compared the first completed version of the Trio in F minor with the published score and had examined the continuous sketch for the B minor Cello Concerto with the work as they had heard it in the concert hall; if only they had pondered over the ten attempts that the Czech composer made to shape the main theme of the G major Symphony's finale to his personal satisfaction, or perhaps had studied the sketch for the Symphony in D minor, op. 70, and taken note of the deletions and revisions in every movement and on every page, they would have known how completely wrong they were. The miracle is that his music sounds so fresh and spontaneous.

Dvořák made three attempts at sketching the beginning of the D minor Symphony, writing twenty-four bars the first time and nearly twice as many the next time, but since neither of these was satisfactory

---

21 Reporting the completion of the symphony to Simrock on 25 March 1885, he said: 'You might be interested to know that there is another new opus in our family (a boy)! So you see a new symphony and a boy as well! How is that for creative energy?' Otakar II was born on 9 February.

he felt obliged to try again. His original version, allowing for some early but comparatively minor changes of mind, was as given here; and below, for comparison, the same passage appears in the form in which we know it today:

The theme occurred to Dvořák after witnessing the arrival of the festival train that brought patriots from Budapest to Prague. The weakness of the original form it took is due largely to its insistence on dominant harmony from the eighth bar onwards. By rejecting this and substituting an ambiguous diminished seventh at that crucial point, he introduced a significant element of instability, and with it a valuable potential for drama. In the recapitulation, which follows an unusually concise development, the first fifty or so bars of the exposition are missing, to good purpose. By leading straight into the *fortissimo* tutti statement of the principal theme, Dvořák ensured there would be no reduction in the dramatic temperature. The Poco adagio, the most profound of Dvořák's slow movements, is based on a pensive melody in F major which becomes impassioned, a theme without precedent in musical literature which seems to plumb the depths of despair, and a horn melody that provides balm. The additional pathos that the countermelody for treble woodwind gives to the second theme on its return cannot fail to attract attention. Conceived originally as a furiant, the scherzo retains strong links with this dance, even though disguised by the 6/4 time signature. Lastly comes the tragic finale, which drives on towards its catharsis in the final bars, marked by a majestic change from minor to major.[22] Without doubt this must surely be Dvořák's greatest symphony.

Dvořák brought yet another friend with him on his third visit to England, the professor of Czech linguistics Dr Josef Zubatý. Their host, Alfred Littleton, and Alexander C. Mackenzie, who had been anxious to meet the Czech composer, met their train on 19 April. The Philharmonic Society concert on the 22nd was attended by the Duke and Duchess of Edinburgh, and was unquestionably a great occasion. Prout observed that 'the enthusiasm at the end of [Dvořák's] work was such as is rarely seen at a Philharmonic concert', and he remarked that 'Dvořák's music is equally interesting, and we may say satisfying, to adherents of the conservative and the progressive schools of art'. Hueffer, the Wagnerian, disagreed with him. According to him, 'The entire work is painted *gris-en-gris*, it lacks the sweetness of melody and light of rhythm, it is lugubrious without that pathos of sadness which is more elevating than joy itself'. Very characteristically, Joseph Bennett found it to be an intensely Czech work; and Bernard Shaw, writing for *Our Corner*, praised it warmly with these words: 'The quick transitions from liveliness to mourning, the variety of rhythm and figure, the

22 The finale's powerful first theme is quoted on p. 60.

spirited movement, the occasional abrupt and melancholy pauses, and the characteristic harmonic progressions of Bohemian music, are all coordinated in the sonata form by Herr Dvořák with rare success.'[23]

After some hesitation, Dvořák decided to extend his stay in London, because Franz Rummel was due to play his piano concerto on 6 May at the next Philharmonic concert, and his patriotic cantata, 'The Heirs of the White Mountain', recently published by Novello, was to be sung by Mr Geaussent's Choir a week later. This meant that he was able to conduct both performances, and still be back home in time for the Prague première of The Spectre's Bride.[24] Dvořák and Zubatý took the opportunity of attending several concerts and listening to English church music in St Paul's cathedral, and they went to see Goring Thomas's Nadeshda at Drury Lane Theatre. They visited friends, going twice to Woolwich to see Zavertal, and Dvořák was the guest of honour at the 147th anniversary dinner of the Royal Society of Musicians. The Raphael Madonna in the National Gallery impressed them greatly when they saw it on one of their sightseeing jaunts, which sometimes occupied the entire day.

Dvořák's second concert was just as successful as the first, and this time Hueffer was entirely satisfied. He described the Piano Concerto as 'one of the composer's most felicitous efforts . . . and infinitely more spontaneous than the symphony'. At the choral concert the enthusiasm does not appear to have been at quite so high a pitch, but the critics offered warm words of praise for this revised version of Dvořák's thirteen-year-old cantata.

Now that Dvořák found it was no longer quite such a struggle to fend for his wife and their still increasing family of five children, he was able to realize his long-cherished dream of buying a modest house in the country where they could all spend the summer months. He purchased a small farmstead consisting of three ground-floor rooms and the land adjoining at Vysoká from Count Kaunitz, and built on to this a room upstairs where he could work when conditions were not suitable for composing in the summer-house. He was blissfully happy in this idyllic spot. He loved wandering through the woodlands early in the morning, he cultivated his land, and in the evenings enjoyed chatting with the

---

23 Shaw wrote this before he decided that it would help his campaign aimed at drawing attention to the gigantic stature of Wagner, if he decried the work of most other composers, including the nationalists and, very naturally, Brahms.

24 Dvořák had conducted the first performance of The Spectre's Bride at Pilsen on 28 March 1885. Knittl conducted the Prague performance.

villagers and miners at the inn. Before long he started on his hobby of pigeon breeding.

Dvořák's relations with Simrock were not nearly so harmonious as they had formerly been. The composer was taken aback that his publisher should have attempted to stop him performing the *Hussite* Overture in London, simply because it had already been performed and was still unpublished. Simrock complained that this Overture, the Violin Concerto, and surprisingly enough even the D major Symphony, were selling badly. He kept on reminding Dvořák of the promised set of Slavonic Dances, and asked if he could have some songs. Dvořák knew that his new D minor Symphony was a finer work than any of his earlier instrumental music, and so asked his publisher to give him 6,000 German marks for it, but Simrock was only willing to pay 3,000 marks. Dvořák objected, saying that another publisher was prepared to give him twice that sum.[25] The composer seemed ready to compromise by allowing Simrock to have four Slavonic Dances in addition if he received the full fee; but the publisher demanded eight dances, which made Dvořák hesitate. In June the two men met at Karlovy Vary (Carlsbad) and struck a bargain, the details of which are unknown.[26]

When the composer made the perfectly reasonable request that his first name should not appear in the German form 'Anton' on the title page of the Symphony, but as 'Ant.', an abbreviation for both the Czech and German forms, Simrock stubbornly refused to comply. Dvořák also asked to have the titles of his works printed in Czech, but Simrock treated this suggestion with levity and added insult to injury by making a gibe at the Czechs. This touched the composer on a very sensitive nerve, and he reacted accordingly. It was more than Dvořák could stand when Simrock next displayed his ignorance about the Austro-Czech political situation and showed his insensitivity to the feelings and aspirations of Czechs, but the composer succeeded in silencing him by a cri de coeur. '*What*', he asked in his letter of 10 September 1885. '*have we two to do with politics?* Let us be glad that we can *dedicate our services solely to the beautiful art*! And let us hope that nations who represent and *possess art* will never perish, even though they may be small. Forgive me for this, but I just wanted to tell you that an artist too has a fatherland in which he must have a firm faith and which he must love.'

25 Dvořák probably had Novello in mind, but it is not known whether Littleton hinted that he might be able to offer so much.

26 Dvořák's valuation of the D minor Symphony is seen in perspective when it is realized that less than four years earlier he accepted 2,000 marks for his D major Symphony.

Travelling alone for the first time, Dvořák arrived in England a full week before the Birmingham Musical Festival was due to begin, so that he could take preliminary rehearsals of the 500-strong chorus at Birmingham and the orchestra of 150 in London. At the weekend he went down to Brighton, where he stayed at the Littleton's seaside mansion. He was much impressed by everything, but was unprepared for such crowds of holidaymakers, and amazed, as he told Rus, to see 'the beautiful English ladies bathing here (*and publically !*)'. Several new works were being performed at Birmingham, including Cowen's *Sleeping Beauty*, Stanford's *The Three Holy Children*, Prout's Symphony in F major and Mackenzie's Violin Concerto, which Sarasate was playing; but the two main attractions were Gounod's *Mors et Vita* and Dvořák's *The Spectre's Bride*. Gounod, however, found it was impossible to be present, so Dvořák's cantata became the focus of attention. It was discussed in detail before the performance in *The Times* and the *Daily Telegraph*, and the *Birmingham Daily Post* and *Birmingham Daily Mail* devoted columns to Dvořák and his new cantata.[27]

At the performance on 27 August 1885, Dvořák experienced a greater triumph than any he had had in his life up to that time. This is how the happy composer described the scene at the end: 'There was such a shindy! They called me and shrieked "Dvořák" without ceasing. The orchestra, chorus and audience were jubilant. The ladies' choir hemmed me in and all of them wanted to press my hand and congratulate me. I didn't know what to do.'[28] The critics, including those who had been hostile to Dvořák, were unanimous in praising the cantata in glowing terms,[29] and Prout fully endorsed a remark he had heard a distinguished musician make during the performance: 'The man is a magician'. Following this phenomenal success, choral societies in the English-speaking countries hastened to prepare and present the new work, and only two and a half months after the English première on 16 November, Providence, Rhode Island, led the way. Eight days later the cantata was repeated at Birmingham and performed by Hallé in Manchester, W. L. Tomlins introduced it at Milwaukee (2 December) and Chicago (6 May), Collinson gave it in Edinburgh (1 February), Mackenzie presented it at St James's Hall, London

---

27 The *Birmingham Daily Post* published articles on 18, 21 and 25 August, and featured the Czech composer at length in two articles in their issue of 28 August 1885.

28 Letter of 2 September from Dvořák to Zubatý.

29 Ferdinand Praeger, who had described the E flat String Quartet as 'Vaudeville music' (*Musical Standard*, 8 January 1881), praised *The Spectre's Bride* very highly in *Neue Zeitschrift für Musik* lxxxi (1885), p. 393.

(2 February) and at the Crystal Palace (13 February), Manns gave two performances in Glasgow (11 and 13 February), and before the season was over Thomas had given it at Brooklyn and it was sung at Philadelphia. Early in the following season it was heard at Melbourne and Montreal.

The rapturous reception accorded to Dvořák's cantata wherever it was sung can be seen mainly as a tribute to the composer's skill and genius in presenting Erben's ballad in so imaginative and musical a form. In the *Athenaeum* Prout compared the work with Raff's *Lenore Symphony*, based on Bürger's similar ballad, pointing out that however wild and terrible the situation described, Dvořák never became ugly whereas Raff frequently did. Yet only eleven years later the English critics were deploring Dvořák's misguided choice of similar subjects from the same source for his symphonic poems, and ignoring their musical qualities. As the lovely melody of the last duet (No. 12) suggests, the demon bridegroom is a persuasive lover. The big soprano aria 'Woeful am I! Where is my Father?' and the maiden's heartfelt prayer to the Virgin, however, remain the favourite extracts. Some of the narrative choral sections unfortunately seem a trifle naïve today, but taste has changed, and consequently a whole cantata on a romantic theme of this sort is no longer as acceptable as it was a century ago.

Before Dvořák left Birmingham, R. Harding Milward, the Festival secretary, asked him if he would be willing to write 'a great sacred work' for their next Festival in 1888, to last a whole morning. The composer promised to think this over.[30] An early answer was out of the question, for at this time he had not even begun to sketch the similar work for the Leeds Festival.

Towards the end of April in the previous year, Littleton had reported to the Leeds committee that Dvořák was thinking of basing the oratorio he was writing for them on an incident drawn from Bohemian history. They were rather uneasy about this, for they were not at all sure that it would be suitable for an English audience.[31] But there was time enough in which attempts could be made to persuade the composer to think along different lines. Littleton attempted to do just this in his letter to Dvořák of 31 March 1885. After inquiring of what subject he

---

30 Letter of 22 January 1886 from Milward to Dvořák (Dvořák's heirs).

31 Spark and Bennett: *History of the Leeds Musical Festival*. In September 1883, Dvořák had anticipated that he might need to write an oratorio for England, due to the success of his *Stabat Mater* in London six months earlier. Inspired by the mounting spirit of patriotism leading up to the festive opening of the rebuilt National Theatre, at which his *Hussite* Overture was to be played for the first time, he considered subjects such as 'St Wenceslas' and 'John Hus'. According to Šourek, the poet Jaroslav Vrchlický gave him a libretto based on the life of St Ludmila.

was thinking, he said: 'In order to make a *certain success* with the English public, it is I think of the *utmost importance* that the subject should be taken from the *Bible*. I hope therefore you will kindly give this matter your most serious consideration and let me know soon what you think about it'. Following this up, Aimée Beringer, wife of the pianist, sent Dvořák some ten weeks later a 'Samson and Delilah' libretto in three parts. Dvořák, however, was awaiting the arrival of Vrchlický's revised libretto of 'St Ludmila', which was the subject on which he had set his heart. Littleton was shown Vrchlický's libretto when the composer was over for the Birmingham Festival, and then wrote to Leeds, saying: 'I find he is determined to carry out his own idea as to subject, and, as he is distinctly proving himself to be one of the greatest musical geniuses we have ever had, he must be allowed to decide for himself'. The oratorio therefore was concerned with Ludmila's conversion of her people to the Christian faith.[32] The composer began setting *St Ludmila* on 17 September 1885.

The Vienna Court Opera, influenced perhaps by the knowledge that they were not going to get a German opera from Dvořák, went ahead after all with preparations for mounting *The Cunning Peasant*. This happened to coincide with increasing anti-Czech feeling in the Austrian capital, and at the opera house there was little or no enthusiasm for the production. The opera was launched on 19 November 1885, at a time when there were student riots in the city. In view of these circumstances, it is hardly surprising that the performance was a fiasco. When four days later the composer completed his sketch of the first part of his oratorio, he wrote on it: 'Finished during the time when "The Cunning Peasant" was murdered in Vienna'.

Dvořák was hard at work on *St Ludmila* throughout the winter and spring. Littleton reminded him periodically that Leeds was needing the printed vocal scores, but publication was held up because the composer was behind schedule. As soon as Dvořák finished one of the parts, he despatched it to London. Soon after reaching the end of Part II, when about to lay his work aside temporarily for the first time, in order to fulfil a promise to conduct his *Stabat Mater* at Kroměříž, Dvořák wrote in deep distress to Rus, fearing he would not have his oratorio finished in time. Frequently he felt like tearing up what he had written. 'The whole thing', he complained, 'is very *unpleasant and worries me greatly*.'[33]

32 At Birmingham, Cardinal Newman gave Dvořák a copy of *The Dream of Gerontius*', but much too late for serious consideration.

33 Letter of 7 April 1886 from Dvořák to Rus; *vide* Šourek :*Antonín Dvořák přátelům doma.*

Fortunately the third part was the shortest, so that two months later, on 30 May, to his very great relief, he reached the end of his laborious task. Working against time, the oratorio had taken him eight and a half months.

The letters that passed between Dvořák and Simrock during these last months show that relations between them continued to be strained. When he was reminded about the Slavonic Dances, Dvořák remarked: 'I havn't the slightest inclination to think about such light music at present. I must inform you that it will not by any means be such a simple matter with the Slavonic Dances as it was the first time. To do the same thing twice over is damnably difficult.' Simrock was incredulous at this, and replied: 'Whoever has as many tunes in his head as you only needs a few days to shake two books of Slavonic Dances out of his sleeve.'[34] To this the composer retorted: '*You imagine composition is a perfectly simple matter; but it is only possible to begin when one feels inspired.* But my dear friend it is difficult to discuss such things.' On belatedly making the discovery that his client was engaged on an oratorio for Leeds, Simrock upbraided him for selling works to an English publisher without first giving him the opportunity to acquire them. This time Dvořák responded in English, doubtless in order to emphasize that he was receiving much more help, encouragement and appreciation from England than from Germany and Austria. In this letter written on 14 April 1886, he wrote:

> I was a little surprised to hear from you, you will have my new oratorio expressly written for the Leeds Festival. I thought you know alredy by the newspapers, that the new great work will be published at *Novello* in London. The people from Birmingham and Leeds and many others, when I was the first time in England, asked me to write oratorios for theirs Festivals and accordingly to this, it could only appear at an english music publisher, as Novello is . . . You see I became quite an Englishman.

Simrock then claimed that by selling his choral works in this manner to Novello, Dvořák was breaking their 1879 contract. This made the composer angry, and he swore he did not know of any such written agreement.[35] He knew Simrock would be pleased when he wrote again

34 Simrock had in mind the eight dances which would form the second set. The first eight, op. 46, were issued for piano duet in two books.

35 This seems to suggest that their original agreement may have been a verbal one. This letter, dated 16 April 1886 and written in German, appears in Šourek: *Antonín Dvořák: Letters and Reminiscences* (Prague 1954).

on 11 June. He told him this time that he was writing those Slavonic Dances and enjoying doing so, and he expected to finish them in about a month. This time, he said, the dances 'are going to be quite different (no joking and no irony)'.

As the time for the mid-October Leeds Festival approached, attention was focused on Dvořák's new work. Among the other works to be performed were Stanford's *Revenge* and Sullivan's *Golden Legend*, but Anton Rubinstein, who had accepted the invitation to compose a cantata, found it impossible to keep his promise. Plans were afoot to present *St Ludmila* at Edinburgh, Glasgow and Dundee early in December, and it was hoped the composer could conduct these performances, if he was able to remain in Britain until then; but there seemed to be little prospect of this. In a letter to Littleton, written in English, Dvořák said: 'You cannot imagine how I long to see Scotland the beautyfull country of Burns—Scott! Really it is very pitty! Canot it be postponed till the spring next?'[36] The *Musical Times* published a much longer article on *St Ludmila* than the one on *The Spectre's Bride* a year before, and when the Festival began, an interview with the composer appeared in the *Pall Mall Gazette*.[37] Just as a key factor in the choice of subject for the oratorio was Dvořák's patriotism, so too the most significant part of the interview revealed the intensity of his national pride. He concluded with these words:

Twenty years ago we Slavs were nothing. Now we feel our national life once more awakening; and who knows but that the glorious times may come back which five centuries ago were ours, when all Europe looked up to the powerful Czechs, the Slavs, the Bohemians, to whom I too belong and to whom I am proud to belong.

The performance, with Albani, Patey, Lloyd and Santley as the soloists, took place on 15 October, the penultimate day of the Festival. It was yet another triumph for the composer, and one he could share with his wife, who accompanied him to England. The audience was in raptures, and the critics praised the music in the warmest terms. Hueffer, it is true, was not wholly satisfied, but he declared, 'his orchestration is always

36 Letter of 4 June from Littleton to Dvořák; and Dvořák's reply of 4 August 1886, formerly in the collection of Richard Border.

37 'From Butcher to Baton', 13 October 1886. The author of the *Musical Times* article noticed Dvořák apparently adapting himself to English taste. He remarked on the simple directness of the massive choruses, which at times reminded him of Handel's methods.

masterly, and his sense of the musically picturesque is keener than that of any living composer'.[38] However, the libretto and Troutbeck's translation were regarded on all sides as unsatisfactory, and there was general agreement that an oratorio which, with the intervals, filled three and a half hours was too long. Bursting with excitement and happiness, Dvořák reported that all the London newspapers agreed that *St Ludmila* was the climax of the Festival, and he was eagerly looking forward to all the principal choral societies of Britain and America performing the new work. He was apparently unaware that Sullivan's *Golden Legend*, performed on the last day of the Festival, was an even greater success than his own.[39]

The composer conducted a slightly cut version of his oratorio at St James's Hall, London, on 29 October, before another large and equally enthusiastic audience, and once again the critics were full of praise. But Dvořák, sensing that all was not well, flatly refused to direct the Crystal Palace performance on 6 November, counting on Mackenzie taking his place. Mackenzie, however, pointed out that unless Dvořák had left London by then, it was absolutely impossible for him to step into the breach.[40] Consequently the composer conducted a more drastically cut version of *St Ludmila* before a little more than half-filled hall on the 6th, and then left for home on the following day.

Seeing the way the wind was blowing, choral societies speedily altered their plans. Glasgow presented *The Golden Legend* and *The Revenge* (14 December), Edinburgh substituted Dvořák's *Stabat Mater* for his oratorio (15 December), and instead of *St Ludmila*, Sullivan's cantata was sung at the Royal Albert Hall (19 January 1887). The sole exception was Hallé's performance of the Czech composer's new work at Manchester on 26 November 1886. Dvořák conducted several performances in Bohemia, but apart from these the only other performance appears to have been given by J. E. van Olinda at Troy, New York, on 9 May 1888, with Lilli Lehmann in the title role. *The Golden Legend*, on the other hand, was seized on by innumerable societies, and was given at Chicago on 11 March, Berlin on 26 March and Boston on 8 May 1887.

Apart from the oratorio's length and poor translation, various

---

38 *The Times*, 16 October 1886.

39 Writing in the *Athenaeum* on 18 October 1886, Prout stated: 'The interest aroused by the other novelties of the week paled before the production of Sir Arthur Sullivan's cantata ... The impression upon the Leeds audience was overwhelming'.

40 A. C. Mackenzie: *A Musician's Narrative* (London 1927), pp. 138–9.

reasons have been offered to explain why *St Ludmila* did not repeat the success of *The Spectre's Bride*. These embrace a belief, contested by Prout, that the composer deliberately aimed to give his English public a work on familiar Handelian and Mendelssohnian lines, whereas it would have preferred one in the modern continuous style, and the feeling that reminiscences of Handel, Mendelssohn, Haydn, Cherubini and others were rather frequent, and that Part II was weaker than the rest. It is understandable that Dvořák's inspiration should have flagged at times in this huge work. But from the delightfully atmospheric Introduction and Chorus suggesting the dawn breaking, through the pagan choruses of varied character, and up to Ludmila's splendid 'I beg thee, on thy dusty feet . . .' (No. 14), there is much to admire. The woodland setting of Part II is sensitively drawn, and Part III gets off to a splendid start with a powerful Kyrie (*Hospodine pomiluj ny*) in Russian style. Provided judicious cuts are made, revivals of this work would be worthwhile in countries with strong choral traditions.

6 New Friendships and a Journey to Russia

Whenever Dvořák started on a new composition, he invariably did so to fulfil a personal need, and, as we have seen, when he accepted a commission to produce a special kind of work, he made certain that this was something which he felt obliged to undertake because of an inner urge. On reaching the end of a large-scale composition, it sometimes suited him to take a complete break from creative work, whereas at other times he turned to writing far more modest things. Simrock often wanted him to compose unambitious and small works when he had bigger things in mind; and when he urged him to orchestrate the new set of Slavonic Dances, Dvořák was not in the mood to do so, and told his publisher later he was prepared to take on this chore, but it would be 'an accursed job'. But he warmed to his work, and was so satisfied, that after trying out some of the dances in their new garb, he declared that they 'sound like the devil'! Earlier on, after finishing the original piano duet version of the dances, he was moved to write something which Josef Kruis, a chemistry student who lodged at the same address, Kruis's violin teacher Jan Pelikán, and the composer himself would enjoy playing together. It was in this way that the delightful Terzetto, op. 74, for two violins and viola, which includes an attractive furiant and an interesting set of variations, came into being. It turned out to be beyond the capabilities of Kruis, so Dvořák set about writing some rather simpler Bagatelles for the same combination, and then immediately rearranged them as the *Romantic Pieces*, op. 75, for violin and piano.

Now that there was such great interest in Dvořák's music, it seemed probable that there would be some difficulty in keeping up with the demand for new works. Consequently Dvořák considered it would be sensible to take another look at some of his earlier compositions, intending, in the more deserving cases, to resurrect, reshape and revise them. So in addition to composing several entirely new works in 1887 and 1888, he recomposed the third act of *King and Charcoal Burner*, using Novotný's revised text, arranged twelve songs from the *Cypresses* cycle of 1865 for string quartet, made some revisions to his Second, Third and Fourth Symphonies (in B flat, E flat and D minor, op. 13), produced a mixed choir version of the 149th Psalm, and also made a number of improvements to the String Quintet in G major, the String Quartet in E major and the Fifth Symphony in F major, ensuring thereby that they would be more suitable for publication and performance.[1]

There was one work, which apparently only required a minimal amount of alteration and some superficial polishing, the splendid *Symphonic Variations* that had attracted so little attention when performed at the end of 1877. The composer conducted a performance in Prague on 6 March 1887, and then immediately offered this work to Hans Richter for his next series of London concerts, mentioning that it was unpublished, but would not remain so for long if Richter launched it. After rehearsing it for the first time, Richter was quite carried away, and declared that it was 'a magnificent work', and after the performance at the Richter concert at St James's Hall on 16 May 1887 he reported: 'Your Symphonic Variations are a great success here, and at the hundreds of concerts I have conducted during my life, no new work has been as successful as yours.'

When the Meiningen Orchestra played in Prague early in December 1884, their conductor Hans von Bülow included *My Home* Overture in his programme, and invited Dvořák to conduct this. The German conductor developed a great admiration for the *Hussite* Overture, and after introducing it at Hamburg on 1 November 1886, he repeated it in various German cities. He was fiercely criticized for playing a work that was so uncompromisingly Czech in character and spirit, but was quite unmoved by this, and continued playing it at his concerts. Dvořák was grateful to him for his devotion and invaluable service in propagating his music in so selfless a manner, and offered to dedicate his F major Symphony to him. In his reply on 25 November 1887, von Bülow said: 'A dedication from you—next to Brahms the most divinely gifted composer of the present time—is a higher decoration than any Grand Cross from the hands of any prince.'[2] He tried to persuade Pollini to mount *Dimitrij* at Hamburg, but was unsuccessful. In October 1887 Dvořák urged von Bülow to introduce the D minor Symphony, op. 70, to Berlin, where it was still unknown, but this was not a suitable

1 Simrock published the Psalm (op. 52) as op. 79, the Quintet (op. 18) as op. 77, the E major Quartet (op. 27) as op. 80 and the F major Symphony (op. 24) as No. 3, op. 76. Similarly the *Symphonic Variations* (op. 38) appeared as op. 78.

2 Simrock published the Symphony early in 1888, and Manns gave the first performance of it in its revised form at the Crystal Palace. Von Bülow conducted it at Meiningen in the following autumn.

time.[3] The composer went to hear his performances of the Symphony in the German capital on 27 and 28 October 1889, and was so delighted by these that he pasted his friend's portrait on the title page of his manuscript score. The two men contrasted strikingly with one another: von Bülow was precise, refined and well groomed, whereas Dvořák, with his shock of black hair and dark piercing eyes, was unkempt and wilder looking, so much so that he reminded the conductor of Caliban.

It was a well nigh impossible task for Dvořák to give satisfaction to all his good friends who clamoured for new and as yet unperformed works. Acting in good time, the Philharmonic Society of London staked a claim for another symphony in the summer of 1886, but the composer had to tell them he was far too busy with an opera (*The Jacobin*) to write one just then.[4] More than a year later news reached the Society that Manns would be presenting a new Dvořák symphony at the Crystal Palace, which puzzled them, for they were sure they had the prior claim. Dvořák replied angrily, but entirely truthfully, on 4 November 1887: 'It is *a lie* if somebody tells you I have a *new symphony* which will be brought out by Manns. I should be so happy if I had one; I should give it to you with pleasure! But unfortunately I have none.' He failed to explain that the work Manns hoped to perform (the F major Symphony) was an old one which he had recently revised. The Society toyed with the idea of presenting an older symphony, but preferred in the end to wait for a new one. Manns had discovered for himself that the F major Symphony was being published.[5] The score and parts reached him only nine days before his concert on 7 April, but he fitted in three rehearsals, and gave a splendid account of the work. Three days earlier Dvořák's last child Aloisie, nicknamed Zinda, was born.

Dvořák was present on 4 December 1887 when Richter gave a highly successful performance of the *Symphonic Variations* in Vienna. Brahms was so delighted by his Czech friend's composition, that he gave him a superb cigar holder. It was fortunate that Dvořák did not return to Vienna when Richter conducted the *Stabat Mater* on 19 February, for strong anti-Czech feeling erupted in the Austrian capital

---

3 There were already enough symphonies in their draft programmes to last the whole season.

4 Letter of 19 August 1886 from Dvořák to Francesco Berger, secretary of the Philharmonic Society.

5 Manns gave almost as many first English performances of Dvořák's music as the composer himself. After this symphony he introduced a selection from the second set of *Slavonic Dances* (21 April 1888), the Mass in D (11 March 1893), *Othello* Overture (24 March 1894) and *Amid Nature* Overture (28 April 1894). He gave the first English performance of *Carnival* Overture (24 March 1894), but Henschel had already presented this at Glasgow five days earlier.

Turnov Castle, where Dvořák's friend Göbl was steward

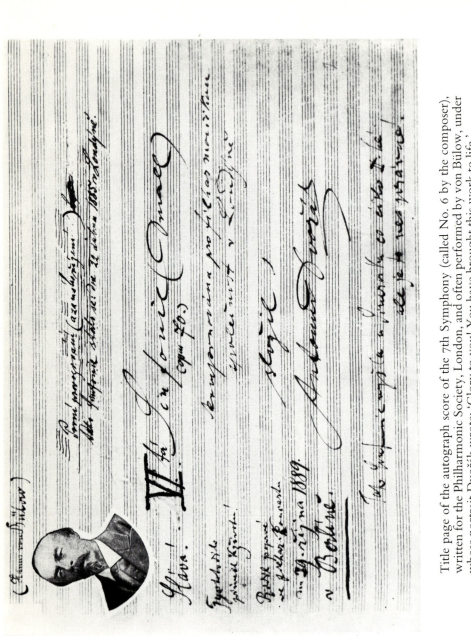

Title page of the autograph score of the 7th Symphony (called No. 6 by the composer), written for the Philharmonic Society, London, and often performed by von Bülow, under whose portrait Dvořák wrote: 'Glory to you! You have brought this work to life.'

just at that time.[6] Deeply moved by Richter's steadfast loyalty, he wrote to him saying: 'Since I have already recovered to some extent from the unpleasant fate of my *Stabat Mater* and the destructive criticism, I am able to express to you my heartfelt thanks for the artistic fervour, courage and devoted sympathy you have so often shown for my sake; in short for everything beneficial you have done for me'.[7]

Towards the end of 1882, when Dvořák's music was scarcely known in Budapest, Sándor Erkel had tried to persuade the composer to direct the performance of his D major Symphony, but he was unsuccessful. The Hungarians knew rather more of his music six years later when Imre Bellowics planned to revive his *Stabat Mater*. Dvořák responded this time to the invitation to present the work himself. This first visit of his to Budapest was most satisfactory, and he was particularly pleased with the excellent preparatory work done by Bellowics.[8]

Not long after composing the Terzetto and *Romantic Pieces*, Dvořák began writing a work which possessed an exceptional significance for him. His architect friend Josef Hlávka, the founder and first president of the Czech Academy of Sciences and Arts, had built himself a private chapel at Lužany castle, and he needed a suitable work for performance at the consecration. Very gratefully Dvořák accepted the commission, and composed the Mass in D major, op. 86, for two solo voices, choir and organ. Later he scored it for orchestra. If, however, the intimate character of the Mass as originally conceived is to be retained, then it will be found advisable to revert to the organ accompaniment.

The composer's next composition was the radiant and much loved Piano Quintet in A major, op. 81. It is very possible that Dvořák composed this delightful work because he knew his attempt to improve his early Piano Quintet in the same key, his op. 5, had not turned it into a work of which he could be proud. If this is the case, then his lack of success led to a most rewarding outcome. It seems as if, when writing the new work, Dvořák may have felt he was being spurred on by his guardian angel. The Quintet possesses a decidedly Czech spirit. There, are, for example, those rapid changes from one mood to another. Right at the beginning and within the space of a few bars the main theme for

6 There was strong resentment because Dvořák's *Stabat*, his new Piano Quintet and several works by other Czech composers were being performed in Vienna within a short period of time.

7 Dvořák dated this letter 9 February 1888, which is incorrect. It was probably written on 9 March or perhaps on 29 February.

8 Letter of 2 April 1888 from Dvořák to Brahms. In Budapest a repeat performance of the D major Symphony was given on 5 April 1886 by Erkel, and he introduced the D minor Symphony on 25 February 1887, and the F major Symphony on 12 December 1888. Bellowics performed *The Spectre's Bride* on 28 January 1889.

the cello changes from the brightness of A major to the more sombre tones of A minor. And in the second movement, a fine example of a Dvořákian dumka, the brooding melody in F sharp minor makes way for a cheerful section in D major, and presently it is again dismissed, this time by a fiery dance, a Vivace in 2/8. The colours and textures are rich, and in the finale there is an irrepressible rhythmic vitality. It is as well to ignore the label 'Furiant' attached to the scherzo.

Several years earlier, directly after his little opera *The Stubborn Lovers* had been given a very warm welcome at its first performance,[9] Dvořák became excited at the prospect of composing another comic opera, but this time one in two or three acts. Although he was faced with several more months of work on *Dimitrij*, he applied to his two librettists, Štolba and Marie Červinková-Riegrová, for a suitable text. Štolba failed to respond, and Mrs Červinková did not think a comic opera was in her line. Nevertheless she produced a scenario for one, which had as its main character a count's son, suspected of being a Jacobin, who returns home from Paris incognito to find that his father has decided to disinherit him in favour of his cousin, the count's nephew. On receiving the composer's approval of this, she prepared the libretto. However, this was less dramatic than he expected, so he laid it aside in the hope of finding something more suitable.

Three years later, while working on *The Spectre's Bride*, his interest in fairy tales was reawakened, and he became convinced that 'The Dragon's Coronet' would make a suitable subject for an opera. He incautiously asked Marie Červinková to write a libretto on this theme, but she flatly refused to do so, because he had not yet used the text he had asked her to write. Thrown back to 'The Jacobin' he persuaded her to make some improvements to Act I, which she did, yet he remained unhappy about this act.

Still hankering after a libretto that was fantastic and romantic, and vainly hoping Mrs Červinková might provide him with one, Dvořák further angered her by telling her that 'responsible gentlemen' were repeatedly advising him against setting 'The Jacobin' and recommending him to wait until he had something finer and more interesting.[10] Replying, she said that if he was not enthusiastic about 'The Jacobin' he had better return it to her, and ask those gentlemen to produce

9 On 2 October 1881, conducted by Moric Anger at the New Czech Theatre.

10 Letter of 26 July 1887 (postmarked 28 July) from Dvořák to Červinková. In her previous letter she had asked for royalties as well as a fee for her work, and Dvořák was not prepared to agree to that.

the kind of thing he really wanted. She could not spare time to prepare another libretto; and besides, if she did so, he and these gentlemen might again be dissatisfied, and then she would be lumbered with a second unwanted opera text.[11] Knowing that a full-length opera would occupy him for a year or more, it was natural that Dvořák should have been reluctant to come to a decision which he might later regret. It was difficult at any time to acquire a good opera text. 'The Jacobin' unquestionably possessed some attractive features, and the one that appealed most strongly to Dvořák was the character Benda, a typical Czech schoolmaster musician, who brought back vivid memories of his former Zlonice teacher and friend Antonín Liehmann. Still keeping his options open, Dvořák composed the Piano Quintet in A, op. 81, and then on 10 November 1887, five weeks after finishing the Quintet, he began work on his eighth opera, *The Jacobin*.

At first his progress was slow. In response to a request from Simrock he wrote the Four Songs, op. 82. He also revised the String Quintet in G and the String Quartet in E major, he paid visits to Vienna and Budapest, and conducted his Mass at Pilsen, *St Ludmila* at Olomouc and *Stabat Mater* at Chrudim. By the time he finished scoring the first act on 18 June 1888, his confidence in and enthusiasm for the new work were growing rapidly, so that he was able to report to Göbl the next day: 'This time I believe that those who have doubts about my *dramatic talent* will be satisfied, if not surprised . . . I believe that *The Jacobin* will be the best of my operas.' He progressed much more rapidly on the remainder of the work. Act Two occupied him until 26 September, and then, showing how eager he was to finish off the work, he sketched and scored the last act simultaneously and completed his task on 18 November. Rehearsals for the National Theatre production began before the end of the year, and Adolf Čech directed the première on 12 February. Early on the following day Dvořák travelled to Maleč to thank Marie Červinková and congratulate her on her libretto, and to inform her that he was extremely satisfied with the reception given to their second joint effort. Within four months there were fourteen performances and another five followed later that year.[12]

Dvořák was fortunate to have a moving human plot as his subject,

---

11 Letter of 1 August 1887 from Červinková to Dvořák; *vide* Bráfová: *Rieger, Smetana, Dvořák* (Prague 1913), pp. 112–13.

12 Ludwig Hartmann, Dresden critic of *Neue Zeitschrift für Musik*, classified *The Jacobin* not as a dramatic or a vocal opera, but as a musical opera, and praised particularly the work's 'exceedingly beautiful orchestration and the masterly treatment of its forms'. Translation in *Musical Times*, xxx (1889), pp. 217–18.

centring on Bohuš, Count Vilem of Harasov's only son, who has returned incognito to Bohemia after a long absence in Paris. The Count, who loves his son dearly, blames Julie, his son's wife, for what he believes will be a permanent separation from Bohuš, whom he is on the point of disinheriting in favour of his nephew Adolf. As a sub-plot, Filip, the Count's pompous burgrave, fully intends to marry Terinka, the daughter of the schoolmaster musician Benda, but he is crossed in love by the young gamekeeper Jiří. A brief melodic fragment associated with Bohuš, played by the flute early in the opera, is the most important recurring theme. There are several closed, or virtually closed forms, and among them Jiří's song (in duple time) taunting Filip, Filip's response to this (a slower triple time transformation of Jiří's theme), Benda's choral Serenade being rehearsed as homage and a welcome to the Count, the Count's broodings while lamenting the loss of his son, and the lullaby the long-deceased Countess used to sing when Bohuš was an infant, which Julie sings within earshot of the troubled Count in order to bring about a reconciliation. Critics had highlighted some weaknesses in the plot when the opera was first produced, so at Dvořák's request Červinková made extensive modifications in the second and third acts in 1894. Dvořák rewrote much of these acts in a slightly Wagnerian manner three years later. He adapted the despondent Count's fine aria, a new addition, from the following orchestral passage in Act Three, scene three of the original version:

Composers with a firmly established international reputation did not very often visit the Czech capital, and when Tchaikovsky did so for the first time early in 1888, his appearance proved to be an event of particular significance not only for Prague music lovers, but also for Dvořák personally. Directly he arrived he asked to meet the Czech composer, and he was also anxious to see his *Dimitrij*, which unluckily could not be performed as announced, due to the illness of Antonín Vavra, the tenor. Tchaikovsky attended the Umělecká beseda concert on 14 February, at which Smetana's String Quartet *From my Life* and Dvořák's new Piano Quintet were played. After having lunch at the Czech composer's flat on the 15th, he wrote in his diary; 'Dvořák is very dear to me and I like his Quintet'. On the following day the two men dined at the Russian Circle. When the distinguished visitor toasted his Czech friend, Dvořák said a few words in Russian about the glory that Tchaikovsky had brought to the Slav nations, with the immediate result that the Russian composer gave him a warm embrace.

Some nine months later Tchaikovsky returned to Prague, to conduct his Fifth Symphony and the first performance outside his own country of the opera *Yevgeny Onyegin*. While he was there he passed on to Dvořák an invitation from the Imperial Russian Musical Society to visit Moscow during the next season, to conduct a programme of Czech music. Dvořák, who never conducted the music of other composers, and was not prepared to undertake the long journey alone, hesitated about accepting. He amused his Russian friend by saying he would have to postpone going until he had had a chance to learn the language.[13] Tchaikovsky believed he could overcome this opposition if Dvořák could be persuaded to conduct one or more of his own compositions, and Karel Bendl would agree to direct the remainder of the programme. In this way, as he admitted when writing to A. O. Patera, 'we would have a fine conductor to perform works by Smetana and other Czech composers, and also the famous Dvořák, whose name will be a great draw on our concert posters.[14] Within a few weeks it was settled that Dvořák would conduct a whole programme of his own music, that the concert would take place on 2 March 1890 (14 March O.S.), and that he would be accompanied by his wife. He was also willing to go on to St Petersburg after the Moscow concert, in order to present two of his compositions there.

A few weeks after Tchaikovsky's departure, Dvořák was asked to become a professor of composition at Prague Conservatory, but realizing how this would restrict his freedom he refused the offer. In America, where there was as much keenness as ever to introduce hitherto unknown Dvořák compositions, the entreprising Kneisel Quartet apparently notched up a world première when they presented the E major String Quartet, op. 80 [27], at Boston on 27 February 1889. Five weeks later, on 4 April, there were simultaneous first English performances of this Quartet by Bauerkeller in Manchester and by Szczepanowski in London. Bauerkeller's programme also included the *Romantic Pieces*, the Terzetto and the A major Piano Quintet, and so he should undoubtedly be credited with the first concert in England devoted solely to chamber music works of the Czech composer.[15] During the latter part of that year two important compositions came into being; first the E flat Piano Quartet, op. 87, and then the Eighth Symphony in G major, op. 88.

13 In his letter to A. O. Patera of 9 January 1889 (21 January O.S.), Tchaikovsky referred to Dvořák as 'simpatichniy chudak', which might be rendered in English as 'the dear funny fellow'. This rambling and interesting letter appears in *Antonin Dvorzhak: sbornik statyei*, ed. L. Ginsburg (Moscow 1967), pp. 212–15. Patera, an active promoter of Russo-Czech relations, was librarian of the Czech Museum in Prague.

14 Loc. cit. Tchaikovsky asked Patera to act as intermediary, and do his best to persuade Dvořák to agree to go to Moscow. He was entirely successful, for on 9 February Tchaikovsky was able to tell P. I. Jurgenson, a fellow director of the Imperial Russian Musical Society, that Dvořák had written to say he was prepared to conduct a whole concert.

15 The Kneisel Quartet played three of Dvořák's compositions when they gave the first performance of the String Quintet in E flat in New York on 12 January 1894. On 27 November 1898 an all-Dvořák concert was given in London in the series of South Place Sunday Popular Concerts. Six members of the talented Grimson family played the String Sextet, two Humoresques, Slavonic Dances nos 4 and 5 (violin solos) and the A major Piano Quintet, and Agnes Witting sang songs selected from opp. 99, 82, 73 and 55.

When the piano gives its bantering reply to the strings' solemn statement at the beginning of the E flat Piano Quartet, the stage is already set for one of the composer's most imaginative and original movements. If attention is drawn to just two of its features, we might consider the persistent whimpering of the cello when the second subject returns in the remote key of B major, and the eerie tremolando version of the main motif that passes from instrument to instrument shortly before the close. Dvořák appears to have been rather less at ease in combining the keyboard instrument with the strings in the Lento than in the other three movements; but the passionate C sharp minor section, and the plaintive theme for the piano in the major mode with a syncopated string accompaniment that follows closely after it, are both convincing and effective. The gracious third movement, with its imitations of the folk instrument the cimbalom, possesses character and style. The Quartet ends with a good-humoured finale which, following a precedent set by Haydn, is in the tonic minor. It deserves to be much better known, but has been overshadowed by the ever popular Piano Quintet.

In March 1889 Dvořák went to Dresden to conduct his second *Slavonic Rhapsody*, the Nocturne for strings and the F major Symphony; but one of the most satisfying events of that year was undoubtedly the award of the Austrian Order of the Iron Cross to Dvořák, which necessitated a visit to Vienna·in December to be received in audience by the Emperor Franz Joseph.

Having succeeded in obtaining Dvořák's acceptance of the Moscow invitation, and settled that he would receive 800 roubles for his honorarium and expenses, Tchaikovsky left the rest of the concert arrangements in the hands of V. I. Safonov. Dvořák suggested that the programme might consist of the first *Slavonic Rhapsody*, the Violin Concerto, which Jan Hřímalý was prepared to play, the *Symphonic Variations*, the *Scherzo capriccioso*, and either the F major Symphony, the D minor Symphony, or perhaps the still incomplete G major Symphony.[16] With the exception of the *Slavonic Rhapsody*, all these works would have been new for Moscow. Safonov thought it might be advisable to include a vocal item, so Dvořák suggested a group of songs or the big soprano aria from *The Spectre's Bride*, but at the same time felt that the programme might then be too long unless another item

16 The Dvořák-Safonov correspondence appears in V. A. Kiselev's 'Perepiska A. Dvorzhaka a V. I. Safonovim', *Kratkiye soobshcheniya*, xvii, Inst. slavyanovedeniya akad. nauk (Moscow 1955). See also my article 'Dvořák's Visit to Russia', *Musical Quarterly*, li (1965), pp. 493–506.

was omitted. In the end the composer chose the 'friendly' F major Symphony, rather than the 'sombre' D minor Symphony, and reserved the first foreign performance of the G major Symphony for the Philharmonic Society in London, feeling no doubt that it was time he showed his gratitude to them once again, in recognition of their earlier kindness to him and their continuing interest in his work. He conducted the Symphony in London on 14 April 1890 after his return from Russia.

This thoroughly Czech work, despite its deep shadows, is one of the composer's happiest creations. Starting with an expressive funereal melody in G minor, the sunshine suddenly breaks through when the flute plays this light-hearted theme in the major key:

followed shortly afterwards by a solemn idea for divided violas and cellos. Dvořák's fecundity is remarkable, but so is the range of mood open to him within a single idea. In the development, for instance, the solemn viola and cello theme appears in F sharp major, while the flute, a favoured instrument in Dvořák's hands, dances high above it. Then again innocuous elements of the same theme, together with the dotted rhythm of the flute theme, are the ingredients for the angry climax leading up to the triumphal return of the G minor melody, richly embellished by the soaring strings. Similarly in the next movement, it is the Adagio's quiet initial phrase which for a while shatters the idyllic peace. A gracious waltz with a rustic trio takes the place of a scherzo; and the work is rounded off with a somewhat freely organized set of variations.

Since Dvořák was eagerly looking forward to renewing his acquaintance with Tchaikovsky, it was a keen disappointment to find on his arrival in Moscow that his friend was in Italy, at work on his new opera *The Queen of Spades*. Dvořák and his wife stayed at the home of a Czech named Ježíšek, where, as Jurgenson had amusingly assured Tchaikovsky, the Czech composer would be as comfortable as if he were in the bosom of the little Jesus.[17] By a stroke of bad luck Hřímalý

17 Letter of 3 February 1890 from Jurgenson to Tchaikovsky. 'Ježíšek' is a Czech diminutive form of 'Ježíš', meaning 'Jesus'.

fell ill a few days before the concert, which had been put forward three days to 11 March, and so it was impossible for the Violin Concerto to appear in the programme. Nor was it possible at such short notice to arrange for an alternative solo item. The Adagio from the Serenade in D minor for wind instruments, which Dvořák seems to have brought with him, served to fill the gap. This was hardly an ideal programme for an audience which normally expected to hear at least one soloist, was accustomed to more varied fare, and who knew Dvořák by scarcely anything besides the *Slavonic Dances*.[18] Even the critics were ill-prepared for a whole concert devoted to the music of a composer whose name was a household word in the west.

The Symphony was fairly well received by the audience, but during the Adagio from the Serenade, which concluded the first half of the programme, it tended to become restive. It thoroughly enjoyed the *Scherzo capriccioso*, but found the last item, the *Symphonic Variations*, too long-winded. The concert was a moderate success according to the critic N. Kashkin, a friend of Tchaikovsky. Nevertheless, such enthusiasm as there may have been was almost entirely due to the reactions of the German and Czech communities, rather than of the Russians. A. A. Komissarzhevsky, by far the harshest of the critics, and G. E. Konyus appreciated Dvořák's technical mastery, but both felt there was something lacking in his works. According to Komissarzhevsky, the spiritual side of creation was closed to Dvořák in his symphonic music.[19] On the other hand Konyus, who thought highly of the first and last movements of the Symphony, nevertheless felt that the work as a whole was deficient in music flowing with life. He found this, however, in the *Scherzo capriccioso*, and remarked that here was a work that could delight and charm the non-specialist listener.[20]

Unquestionably the staunchest of Dvořák's supporters in Russia was Johannes Bartz, the German organist of the Moscow Lutheran church of St Peter and St Paul. He and his Gesangverein were about to give the first performance in Russia of Dvořák's *Stabat Mater* on 23 March, too late unfortunately for the composer to be present. Bartz was very distressed to discover that because of poor organization, Muscovite

18 Moscow heard the E flat String Quartet in 1882, the first *Slavonic Rhapsody* in 1884 and the *Hussite* Overture in 1887. Any other performances which may have taken place in Moscow have not yet been traced.

19 *Moskovskiy listok*, 3 March 1890 (O.S.). Komissarzhevsky admired the *Slavonic Dances*, but found Dvořák's ideas 'vulgar and common', his orchestration 'ponderous and pompous', his form 'artificial and diffuse'. But he praised 'the many harmonic beauties', 'the solid contrapuntal technique' and 'a sort of orchestral piquancy'.

20 *Moskovskiye vedomosti*, 2 March 1890 (O.S. date).

indifference, or possibly a deliberate intrigue, the plan to give their Czech visitor a silver wreath, similar to the one presented to Tchaikovsky in Prague, had misfired. He therefore did his best to make amends and show that there was loyalty in German circles by presenting Dvořák with a laurel wreath from the Gesangverein when he attended a rehearsal of his *Stabat*. Dvořák, who was aware of the situation, was deeply moved by this gesture of friendship and appreciation.[21] A few days earlier, when Dvořák was the guest of honour at a party given by Moscow's Czechs and Austrians, they gave him a fine silver coffee set of Russian design.

At St Petersburg things worked out rather better than in Moscow. The Imperial Russian Musical Society concert on 22 March began with Schubert's 'Unfinished' Symphony and Max Bruch's *Scottish Fantasia*, with Leopold Auer as the soloist, and then Dvořák introduced two well-chosen works of his, the Sixth Symphony in D major and the *Scherzo capriccioso*. The audience applauded at the end of each movement of the Symphony, but enjoyed the *Scherzo capriccioso* even more. As is so often the case, the critics disagreed with each other. P. P. Veymark advised Dvořák to restrict himself to ballet music,[22] while D. P. Nikolsky regarded him as the Bohemian Brahms, but also the possessor of an even finer and more significant talent.[23] At the Moscow concert Konyus had been entirely satisfied by the signs of the Czech composer's nationalism, whereas Komissarzhevsky, recognizing that Dvořák had adopted cosmopolitan techniques, believed that in consequence the spirit of his music was not a genuine outcome of social conditions and national peculiarities. In an attempt to put his finger on the reason why the Petersburg concert was no more than a *succès d'estime* for their visitor, H. A. Laroche, known as the 'Russian Hanslick', remarked: '... the mixture of Brahmsian texture with a melodic content of a very distinctive Czech character puzzled us by its novelty, and was not understood by us'.[24]

On the evening before his concert the Czech Aid Society invited all the leading Czechs of the city to a banquet to meet their distinguished

21 Dvořák touched on the subject in his letter to Gustav Eim of 23 March 1890; *vide* Šourek's *Antonín Dvořák: Letters and Reminiscences*, pp. 127–8. For a fuller account, see Přenosil's article, 'Dvořák v Moskvě', *Dalibor*, xxx (2 May 1908), p. 264.

22 Veymark's critique appeared in three papers: *Minuta* (12 March 1890); *Syn otechestva* (12 March 1890); *Bayan* (15 March 1890); all dates O.S.

23 *Grazhdanin* (14 March 1890).

24 *Moskovskiye vedomosti* (30 April 1890), O.S. His feuilleton is entitled 'A Musical Letter from St Petersburg'.

countryman. Dvořák was given a splendid silver goblet neatly orna-
mented in gold with a lyre and a monogram. His health was proposed
by Eduard Nápravník, the conductor of the Imperial Opera. There was
also a brief party after the concert, at which Rubinstein, the president of
the Russian Musical Society, proposed the main toast, and Laroche
praised the small nation of Czechs for their achievements in art and
science.

Dvořák's visit to Russia did little apparently to stimulate interest in
his music. Performances of his compositions were extremely scanty
until five years later, when the Bohemian Quartet began making
annual visits, and even then Dvořák's orchestral works were rarely
played. Commenting on the rather general lack of interest displayed by
Russians, Laroche remarked in his feuilleton: '. . . racial sympathy has
influenced our public just as little as racial differences have prejudiced
his success in Germany.'

7 From Discord with Simrock to Concord with America

Ever since Dvořák's first visits to England he had been able to live without undue financial worries, although it would be wrong to imagine that he was at all prosperous. If, as had recently happened, he felt impelled to spend many months composing a really big work, it became a virtual necessity to ensure that fees of one kind or another would be forthcoming during that time. This helps to explain why he interrupted work on the first act of *The Jacobin* to compose the *Four Songs*, op. 82, and revise the G major String Quintet and the E major String Quartet for publication. Having finished his opera he completely revised eight songs from the *Cypresses* cycle of 1865, transforming them into the *Love Songs*, op. 83. Next, after an interval of four months, he composed something which he knew would be of interest to his publisher, the set of *Poetic Tone Pictures*, op. 85, for piano. Confessing that he loved Dvořák's music as a whole and was strongly attracted by some of these pieces, Simrock, the cautious publisher, added that he did not expect them to be very accessible musically or to be very popular.[1] The composer had hoped to receive 3,000 German marks for the set, but he was satisfied when Simrock offered him 2,400. This must have been considerably more than he received for his next work, the Piano Quartet in E flat major, op. 87, even through Simrock had been demanding one for some time.

On New Year's Day 1890 Dvořák told his publisher that his new G major Symphony would be performed in Prague on 12 January,[2] and that Richter was planning to conduct it in Vienna at the end of the month. Simrock did not take at all kindly to any of Dvořák's compositions being performed a second time before he had a chance to publish them. Six years earlier he had raised a similar objection to his client con-

---

1 Letter of ca. 9 July 1889 from Simrock to Dvořák.

2 The performance was postponed until 2 February, because Dvořák's whole family went down with 'flu.

ducting his *Hussite* Overture in London; but he had given way when Dvořák pointed out how essential it was for him to be able to present a new work when he appeared in London for the first time.[3] When objecting to the Richter performance, Simrock enquired how much the composer wanted for his Symphony, but Dvořák refused to be the first to name a price. He then warned the publisher: 'If we can't agree about an honorarium, I suppose I could look out for another publisher for the symphony, but I should prefer not to do that ... Since you left me in the lurch with the Mass, that could happen with the symphony as well.'[4] Simrock countered this by saying he was losing thousands of marks on Dvořák's symphonies. Von Bülow persisted in playing the *Hussite* Overture, which the public did not like, and it had been far from easy to persuade him to perform the D minor Symphony. As for the F major Symphony, that, he said, had not yet been heard in Germany.[5]

Dvořák was convinced that Simrock did not want to risk buying any of his big works, but he gave him until the autumn to make him an offer. After biding his time, he wrote again on 7 October, saying that unless he received more than Simrock had given him in the last two years, it would be impossible for him to meet the expense of educating his growing family. And two days later he pointed out that 1,000 marks would be inadequate payment for a work which took him three months to write. If another publisher were to buy his symphony, he said, it might no longer be possible for him to let Simrock have those lucrative small compositions, and doubtless everyone would be curious to know the reason he had refused to take the symphony. In conclusion he said:

Since you again saw fit to refuse my Symphony, I shall not offer you any more big expensive works in future, for I shall know in advance, because of what you say, that you cannot publish works of that kind. You advise me to write small things; but that is difficult, for how can I help it if I am not able to think of a theme for a song or a piano piece? *And just at present my mind is full of big ideas—I shall do as the good Lord wills.* That will certainly be best.

3 Letter of 10 March 1884 from Dvořák to Simrock.

4 Letter of 3 January 1890 from Dvořák to Simrock.

5 Simrock was wrong. During the previous season this work was performed at Kiel, Meiningen, Mannheim and Dresden.

Simrock was greatly perturbed by this letter. In his reply he sternly reminded Dvořák that according to their agreement of 1879 he had granted Simrock the prior right of publication for all his new compositions. In doing so he raised the spectre of possible legal proceedings. This made Dvořák extremely angry, and on 11th October, by return of post, he sent the following reply:

> You too seem to be amazingly logical: you want me to offer you compositions—and then you just reject them! After refusing the *Mass* for chorus and organ last year and doing the same now with my new Symphony, I am bound to assume that you are not considering my *major works* because the fee would have to be high. Well, I don't intend to let myself be fooled! And if you begin to *threaten* me I shall then be obliged to increase my demands considerably. All the more so, because you always fall back on your rights regarding priority. I too should be sorry if you were to prosecute me, but I shall always know how to defend my *spiritual* property. Over this surely the world will be on my side, and I am at liberty to demand what I like for it. Nobody can stop me from doing that. I have not yet proposed a fee for the Symphony, but if you speak in that manner I shall not even give you the work for *ten thousand* marks; and judging by your letter you have refused the Symphony and I shall do with it whatever I can . . .

Writing in a more conciliatory tone on 28th October, Simrock enquired whether Dvořák would consider writing a piano concerto for him. The quarrel, however, had already gone too far, and the composer saw no point in replying. The rupture in their business relationship was complete.[6]

Having been unable to persuade Dvořák to compose a new choral work in 1888, the Birmingham Musical Festival had high hopes of securing one in time for their next triennial festival in 1891. They did not mind whether it was a sacred or a secular work, and invited him to conduct it. Anticipating that he would be publishing the work if it materialized, Littleton expressed the hope that it would not be too difficult for the orchestra, and, without making any direct reference to *St Ludmila*, asked the composer 'in any case to write only Dvořák'.[7]

6 Due to this break, further performances of the Symphony were possible while it was still in manuscript. Richter repeated it in London (7 July 1890), and it was conducted by Dvořák in Frankfurt-am-Main (7 November), by Richter in Vienna (4 January 1891) and Manns in Edinburgh (12 January).

7 Letter of 16 May 1889 from Alfred Littleton to Dvořák.

The composer was much keener on writing chamber music and a symphony at that time, and so would not promise anything, yet he had no wish to disappoint his English friends. He took a few weeks break after completing the G major Symphony, and then on 1 January 1890 he started sketching the Requiem Mass for Birmingham.[8] He worked steadily on this, except during his four-week trip to Russia and shorter absences from home, and finished it on 18 July. He began work on the full score a fortnight later and completed the whole work by 31 October.

When Dvořák named his price for the Requiem, Littleton thought he was asking too much, and made an offer of £650, which the composer felt was inadequate. Even so he must have been somewhat relieved to find that Littleton was showing a cautious interest in the Symphony which Simrock had rejected.[9] By the end of February Birmingham was becoming seriously worried over the failure of the composer and publisher to agree on terms, and wondered if they would be obliged to find an alternative work. Littleton drew Dvořák's attention to the fact that the Requiem was only half the length of St Ludmila, for which he had given a similar sum, and the composer for his part obviously did not cherish the idea of stowing away the scores of the Requiem and Symphony in a trunk, along with his other unpublished compositions. After pondering about it for well over a month, he finally agreed to accept £650 for the Requiem, £100 for the G major Symphony, and a further £50 for orchestrating the Mass in D; and so at last Novello were able to go ahead with preparing the Requiem for publication.[10]

While engaged on the sketch of the Requiem, Dvořák was elected a member of the Czech Academy of Sciences and Arts. Shortly afterwards, while he was in Moscow, news reached him that the Charles University, Prague, wished to confer on him the honorary degree of doctor of music. This, however, was impossible, for no such degree existed in the Austrian Empire. He was again invited to become a professor of composition at Prague Conservatory, and this time he

8 Dvořák deliberately concealed from Simrock that he was writing a huge work for England; but he made an oblique reference to the Requiem in his letter of 9 October 1890, when he said: 'just now my mind is full of big ideas'.

9 Letter of 19 November from Littleton to Dvořák. The publisher pointed out that Dvořák would receive £100 for conducting the Requiem at Birmingham if this was to be the world première. He offered to pay £100 for the G major Symphony with rights for all countries.

10 Littleton acknowledged Dvořák's acceptance of his terms on 13 April 1891. Birmingham's committee chairman, Charles Beale, wrote to Dvořák on 25 February. Littleton wrote to Dvořák on 31 December 1890, 5 and 16 February, 3 March and 13 April 1891.

agreed to do so, commencing his duties in January 1891. He was greatly
excited in November when Stanford wrote to him, asking if he would
accept a MusD, *honoris causa*, of Cambridge University, and on the
same occasion conduct there his *Stabat Mater* and one of his symphonies.
Dvořák accepted with alacrity, and it was then arranged for him to be
at Cambridge on 15 and 16 June 1891. Prague University, not wishing
to be forestalled by Cambridge, immediately decided to confer an
honorary PhD on the composer in mid March.

From time to time Dvořák suffered from anxieties of one kind or
another, and these were often connected in some way with the unknown. When going on a long journey he liked to have a companion,
and he needed to be assured well in advance about travelling instruc-
tions. He took a long time to reach a decision when invited to America,
and in later life showed signs of agoraphobia.[11] He was also apt to be
concerned about his family's and his own health; and when it was
suggested that he should go to Moscow a little earlier than originally
planned, he said: 'I have no objection to changing the date of the
concert to February, although I fear that the cold weather in Russia
might affect my health . . . [12] He was disturbed by the report that there
was an influenza epidemic in England three weeks before he was due to
go to Cambridge, and he gave Stanford a fright when he wrote: ' . . . on
acout [sic] of that I and my wife are afraid to come there. The journey
from Prague to London is very long and if we had a bad weather we
can easy take cold—and what shall we do then? Please tell me what is to
be done.'[13] Stanford immediately reassured him by saying that there
was no longer any risk, that the weather in Cambridge was glorious,
and as regards health he would probably be safer in Cambridge than in
Prague. He also stressed how extremely embarrassing it would be if
Dvořák failed to appear, for Albani, Lloyd, and Henschel had promised
to give their services free, practically all the tickets for the concert had
been sold, and for the degree ceremony there were distinguished men
coming from Germany, Russia and Rome.[14] In Dvořák's reply he
said ' . . . I with pleasure see that no danger is to the influenza. When all
is right I arrive in London Friday morning [12 June] Charingcross. I
would be very glad if I meet you there because I don't know how a
[sic] find my way to Littleton or anybody else . . .'[15]

11 He placed reliance on one of his students helping him to cross the street in Prague.
12 Letter of 2 October 1889 from Dvořák to Safonov.
13 Postcard of 26 May 1891 from Dvořák to Stanford.
14 Letter in German of 28 May 1891 from Stanford to Dvořák.

The *Stabat Mater* was greatly appreciated at the afternoon concert. The duet 'Fac ut portem' was warmly applauded, and the composer was given a rousing ovation at the end. Emma Albani sang 'Where art thou, father dear?' from *The Spectre's Bride* between the two main items, the second of which was the G major Symphony. In a letter to Rus next day, Dvořák said it was 'very tiring, with enough music to give one indigestion', and then he added: 'The glory was quite frightening'. At the degree ceremony, dressed up in the splendid robes which had been presented to him by the ladies of the Cambridge University Musical Society, he was astonished and disconcerted to find that the only language spoken was Latin, and it took him a little time to realize when he was being addressed in this archaic tongue. In later years he comforted himself with the thought that after all it was better to have composed a *Stabat Mater* than to be able to understand Latin. Stanford, who gave the Dvořáks hospitality during their stay at Cambridge, was surprised by various things that Dvořák said in conversation.[16] He was also taken aback when he 'heard a noise in the garden in the small hours, and saw the pair sitting under a tree in my garden at 6.00 a.m.'

Special performances of Dvořák's music were arranged in Prague for the months up to the composer's fiftieth birthday. *The Jacobin* was given and a new production of *Dimitrij* was mounted, Ondříček played the Violin Concerto, the 149th Psalm was sung and Dvořák conducted his D major Symphony. At the time of the actual jubilee he was at Vysoká, and although a repeat performance of *Dimitrij* was taking place, he had no intention of forsaking his beloved retreat for that.

Dvořák returned to England early in October for his important contribution to the Birmingham Festival. The programme included new works by Mackenzie and Stanford, but the new Requiem Mass, performed at the conclusion of the Festival on the 9th, attracted the most attention. It was warmly welcomed by the public, and made a deep impression on several of the critics. They were curious to know whether the syncopated chromatic motto theme symbolized supplication, personal grief, or perhaps even the deprecation of divine wrath,

15 Postcard of 30 May 1891 from Dvořák to Stanford. The Dvořák-Stanford correspondence appears in my article 'Dvořák at Cambridge', *Monthly Musical Record*, lxxxix (1959), pp. 135–142. Dvořák stayed two nights at the Charing Cross Hotel. Although he usually arrived at Victoria, it is strange that he was anxious about finding his way from Charing Cross, which he must have known quite well.

16 The only living composer about whom he seemed at all enthusiastic was Verdi; and he said very little about Brahms, and in any case not what Stanford had expected him to say. C. V. Stanford: *Pages from an Unwritten Diary* (1914).

but none of them commented on the fact that the melodic outline is similar to the initial bar of the second Kyrie of J. S. Bach's B minor Mass:

During the unorthodox repetition before the Agnus Dei of the concluding prayer ('Pie Jesu') of the Dies irae, the composer became so carried away by his own music that he unfortunately failed to steer the huge chorus safely through a tricky unaccompanied passage. The situation was saved by the organist, and afterwards the composer confessed frankly that he alone was to blame. Towards the end of that season the Requiem was performed by R. H. Warren in New York, by Hallé at Manchester and Liverpool, by Barnby in London, and then at Olomouc, Kroměříž and Prague.

Dvořák's noble and deeply felt setting of the Mass for the Dead, which Birmingham gave him the opportunity of writing, was not written apparently with the funeral rites of any particular person in mind. On the contrary it was the fruit of a powerful inner urge of a devout Catholic, at the peak of his powers in the last decade of the nineteenth century, and when he was nearing his fiftieth birthday. It was evidently incumbent on him to provide a monumental work to stand beside his *Stabat Mater* and the rather more modest Mass in D major. The joyful fugue subject, 'Quam olim Abrahae', is an adaptation of a favourite early fifteenth century hymn of praise, 'Vesele spívejme, Boha Otce chvalme':

And since he had a fascination for allusions, Dvořák introduced in a perfectly natural manner near the beginning of the Tuba mirum a conspicuous reference to *Tristan and Isolde*. In an age when individualism flourished, it is only natural that the Czech composer's setting should differ greatly from those of Berlioz, Verdi and Fauré. As a whole, Dvořák's Requiem impresses us with its convincing sense of balance, its restraint and a feeling of awe, coupled with an avoidance of the unduly dramatic. His sympathetic and sensitive response to the Latin text reflects what Burghauser rightly refers to as his contemplation of the mysteries of human existence, of life and of death.

Adelina de Lara, who met Dvořák during the Festival, described him as 'a jolly good fellow' but rather quaint. He had a broad face and very bright eyes above a squat nose and a closely trimmed beard. The huge silk bow he wore with his velvet jacket seemed to her to be out of place with the rest of his appearance. As he strolled about with his hands in his pockets he would whistle or hum. He offered the nineteen-year-old Adelina a halfpenny if she played Chopin's Ballade in A flat for him, and she did so. After a long interval he returned with the promised coin, on which he had scratched 'Dvořák', 'Birmingham', 'October '91' 'Adelina' and 'Ballade'.[17]

On the other side of the Atlantic preparations were in full swing in 1891 for the celebrations being held in the following year to mark the Fourth Centennial of Columbus's discovery of America. Mrs Jeannette M. Thurber, the wife of a millionaire New York grocer, and a philanthropist who had founded the American Opera Company (later known as the National Opera Company) and in 1885 the National Conservatory of Music of America, saw this as a splendid opportunity to attract one of the foremost European musicians to act as the titular head of her National Conservatory. Her choice fell on Dvořák,[18] whom she was confident could realize her dream of bringing into being a national American school of composition. A friend of hers who tried to sound Dvořák on the subject in the spring received no response, so while in Paris Mrs Thurber sent him this cable on 5 June: 'Would you accept Director National Conservatory of Music New York October 1892 also lead six concerts of your works.' She followed this up with a letter which he did not see until he returned from Cambridge. In this she asked him to be the Director of the National Conservatory and the conductor at ten concerts, for eight months, followed by a four-month vacation, at an annual salary of 15,000 dollars. She probably assured him that his duties would not be onerous, so that he would be left with

17 A. de Lara: *Finale* (1955), pp. 62–65.

18 There does not appear to be any plausible evidence to support the oft-repeated statement that she considered Sibelius as a possible alternative. Sibelius was 25 in 1891 and hardly known outside Finland.

ample time for composition.[19] The composer was excited by this attractive offer, but before he could commit himself he needed to find out more details and see the draft contract, to consult his friend Judge Rus, and find out whether Dr Tragy, who happened to be a Doctor of Jurisprudence, would be prepared to give him leave of absence from Prague Conservatory. It was also essential for him to see whether satisfactory arrangements could be made for the custody and education of his six children, and consider whether he could bear to be parted from them for so long.[20]

Alfred Littleton, who was asked by Mrs Thurber to negotiate with the man of her choice, reported on 25 June that Dvořák still appeared to be suspicious and very cautious, but he was confident that in his own good time Dvořák would accept her offer. By 10 July she agreed to his request to have half his salary deposited in Prague before he sailed.[21] She wished it made clear that she wanted him for two years, not merely for the eight months that Dvořák referred to, and thought that if Littleton went ahead with preparing a contract, it would be easier to overcome the composer's opposition. According to the draft contract, which reached him on 31 July, Dvořák was to have three hours of teaching and other duties from Monday to Saturday, and would conduct four students' concerts and six concerts which would feature his own compositions. In a number of ways he was not satisfied. He wanted the second half of his salary to be paid in eight monthly instalments in advance, and not spread over the whole year, he asked for more favourable conditions about the payment of his salary if he were ill, and insisted on being free to terminate his contract if the climate proved to be injurious to his health. He was prepared to teach composition and orchestration, but only to the most promising students, and was not willing to give instruction 'in other branches of music'.[22]

By accepting all these proposed changes, Mrs Thurber was so certain that the matter was settled, that she cabled to New York early in September with the news of Dvořák's acceptance. Then on the 17th she sent him copies of the revised contract in English and German for his

19 Mrs Thurber's letter is missing, but Dvořák outlined the details in his letter to Göbl of 20 June 1891.

20 Since his family meant so much to him, he would have been particularly sorry not to be with them at Christmastime. Cf. Dvořák's letter to Richter of 1 January 1881.

21 She would not agree to Tragý's proposal that he ought to receive a salary of 20,000 dollars to help him to maintain three homes, and said he had already accepted the earlier figure.

22 The alterations needed by Dvořák are set out in a memorandum in German discovered by M. R. Aborn. It is evidently the work of one of the composer's lawyer friends, and very possibly Judge Rus.

signature. The composer, however, had no intention of being hustled. After demanding some further amendments, and being sent the new draft in the second half of October, he returned this to Littleton asking for a few more adjustments to be made.[23] Although he was becoming excited about the prospect ahead, and looking forward to meeting Czechs who had settled in the United States, he still hesitated a little before committing himself irrevocably, and delayed giving his formal acceptance until 12 December. Writing on that date to Mrs Thurber he said:

> Mrs Dvořák and my eldest daughter Otilka are very anxious to see Amerika, but I am a little afraid that I shall not be able to please you in everything in my new position. As a teacher and instructor and conductor I feel myself quite sure, but there [are] many other trifles which will make me much sorrow and grieve—but I rely on your kindness and indulgence and be sure I shall do all to please you.

Littleton posted the contract in its final form to Dvořák on 21 December, and no doubt the composer was glad to be able to return the completed document before Christmas. After hearing that everything was settled, Mrs Thurber wrote on 29 December asking for signed photographs, autographed manuscripts and biographical details, to contribute towards the publicity she was planning.

In her letter to Littleton of 17 September Mrs Thurber mentioned that she wanted Dvořák to compose a work which would have its première at his first concert in New York. For nine months no more is heard of this idea, but then she made her wishes known. She was having difficulty in finding a suitable text for the short cantata she wanted, and if none was forthcoming she suggested Dvořák might set the 'Te Deum laudamus' or the 'Jubilate Deo'.[24] They sent Joseph Rodman Drake's poem 'The American Flag' a fortnight later, but by the time that reached Dvořák he had already completed the sketch for his *Te Deum* and had begun working on the full score.

After severing relations with Simrock, Dvořák had composed a work which is highly characteristic of him, the *Dumky* Trio. Two months

---

23 In his letter of 24 October to August Bohdanecký, Rus's son-in-law, he said: 'Yesterday I sent off the contract to London, revised for the third time, and if they agree to my alterations—then I shall sign it.' 'Šourek was mistaken in assuming that Dvořák signed the contract soon after writing this letter.

24 Mrs Thurber's wishes are stated in the letter of 10 June 1892 from B. Bachur of the New York branch of Novello, Ewer & Co. to Littleton in London.

after writing it, he, Ferdinand Lachner and Hanuš Wihan launched it in Prague on 11 April 1891. When Dvořák wrote his earliest dumkas he was not sure of the exact meaning of this term, even if he may have linked it in some way with a poetic or sung form concerned with brooding over heroic deeds of bygone days. It is more important to recognize that he transformed the dumka into something rather different, a musical form that embraces both brooding melancholy and the gaiety of the dance. Instead of conforming to classical models the *Dumky* Trio consists of a series of six dumkas in different keys. Alternations of the minor and major modes occur frequently, but as the third section makes clear, the dumka portion may be in a major key and the vivacious dance in a minor key. A striking feature of this attractive and indeed magical work is the ease with which the composer contrasts one melancholy mood with the next, and we can hardly fail to notice, in the second section, how a mood may be changed by means of a momentary blossoming of melody:

At the end of March 1891 Dvořák began work on another large-scale orchestral work, in this case a Triple Overture, with the general title 'Nature, Life and Love', the three parts of which were renamed *In Nature's Realm* (op. 91), *Carnival* (op. 92) and *Othello* (op. 93). These overtures present three aspects of the divine life-giving force's manifestations, a force which the composer designated as 'Nature', and which not only served to create and sustain life, but also, in its negative phase, could destroy it. In order to emphasize that these had a common root, he linked the three overtures with a single Nature theme, which in the first two works is presented in a pure diatonic form, and acquired a somewhat distorted shape in the third.

In Nature's Realm might very easily be thought to represent the awakening of Nature on a spring morning. This interpretation, however, must be rejected, because the sketch reveals that at that early stage Dvořák was considering calling the work 'In solitude' or 'Summer night', as alternatives to the title it now bears. Šourek therefore suggested it represents Man's gradual awareness at the end of the day of the vibrations of the inner voice of Nature, which eventually burst forth in the expression of unrestrained joy. *Carnival*, Dvořák's most popular overture, possesses an irresistible brilliance and verve. At one point the composer hints that the delights of the Venusberg are linked with the spirit of revelry. The Nature theme is referred to briefly, but only in the delicately scored G major interlude. Although *Othello*, surely the finest of the composer's overtures, begins as if it were a sonata form structure, with the jealousy motif as the main Allegro theme, it was necessary to abandon this scheme half way through because Dvořák wanted to give a musical impression of the two main protagonists in their final scene. His pencil comments in the score indicate the sequence of events.[25] In addition, a few bars after the passage marked 'They embrace in silent ecstacy', we recognize Wagner's Magic Sleep motif (bar 261); and shortly after Othello becomes consumed with jealousy and desire to have revenge, a reminder of the Requiem Mass motif hints at what lies ahead. When Desdemona expires, the love theme is heard again, to which tremolando *sul ponticello* strings contribute a chilly atmosphere. Due to his remorse Othello prays (a chorale indicates this), for which there is no precedent in either Shakespeare or Verdi.

As soon as the Philharmonic Society of London heard that Dvořák was writing something for orchestra, they asserted that they, rather than Richter, Henschel or Manns, had the strongest claim to present it for the first time in England. Berger was piqued when the composer eventually scribbled a hasty reply giving an evasive answer, and, not understanding what Dvořák meant by the 'element of the publishers', asked how many of the overtures were available in print. They were not published until early in 1894, and then, ironically enough, Henschel presented *Carnival* Overture first at Glasgow on 19 March, and Manns performed *Othello* on 24 March and *In Nature's Realm* on 28 April at the Crystal Palace. The Philharmonic Society did not perform any of the overtures until 1907.

During the first five months of 1892 Dvořák undertook an extended farewell concert tour of almost forty Bohemian and Moravian towns, taking with him his friends Lachner and Wihan. Wherever they went the main item in their programme was the *Dumky* Trio. Apart from the

25 The composer's notes are quoted in the Editor's Notes of the Artia (Complete Edition) full and miniature scores.

Mazurek and *Romantic Pieces* for violin and piano there was nothing suitable for his two companions to play; so before they set off Dvořák composed a Rondo for Wihan, and arranged the E minor *Slavonic Dance* for violin and piano, and the G minor *Slavonic Dance* and 'Silent Woods' from the piano cycle *From the Bohemian Forest* for cello and piano. The whole tour was planned by the music publisher Velebín Urbánek. While it was in progress the composer found time to conduct the Olomouc Žerotín choral society in two performances of the Requiem Mass, and on 28 April he directed the first performances of his three new overtures at a farewell concert in Prague.

Immediately after the tour was over, Dvořák was shocked and saddened to hear of the disaster in the silver mines at Příbram and Březové Hory. Some of the men involved used to frequent the inn at Vysoká and the composer had been on very friendly terms with them. Whatever pleasure he may have taken in the news that the Prague National Theatre company had staged *Dimitrij* at the International Exhibition in Vienna two days later, was overshadowed by his concern over this calamity.

Dvořák completed his *Te Deum* for soprano, bass, chorus and full orchestra on 28 July 1892, several weeks before his departure for New York, and obviously enjoyed writing it. His approach to the text was certainly novel, and resulted in a delightful blend of simple and direct diatonic writing, verging on the primitive, coupled at times with sections that are adventurous in both melody and harmony. The cantata opens with a forthright display of jubilation that reminds us of a peal of bells, set against a conflicting triplet rhythm for the kettle drums. In the second part the noble bass solo, 'Rex gloriae', is set between fine passages for bass choir; and the section 'Te ergo quaesumus . . .', a verse which affected the composer deeply because of the phrase 'redeemed by Thy precious blood', is entrancingly set for sopranos and altos over a pulsing accompaniment, and with violins soaring above like an angelic choir. The third part turns into a kind of dance, with perhaps a suggestion of the gamboling of forest fairies. In the final section the opening material returns to become the basis for an ecstatic conclusion.

His last task before departing for America was to sketch in full the cantata *The American Flag*, but it was quite impossible to have it ready for the first concert. So he laid it aside and completed the score in New York during the winter months. Two months before sailing a splendid idea occurred to him. Josef Jan Kovařík, a young Czech whose home was at Spillville, Iowa, had just completed his violin studies at Prague

Conservatory, and was due to return to America. Dvořák liked him and, thinking how useful he might be to him when he reached New York, invited him to be his secretary and live with them as one of the family. Kovařík agreed very readily to this plan.

Leaving four of his children in the charge of his mother-in-law, Dvořák left home on 15 September 1892 with his wife Anna, fourteen-year-old Otilka, nine-year-old Antonín (Toník) and Kovařík. It was unfortunate that he had to be parted from his other children, he knew he would miss his friends and the country which he loved so much, and he was unsure about what lay ahead. On the other hand he realized there were bound to be many valuable and interesting experiences in store for him, and it seemed almost certain that there was much to be gained by plunging in this way into the unknown.

8 The First Year in the New World

Thanks to the pioneer work in the first place of such men as Theodore Thomas, Anger Hamerik, Walter Damrosch, B. J. Lang, W. L. Tomlins and Wilhelm Gericke, the main cities of the eastern and mid-western states of America were given excellent opportunities to become familiar with Dvořák's work, and in the years that followed their appetite for his vital, fresh, colourful and highly characteristic music grew steadily. R. H. Warren's Church Choral Society of New York must be given the credit for giving the second performance of the Requiem Mass, on 24 February 1892, not long before the Czech master's arrival. This work was heard again three months later at the 10th Biennial Festival at Cincinnati directed by Thomas. Dvořák's other recent work, the G major Symphony, was presented by Nikisch and the Boston Symphony Orchestra on their home ground on 27 February that year, and then within the next two months they repeated it at Washington, Baltimore, New York[1] and Buffalo. However, during the years 1889 to 1892 the work which had the most outstanding success was the *Scherzo capriccioso*. The Boston Symphony Orchestra, directed by Gericke at first and later by Nikisch, played it in more than a dozen cities when on tour, and simultaneously Thomas gave it in New York, Brooklyn, Chicago, Cincinnati and St Louis.

On the afternoon of 27 September, after a stormy voyage in which there was one day when the captain and Dvořák were the only two to appear in the dining saloon, S. S. *Saale* berthed at Hoboken, N.J. The composer was met by Edmund Stanton, the secretary of the National Conservatory, but he was particularly delighted to see that a group of Czechs had gathered there to greet him. At first Dvořák's party occupied six rooms at the Clarendon Hotel, with a pleasant view across Union

---

1 Seidl had previously given it in New York at the Philharmonic Society concert on 12 March 1892.

Square. This, however, was rather noisy and more expensive than the composer liked, and so after a couple of weeks they moved into three rooms at 327 East 17th Street, very close to the National Conservatory.[2] On 1 October Dvořák went to the National Conservatory, where he was warmly welcomed by Mrs Thurber and introduced by her to the numerous professorial staff.[3] These welcomes, however, were completely eclipsed by the banquet that took place at the Central Turn Verien Opera House on the 9th. When the composer and his family entered the 3,600 Czechs all rose to their feet, waving wildly and crying out enthusiastically. He was hailed as the man who would give birth to American national music, and was presented with a silver wreath. It was a most moving experience, and wonderful to find himself surrounded by a host of friends, who were far better acquainted with his music than he had dared to hope.

Several years earlier Mrs Thurber had created an American School of Opera which trained singers and performed operas in English. When this failed to live up to her expectations she devoted her entire energies towards establishing an institution, similar in type to the Paris Conservatoire, which would make it unnecessary for talented young Americans to go to Europe for their training. With the aim of fostering musical talent which came to light in any part of the United States, she was prepared to accept students free of charge, but expected those she helped to repay a portion of their earnings to the National Conservatory during the first five years of their professional life. She made strenuous efforts to obtain governmental recognition and support for her work, but as she was unsuccessful she was obliged to bear the greater part of the financial burden herself.[4] As the founder, the principal benefactor and the president of this enterprise, she quite naturally made sure, with the cooperation of the vice-president, secretary, treasurer and a score of trustees, that the National Conservatory was run in accordance with her aims and wishes. She appointed Dvořák as her Director for the lustre that his name, reputation and presence would bring to her institution and to prepare the ground for that American national school of composition that she dreamed about. She was prepared to listen to his advice on artistic matters, but never

2 He was paying 70 dollars a week at the hotel, almost a quarter of his total salary, and nearly half the amount he was receiving in New York. At East 17th Street he paid 55 dollars a week.

3 Since 1890 the staff had increased from 22 to more than 50.

4 Only 21 of the 258 students enrolled in 1890 paid tuition fees. During the National Conservatory's first year Mrs Thurber contributed about 100,000 dollars towards the costs, and during her lifetime she is believed to have spent ten times that amount in order to keep it solvent.

considered him in the light of a day to day director and administrator.[5]

Dvořák was glad that his responsibilities were limited in this way, and pleased to find his duties were lighter than those set out in his contract. On Monday, Wednesday and Friday morning he spent two hours teaching composition to eight selected students, only two of whom he considered to be really promising, and on two afternoons each week he conducted the students' orchestra. During his first term the most formidable task facing him appeared to the judging of the prize competitions, for which works were submitted from all parts of the United States and he was on every jury. One thousand dollars was being offered for a grand or comic opera, 500 dollars for an opera libretto, an oratorio and a symphony, 300 dollars for a cantata and a suite, and 200 dollars for a piano or violin concerto.[6] He soon discovered, however, that a glance at the first page of a composition revealed whether it was the work of a dilettante or an artist. Several prizes were given, including one to Horatio Parker for a cantata, but Mrs Thurber must have been disappointed that no opera was considered worthy of an award.

As the *New York Herald* expressed it, the huge audience that packed the Carnegie Music Hall on 21 October, when Dvořák appeared in public for the first time, was 'representative of the best elements of artistic and social New York'. 'My Country, 'tis of Thee', sung to the tune of 'God Save the Queen', opened the proceedings. This was followed by an oration by Colonel Thomas Wentworth Higginson, the author, who mistakenly imagined music, the youngest of the arts, did not blossom until after Columbus had discovered America, and so entitled his speech 'Two New Worlds—the New World of Columbus and the New World of Music'. Next Seidl conducted Liszt's *Tasso: lamento e trionfo*, and finally Dvořák presented the three overtures, *In Nature's Realm*, *Carnival* and *Othello*, followed by the first performance of the *Te Deum*, composed especially for the occasion. The critics were not as impressed by the overtures as one would have expected—Krehbiel expressed disappointment at 'their paucity of ideas of real beauty'—but the *Te Deum* was warmly praised. In this

---

5 M. R. Aborn states that Dvořák never attended a meeting of trustees during his period of office, and, more curiously, at no time is he referred to in the minutes of their meetings. *Vide:* Aborn's PhD thesis, *The Influence on American Musical Culture . . .* Ann Arbor (1966).

6 These figures, taken from the National Conservatory prospectus for 1892, are more reliable than those quoted by Dvořák in his letter of 27 November 1892 to the Hlávkas. The juries included leading musicians from as far afield as Boston, Chicago and Washington, and among them were Nikisch and Seidl (Grand Opera) and Rafael Josefffy and Scharwenka (Symphony, Suite and Concerto). There is no mention of these competitions in Dvořák's contract.

Krehbiel found 'much greater forcefulness and loveliness of thought', and while admitting that it was not particularly churchy, he declared that it was 'impressive throughout and sometimes eloquently expressive'.[7]

Several other chances arose for Dvořák to present his own works to the public, the most important of which was at Boston. When the Cecilia Society and Boston Symphony Orchestra combined to perform the Requiem Mass, he directed the public rehearsal for workers on 29th and the performance 'for the wealthy and the intelligentsia' on 30 November. The composer was frequently applauded between numbers and given a most enthusiastic ovation at the end. Philip Hale, for many years the arbiter of musical taste in Boston, regretted that a work of this kind should have been performed in a brilliantly lighted concert hall, before an audience with an animal curiosity concerning their Czech guest and a desire for amusement of a high order. In his view the strength of the Requiem lay in its orchestration, and its weakness in the treatment of the voices as if they were orchestral instruments.[8] Dvořák also conducted the D major Symphony at the New York Philharmonic Society's concert on 17 December,[9] and if Mrs Thurber had not had a quarrel with Emmy Juch, the solo singer, he would probably have directed the Church Choral Society's performance of the *Stabat Mater*, or the Brooklyn Choral Society's performance of the same work, at the end of February 1893.

In earlier years *The Spectre's Bride* had been sung in various American cities, and on 20 March 1886 Theodore Thomas had introduced it at Brooklyn, but strangely enough it had never been given in New York. Feeling it was time to remedy this situation, R. H. Warren arranged for it to be performed by the Church Choral Society, with the support of Damrosch's Symphony Society orchestra, at a charity concert to be held at Carnegie Music Hall on 6 April. Warren directed the performance, but invited Dvořák to open the concert by conducting his *Hussite* Overture. It was hoped that the composer would direct the Chicago Apollo Club's Requiem performance on 11 April, but it is possible that Mrs Thurber may not have wished to spare her Director just then. Theodore Thomas filled the breach.

7 *New-York Daily Tribune*, 24 October 1892.

8 *Boston Morning Journal*, 1 December 1892. On the same day Hale contributed a biographical sketch of Dvořák to the *Boston Globe*.

9 Not 17 November, as Dvořák incorrectly stated on 1 January 1893 in his letter to Rus.

During that season Dvořák attended New York Philharmonic Society concerts regularly and was present at Walter Damrosch's performance of the *Hussite* Overture on 7 January. He may have heard his E flat Piano Quartet played by the Beethoven String Quartet led by G. Dannreuther (17 November), and he heard the Kneisel Quartet when they were in New York for their periodic recitals. Although he was keenly interested in opera, he avoided going to the Metropolitan Opera because of the expense. When Seidl discovered in the following winter that Dvořák did not know Wagner's *Siegfried* well, he gave him complimentary tickets for his next performance. Knowing little or nothing about performances there, the composer and Kovařík arrived long before the rest of the audience, and were shown into their box by a puzzled attendant. When the auditorium began to fill, he found to his horror that their box was in the 'Diamond Horseshoe' and that the occupants of the other boxes were in full evening dress, whereas he and his secretary were wearing lounge suits, and Kovařík's was a very pale colour. They moved to the back of their box, where they were less conspicuous, and left after the first act. When Seidl enquired what he had thought of *Siegfried*, Dvořák admitted that he had left early and offered the lame excuse that he had had enough of that ubiquitous anvil rhythm, which in any case was very probably true.

The composer's first impressions of the American capital were most favourable, and in his letters to his friends he continued to give cheerful accounts of his life there. He often visited the pigeons in the small zoological gardens in Central Park, but never regarded them in any way as the equal of his Pouters and Fantails at Vysoká. Since visitors were not allowed at the Central Station, and travelling to the vantage point from where he could watch the Boston and Chicago expresses go by was very time consuming, he was obliged to abandon his hobby of train spotting and turn his attention instead to the trans-Atlantic liners. He made a habit of inspecting from stem to stern every ship bound for Europe, made friends with their captains, and when the *New York Herald* was delivered he invariably turned first to the shipping intelligence. The departure of the ships served as a sharp reminder of his home and family, and, as Mrs Thurber noticed, this brought tears to his eyes.[10] She claimed that on one of these 'steamer days' she attempted to dispel his mood of nostalgia by suggesting he should compose a symphony, and that the outcome was the 9th Symphony *From the New World*. But it was more than three years since he had written one, and he can

10 J. M. Thurber: 'Dvořák as I knew him', *The Etude*, xxxvii (Philadelphia, 1919), pp. 693–4.

hardly have needed any prompting from her. Besides, he did not launch out on a new work until he was convinced that he was ready to do so.[11]

On reaching America he had been astonished to hear himself hailed as the man who would lead the music of that country to a glorious future. He considered that his rôle was a more modest one, to instil ideas of musical nationalism into his students at the National Conservatory, in the hope that in this way the foundations might be laid for an art having roots in the soil of its origin. As a preparation for this he began to explore the indigenous music of the United States, and was attracted most of all by the spirituals and the plantation songs of the southern states. As soon as he discovered that there was a talented black singer named Harry Thacker Burleigh among the National Conservatory students, who was not a member of his class, he invited him to sing many of these songs to him on a number of occasions.[12] As the partial quotation of 'Swing low, sweet chariot' and the character of the cor anglais theme of the Symphony's Largo show, Dvořák's conception of his first American composition was affected a little by what he had heard.[13]

Mrs Thurber encouraged Dvořák to compose an American opera, and finding he was prepared to write one on the subject of 'The Song of Hiawatha', which he already knew from the translation into Czech, she tried to find someone who would prepare a libretto. Meanwhile, wishing to give him some suitable ideas for the opera's ballet, she took him to see Buffalo Bill's Wild West Show. Although there is not the slightest hint of Indian music in the Symphony, it is closely linked with this opera project, for the composer described the Largo as a study or sketch for a Hiawatha work, and said the scherzo was suggested by the scene at the feast in 'Hiawatha' at which the Indians dance.

Josef Jan Kovařík, whose father Jan Josef Kovařík was a schoolmaster, spoke from time to time about his north-east Iowa home at Spillville, a settlement of Czechs who conversed with each other in their native tongue. Dvořák wanted to know more about this place and plied

11 Most of the themes for the E minor Symphony appear in the American sketch books; the main theme of the Largo appears first and is dated 20 December 1892. Dvořák finished scoring *The American Flag* on 8 January 1893 and began sketching the Symphony on the 10th.

12 In his article 'The negro and his song' Burleigh states that he was not sufficiently advanced to be a member of Dvořák's class. *Vide* H. G. Kinscella: *Music on the Air* (New York 1934), p. 188.

13 Dvořák is reported to have said, when discussing his teaching aims at the National Conservatory: 'In the negro melodies of America I discover all that is needed for a great and noble school of music. They are pathetic, tender, passionate, melancholy, solemn, religious, bold, merry, gay or what you will . . . There is nothing in the whole range of composition that cannot be supplied with themes from this source.' Interview with the *New York Herald*, 'Real Value of Negro Melodies', 21 May 1893.

his secretary with questions. But it came as a complete surprise when he announced, possibly in the first half of February, that instead of returning to Bohemia for the summer vacation, he was going to Spillville. He had decided to arrange for the rest of his children to be brought to America, so that they could all go together to this idyllic spot. Some time before this he had been invited to visit Edward Rosewater, the proprietor of the Nebraska newspaper the *Omaha Bee*, who came from Bukovany, and now there was a chance of accepting. Besides this there was the further attraction of the World's Columbian Exposition in August at Chicago, where he knew there was a large Czech population and a Czech Day was being arranged. He was looking forward to seeing more of America and decided it would be simple to make a detour on the return journey, via Buffalo, so that they could see Niagara.

According to Kovařík, Dvořák became so excited when he heard that his four children had reached Southampton, that he forgot to fill in the trombone parts in the last bars of his new Symphony, and it is often stated that the omission was not discovered until the work was being rehearsed. Attractive as this story is, it will not stand close examination and must now be discarded as a myth. The inscription on the final page of the score reads, 'Praise God! Completed 24th May 1893 at 9 o'clock in the morning. The children have arrived at Southampton (a cable came at 1.33 pm)', showing that the work was finished before the cable arrived. Neither were the trombone parts inserted later, as Burghauser has now shown.[14] Kovařík's memory was unreliable, and he may have been confusing this and other episodes.

Anna, Magda, Otakar and Zinda, accompanied by their aunt Terezie Koutecká and a maid, reached New York on 31 May 1893, and three days later the whole party of eleven set off on the long trip to Spillville. Dvořák's interest increased with each successive stage of their journey. They stopped for a few hours at Chicago, and drove round the city, and at breakfast time the next day they arrived at McGregor, Iowa, from where they gazed in wonder at the great Mississippi river. At Calmar they were met by Jan J. Kovařík, Thomáš Bílý, the parish priest, and also by the priest from the neighbouring Czech settlement of Provitín, and then drove the last few miles. They were given accommodation at Spillville by J. Schmidt, who was German in origin.[15]

14 Introductory notes to the facsimile edition of the manuscript score of the 9th Symphony *From the New World* (Prague 1972). Burghauser is convinced that the same pen and the same ink were used for this last page, and that Dvořák completed the page from the top in three stages, blotting each section before starting on the next. Kovařík had claimed that he noticed the trombones were missing while making a copy of the score at Spillville.

15 His house, now the Bílý Clock Museum, includes two rooms which serve as a small Dvořák museum.

Signed portrait given to Dvořák by Tchaikovsky

Dvořák (centre), Wihan and Lachner (seated) at the time when they toured
Bohemia and Moravia playing the Dumky Trio

Dvořák immediately felt completely at home in his new surroundings. On rising at around 4 o'clock next day, he became very excited while walking through the woods by the Little Turkey river to hear the birds singing, which was something he had missed during his eight months of city life. The birds were different from those he knew, and he was especially interested in a small red bird with black wings with a very rapid song. He jotted down the song, and introduced it into the scherzo of the F major String Quartet, which he was about to compose. The bird was a scarlet tanager. Early morning mass at St Wenceslas church was invariably celebrated without music, but on this first day the congregation were greatly astonished when Dvořák seated himself at the little organ and played the favourite Czech hymn 'Bože, před tvou velebností' (God, before Thy Majesty'). Every day after that he played the hymns which meant so much to the folk of Spillville.

Dvořák became extremely friendly with Father Bílý, and the children had fun riding on the priest's ponies. He would listen for a long time to what the older people had to tell him about their early experiences in America. They were poor when they settled in the area some forty years before, but after many years of struggle they had become quite prosperous. The composer was surprised to find that one farmer in the prairies might be four miles from his nearest neighbour, and that the cattle were milked wherever they grazed, and remained there throughout the year. Since Dvořák needed contact with people, and here one could go miles without meeting a soul, he was saddened by the loneliness of the life that these farmers lived.

With the single exception of the excessive heat at the height of the summer, all the conditions at Spillville were ideal for Dvořák. He was able to relax and enjoy the peaceful atmosphere to the full, surrounded by his family and his fellow countrymen, and at no time during his stay in the United States was he happier than here. Finding everything so congenial, he felt moved to start composing on 8 June, and by the third day he had completed the sketch for the String Quartet in F major, op. 96, *The American*. Pleased with his rapid progress, he wrote at the end of the sketch: 'Thanks to the Lord God, I am satisfied, it went quickly. Completed 18 $\frac{10}{6}$ 93'. He was occupied with the score until 23 June.

The F major String Quartet has undeniably earned its great popularity because of its lively rhythms, its predominantly major keys, its appealing Lento in D minor, and because it makes no great demands on the listener and is easy on the ear. For the most part the moods are gay, phrase structures are simple, verging on the primitive, and there is a tendency for themes to be pentatonic and to have flattened sevenths in place of leading notes. Even though, it hardly qualifies as one of the composer's best products, it possesses a remarkable freshness. It brims over with the joy and good humour that marked Dvořák's first days at Spillville, and in the finale (Meno mosso, bar 280) reminds us of the little organ there in the church of St Wenceslas. Spillville is the only place where the Quartet could possibly have orginated.

Just at this time a party of Indians selling medicinal herbs visited the little town. Their leader, Big Moon, was apparently a Kickapoo, and John Fox, their legal adviser, was a Yankton Sioux, but it is not known what the tribes of the rest of the band may have been.[16] The composer welcomed this unexpected opportunity to become better acquainted with Indian art, and so he invited them to give performances of their dancing and singing at the inn several times while they remained in the neighbourhood. Kovařík (presumably the younger Kovařík) noted down a brief snatch of one of their songs, and Dvořák worked it into his next composition, the String Quintet in E flat major, op. 97.[17] In the slow movement of this same work he used a tune of his to which the anthem 'My Country, 'tis of Thee' could be sung. He sketched and scored the Quintet between 26 June and 1 August.

Since Dvořák began sketching the E flat String Quintet only three days after completing his Quartet, it is not surprising that the two works should have stylistic features in common. Nevertheless the Quintet is planned on quite different lines. The fragment of Indian melody utilized for the first movement's subsidiary theme in G minor, lost its Indian flavour when Dvořák provided it with a new rhythmic shape. Šourek was wrong in imagining the finale's second theme possessed an Indian colouring, and equally incorrect in his belief that there were Indian drum rhythms in the three quick movements. Dvořák used countermelodies to enrich the rhythmically austere Allegro vivo (¢), a substitute for a scherzo, and in the Trio the first viola is given a glorious soaring melody:

16 Jan J. Kovařík very misleadingly stated that these Indians were 'the kickapoo and belonged to the Iroquois tribe', but the Kickapoo, a small and insignificant tribe belonging to the Central Algonquin group, are entirely unrelated to the Iroquois, who are a linguistic group, not a tribe! The matter is discussed more fully in my article 'Dvořák and the American Indian', *Musical Times*, cvii (1966), pp. 863-7.

17 Due to the modifications made by Dvořák, this theme loses its Indian character. Indian influence on his music is minimal, as I have attempted to show in my paper 'Indian Influence in Dvořák's American Chamber Music', *Colloquium Musica Cameralis, Brno 1971* (Brno 1977), pp. 147-156, 525.

The most impressive movement, however, is the Larghetto, a set of variations on a pair of themes, in A flat minor and major, the second of which may be fairly described as Beethovenian. The sketch of this double theme, dated 19 December 1892, is the very first of the composer's American sketches.

During the two previous years there had been a slight thaw in Dvořák's relations with Simrock. When the Berlin publisher enquired if he was already in America, or going there or actually dead, the Czech composer replied that he was glad to have heard from him, and raised his hopes that he might be able to offer him one of his compositions before long.[18] His next letter mentions that the *Dumky* Trio and the Rondo in G minor for cello were both ready, but he insisted that he was in no hurry; and when Simrock asked to see the manuscripts and to hear what he wanted for them, the composer refused to respond. He evidently wished to entice Simrock with his wares but withhold them from him. After a year he wrote to Littleton, offering to sell him seven of his compositions for £600; but the latter was only interested in the two choral works, which did not suit Dvořák.[19]

The signs are that Dvořák dismissed the possibility of approaching Bote & Bock, Schlesinger or other publishers, because he felt the time was drawing near when he would be able to resume normal relations with Simrock on his own terms. The longer he delayed doing so, the more unpublished works there would be. He would not have had any difficulty in getting the *Dumky* Trio, the F major Quartet, the cello Rondo and the two cantatas published, but he did not relish the idea of having the three overtures and the new symphony left on his hands. While enjoying himself at Spillville Dvořák received an impatient letter dated 6 June from Simrock asking why he had still not received the Trio, Overtures and Rondo, which the composer had known he wanted to publish ever since early in January 1892. The time at last appeared to be ripe for Dvořák to, as it were, bury the tomahawk and smoke the calumet with his publisher.

18 Letters of 17 and 22 November 1891 between Simrock and Dvořák.
19 The works were the *Te Deum*, *American Flag*, the Triple Overture, the *Dumky* Trio and the Rondo.

In the long and cordial reply that the composer sent to Simrock on 28 July 1893, he remarked that he was composing simply to please himself because his good salary made him independent, and due to this he was in no hurry to publish his compositions. He mentioned all that he had to offer, including piano duet versions of the three overtures, and said he did not expect to receive more for them than Simrock had been accustomed to pay. He asked for 2,000 marks for all three overtures, and the same amount for the *Dumky* Trio and also for the 9th Symphony, and would be satisfied with 500 marks each for the Rondo, the arrangement of *Silent Woods* and the F major String Quartet, a total of 7,500 marks in all. Simrock immediately agreed to take all these works, and asked to have the E flat String Quintet as well.[20] Obviously very satisfied with this new turn of events, the composer commented to Rus on 17 August: 'At last Simrock has eaten humble pie, and says he will take all my works. I was sure he would have to come to me first, and not I to him. So after all by waiting I have punished him.' In pulling off this deal, Dvořák had been successful in getting Simrock to agree to publish these works with the titles in both Czech and German, which was a small but significant victory.

Dvořák took his whole family and Josef Kovařík with him when he went to Chicago for a week in August. When they arrived at 8 am on the 6th they were met by a group of local Czechs, and later that day Theodore Thomas and other leading musicians of the city called at the Lakota Hotel to wish Dvořák a very warm welcome. There was much of interest at the huge World Columbian Exposition, but for them all 'Bohemian Day' on 12 August crowned everything. Thirty thousand Czechs and Moravians marched in the two or three-mile-long procession from the city's downtown to the fair grounds, and among them musical societies, Sokols (athletic organizations), school leagues, sharpshooters, secret societies, benevolent associations, labour unions and a host of other groups added colour and swelled the throng. The main event of the day was the concert which followed the speech of Lieut.-Governor Charles Jonáš of Wisconsin. The conducting was shared by Dvořák and Vojtěch Hlaváč from St Petersburg. When the composer appeared to present his G major Symphony the audience of 8,000 gave him a rousing storm of applause which lasted almost two minutes, and they were spellbound while the orchestra of 114 played the Symphony.[21]

20 Simrock agreed to pay additional fees for the piano duet version of the *Dumky* Trio, and the orchestral versions of the cello Rondo and *Silent Woods*. He was prepared to take all the works he was buying on trust, without seeing any of them.

Dvořák went on a 1,200-mile trip from Spillville with his wife and Josef Kovařík at the beginning of September. They went first to Omaha, where they had a very warm reception from Edward Rosewater, the newspaper proprietor and friend of Presidents Harrison and Cleveland. On the first evening they were serenaded by a number of Czech instrumentalists, a huge banquet was arranged in the composer's honour, and when they departed at the end of their short stay an American band gave a little performance. At the invitation of Father J. Rynda, whom Dvořák had met at Chicago, they then went on to St Paul, Minnesota, another city where there were many Czechs. Rynda, a Moravian from Kojetín, took them to see the beautiful Minnehaha Falls, the sight of which gave the composer an inspiration for a melodic theme. For want of a piece of paper, he wrote this down on his starched cuff, and it later became the theme for the Violin Sonatina's Larghetto.

The memorable holiday at Spillville came to an end on 17 September, and the family had what the composer describes as a troublesome journey back to New York, but he was relieved that the children were so cheerful. He found the Niagara Falls absolutely incredible, and after gazing silently at them for five minutes, he exclaimed 'Crikey!²² That will be a symphony in B minor!'

21 In the second half of the programme Dvořák conducted his *My Home* Overture and the *Slavonic Dances*, op. 72, nos 6, 2 and 3. Hlaváč conducted *The Bartered Bride* Overture, Bendl's *Bohemian Chorale*, the Funeral March from Fibich's *Bride of Messina*, Nápravník's *Spanish Fandango* and some pieces of his own. *Chicago Tribune*, 13 August 1893.

22 The word he used was 'Kakra', a corruption of 'sakra', which is equivalent to 'sakrament(e)'.

9 The Fickleness of Fortune

After returning to New York, Dvořák was very much happier than he had been during his previous eight months in the city, or at least he was for the first few months. This was because, having been successful in uniting his family in America, he had no intention of sending any of the children home again before the next spring. Having them all around him outweighed his longing to see his homeland and his friends. When his contract expired they would all return to Bohemia together, and then he could enjoy a peaceful summer at Vysoká. They settled down in New York, the children went to school and young Toník outstripped the others in learning English.

Work went on much as before at the National Conservatory, except for the implementation of the new policy of training black students to qualify for membership of the professorial staff. Dvořák's duties remained virtually unchanged. It is not known whether he arranged more than one students' concert in his first year, possibly only that on 8 May 1893 at which his composition class presented several of their own compositions. In his second year, however, he arranged three concerts, in all of which the Conservatory orchestra, which he was training, seems to have participated. No professional stiffening was possible when the orchestra played, due to union rules, a factor which could easily account for the composer's excessive nervousness during the first of these programmes.

There was a very striking change, however, in the position over public concerts. Clearly Mrs Thurber to a large extent justified providing her Director with a generous salary because she wished him to present his own music personally at concerts in New York and other American cities, which would lead to publicity and reflected glory for her National Conservatory. If she organized one of these events herself, as she had in the case of Dvořák's inaugural concert, then he would need no fee, and if he was invited by some other body, such as the Cecilia at Boston and the Philharmonic Society of New York, then presumably the fee which they offered him would go to her.[1] During this second year Dvořák did not conduct a single concert of this kind. When the 9th Symphony *From the New World* received its première, Seidl conducted it, and a fortnight later when it was introduced by the Boston Symphony Orchestra at Boston, it was directed by Emil Paur. Other works by Dvořák were performed that season in New York and Boston, but the composer does not seem to have been asked to conduct any of these.

There is more than one possible explanation for this. At this time Mrs Thurber was chary of organizing anything that might lead to a financial loss.[2] For their part professional bodies would very probably have held back if they suspected that Dvořák's participation might not turn out to be a sufficient draw to offset the additional expense of engaging him, and also possibly if they considered that their own regular conductor would be likely to achieve a more polished performance. The critics were not unanimous about Dvořák's efficiency as a conductor, but it may be assumed that he lacked professional skill.[3]

Long before this, on Christmas Eve 1892, Alfred Littleton had written with a request for an oratorio for a festival in 1895. The composer appears to have been more ready to write a cantata, but was unwilling to commit himself in any way, which the Cardiff Musical Festival committee found very frustrating. The months passed, until in November Littleton wrote again, saying that the committee had heard he was at work on a cantata and wanted him to promise them the first performance. It is true that Dvořák had become enthusiastic at Spillville about setting Erben's ballad 'Záhoř's Couch',[4] but he had not made a start on this. Replying to Littleton on 17 November 1893, he said he had a very good subject and was prepared to grant Cardiff's request,

1 It is uncertain whether there would have been a fee when Dvořák conducted the *Hussite* Overture at R. H. Warren's concert on 6 April 1893 in aid of the Women's Auxiliary of the Saturday and Sunday Association. Dvořák's Chicago concert fell during the vacation and so did not concern Mrs Thurber. When Dvořák's first and second American contracts are compared, it can be seen that Mrs Thurber considered that her Director's services as the conductor at up to six public concerts were worth approximately 5,000 dollars to her.

2 The justification for this remark will become clear later. Aborn found a rather casually worded memorandum among Mrs Forell's papers which cannot be exactly dated, but refers to a concert that Dvořák gave which made a loss. This may perhaps have been the inaugural concert for which Mrs Thurber engaged the Metropole Orchestra, hired the Carnegie Hall, and relied on Seidl to share in the conducting. The document may antedate the only other known outside concert, the Conservatory students' concert on 9 May 1894, and seems to indicate clearly that the loss was made at a concert that included his own compositions.

3 The *New York Herald* considered him an excellent orchestral leader (22 October 1892), but the *New-York Times* said it was impossible for players to follow his uncertain beat with confidence (22 October 1892). Philip Hale described his beat as 'plain', and the *Chicago Tribune* remarked: 'As a conductor Dr Dvořák is by no means graceful, but in his every movement there is meaning.' (13 August 1893).

4 Letter of 15 September 1893 from Dvořák to Kozánek.

but he did not feel inclined to start on something which was likely to take a year to write unless he was sure it would be published.[5] Littleton then asked what the composer's terms would be, and wanted to see the libretto. Dvořák, however, had something else on his mind: before coming to any decision about the cantata, he wanted to find out whether Littleton would purchase the *Te Deum* for £150,[6] evidently thinking that this would provide some indication of the fee he could expect for the cantata. Even though Dvořák reduced his demand six months later to £120, Littleton still thought this was too much.[7] The composer abandoned his plan to set Erben's ballad, and Cardiff's hopes for a cantata were dashed.

Towards the end of 1893 Dvořák hit upon a delightful idea, to compose a modest work for his own family which Otilka and Toník would be able to play. With his E flat String Quintet he had already reached op. 97. He decided for the moment to keep the next two numbers in reserve, so that he could designate the new work Op. 100. It was in this way that the Sonatina in G major for piano and violin came into being. The new work, begun on 19 November and finished on 3 December, is inscribed: 'Dedicated to my children Otilka and Toník, Aninka, Mařenka, Otakar and Zinda to commemorate the completion of my hundreth work.' Soon after this he made a choral arrangement of 'Old Folks at Home', and then composed the piano Suite in A major, op. 98.

His next work, composed during March, was prompted by external events and a strong inner compulsion. It need not be assumed that he had been much affected by the death of Gounod, for whom he had no great admiration, but he felt the loss of his friends Tchaikovsky and Hans von Bülow intensely, and just at this time his own father lay seriously ill. He died just two days after Dvořák had finished writing his *Biblical Songs*, op. 99. These settings of selected verses from the Book of Psalms, drawn from the old Bible of Kralice, must be recognized as a sincere and devout reaffirmation of the Czech composer's unshakable faith in the divine wisdom and love of the Almighty. There was an additional reason at that time why it should have been such a comfort for Dvořák to commune in this way with God. As will become clear

---

5 Letter formerly in the collection of Richard Border.

6 Dvořák wrote to Littleton on 3 March 1894. The content can be gathered from Novello's reply of 15 March.

7 Letter of 25 September 1894 from Dvořák to Novello, Ewer & Co. The *Te Deum* was eventually bought by Simrock and published in 1896.

presently, he was faced with a dilemma over the possibility of resuming his post as Director of the National Conservatory after the summer recess.

In setting these verses, Dvořák, a Catholic, showed his affection for the old Czech protestant Bible by relying largely on a simple and expressive vocal line. In 'I will sing a new song unto thee' (No. 5) and 'O sing unto the Lord a new song' (No. 10) he even resorts to pentatonicism, but for strength of line the following cry from 'By the rivers of Babylon' (No. 7) cannot be bettered:

Rather earlier than this the première of the Symphony *From the New World* had caused a considerable stir in New York. A half-column interview with the composer, headed 'Dvořák on his New Work', appeared in the *New York Herald* on 15 December 1893, the day of the public rehearsal, and on the same day Krehbiel devoted two and a half columns of the *New-York Daily Tribune* to an illustrated discussion and description of the new symphony. The rehearsal itself was quite an event, but since Dvořák had given his tickets to someone who was most anxious to be there, he was not present himself. As it was an afternoon rehearsal the audience consisted mainly of women, whose enthusiasm for the new work was unbounded. At the performance on the 16th, Dvořák, his wife and Otilka shared a box with Mrs Thurber, Adele Margulies and Dvořák's two favourite pupils, Harvey W. Loomis and M. A. Stratthotte. Undoubtedly the composer was keen for his students to observe how what he claimed to be the spirit of indigenous American music could serve as a basis for a symphonic work, and invest it with a national character. Krehbiel, who like Philip Hale, thought that English influence on Dvořák had been harmful, was convinced that American influence was beneficial. While the pundits continued to argue that national American music was an impossibility, the composer, using ears of genius, demonstrated that it was a reality.[8] He wondered whether the Czech composer's example would be followed.

Every movement of the Symphony was greeted with a storm of applause, and the Largo made such an impression on the packed hall that the composer was obliged to rise to his feet and bow from his box, 'like a king—alla Mascagni in Vienna', as he remarked to Simrock. On this occasion, as Krehbiel noted, 'the staidness and solemn decorum of the Philharmonic audience took wings'. Without question this was one of the greatest triumphs, and very possibly the greatest triumph of all that Dvořák experienced in the whole of his life. When the work was published it was seized on by conductors and orchestras in many parts of the world. Mackenzie gave the first performance in Europe at the Philharmonic concert in London on 21 June 1894, and repeated it at the Crystal Palace on 20 October. Labitzký introduced it to Bohemia at Carlsbad on 20 July, following this with a second performance there on 2 August. Dvořák himself presented it in Prague on 13 October. Richter took it to Vienna on 16 February 1896. Mengelberg played it at Amsterdam early in 1898, N. S. Klenovsky apparently introduced it to Russia at Tiflis on 7 February 1899, and Toscanini almost certainly gave the first Italian performance at Milan on 27 April 1900. But at that time Dvořák's former pupil Oscar Nedbal did most to make the Symphony known. Paris first heard it under his direction at the Exposition Mondiale on 23 July 1900, and later that year he presented it at Pavlovsk, near St Petersburg. This work, the title of which Dvořák explained simply meant 'Impressions and greetings from the New World', had already become one of the most popular symphonies of all time.

This Symphony caught the imagination of the musical public in a most remarkable way. At a time when Dvořák's major compositions were being welcomed in some ten countries at the most, this was the work that penetrated to those lands where his music was being received coolly or ignored altogether. Today the Symphony is a universal

8 *New-York Daily Tribune* 17 December 1893. Krehbiel rejected Dvořák's rash claim to have conveyed the spirit of Indian music in this work, but conceded that its mood could have been inspired by Indian legend and romance; *New-York Daily Tribune*, 15 December 1893.

favourite. It is performed more frequently than any other symphony at the Royal Festival Hall, London, and is in tremendous demand in Japan. The imaginative title 'From the New World' gives the work an initial advantage, but it is the quality of the colourful music itself that has set the seal on its widespread acceptance. It was written by a fully mature and greatly experienced composer at the peak of his powers for an eager new public whose expectations ran high. Even if the Symphony cannot be claimed to be an unflawed masterpiece, it displays great fertility and originality of musical thinking, a directness of utterance, and at the culmination of the work an overwhelming dramatic power. The piquant scherzo was inspired by the dance of Pau-Puk-Keewis in *The Song of Hiawatha*, and the Largo too was also suggested in some way by Longfellow's poem, although it is uncertain which episode he had in mind. The beautiful slow movement melody could almost have been a spiritual, which it virtually became soon afterwards when it was provided with words and the title 'Goin' Home'. It must be recognized, however, that in general the work is decidedly Czech. Hitherto Dvořák had been sparing with thematic cross references, but in this case he relied on a motto theme which, in contrast with normal practice, plays a significant role in every movement.

Shortly after the Symphony was launched, the Kneisel Quartet gave the premières of the two works composed at Spillville. Boston heard the F major Quartet on 1 January 1894, and on the 12th they played the E flat String Quintet in New York, together with the new Quartet and the String Sextet. In each case Krehbiel provided detailed illustrated descriptions of the two works, just as he had previously for the E minor Symphony.[9]

Mrs Thurber, eager to show the first fruits of her policy of giving greater encouragement to black students, planned a concert in which most of the participants were black. It took place on 23 January at Madison Square concert hall. The programme included Dvořák's 'Inflammatus', sung by the black singer Sissieretta Jones, and *American Plantation Dances*, composed and conducted by the black student Maurice Arnold, and it ended with Dvořák's arrangement of *Old Folks at Home*. The soloists in this were S. Jones and H. T. Burleigh and there was an entirely black choir, but since the Conservatory was very short of male students, they were helped out by the St Philip's Coloured Choir.

When Mrs Thurber broached the subject of Dvořák staying on as Director of the National Conservatory for another two years, he seemed

9 *New York Daily Tribune*, 1 and 7 January 1894.

quite prepared to do so, provided Dr Tragy was willing to spare him
for a further period; yet he was in no hurry to commit himself. He
and Otilka were subject to severe waves of nostalgia, but there was
another factor that needed to be taken into consideration. There had
been an immediate panic when it was disclosed on 21 April 1893 that
the nation's gold reserves were below the safety level, and the conse-
quent run on the banks placed even the richest people in a very pre-
carious position. Due to this calamity the eighth instalment of the
composer's salary arrived two months late, and, even worse, the draft
for 7,500 dollars which reached his Prague bank at the end of that
year, three months late, was not honoured. By the second half of
January Dvořák became extremely worried. Several weeks later, on 17
March 1894, Mrs Thurber said she would be able to give him some
money in the following week, she would try to give him the balance
of his monthly salary before he sailed in May, and she could give him a
promissory note payable on 15 October for the 7,500 dollars on which
she had defaulted. During this difficult time it must have been a great
struggle for the composer to make ends meet. Driven to desperation, he
sent Mrs Thurber a threatening letter on 5 April, which ran as follows:

> I love the American people very much and it has been my desire to help
> Art in the United States, but the necessities of life go hand in hand with Art,
> and t[h]ough I care very little for worldly things, I cannot see my wife and
> children in trouble. If circumstances are such that I cannot receive my
> salary according to the Contract I shall submit the case to the 'Board of
> Trustees' and if I can not have *immediate* attention from them I will
> publish my situation to the world.
>
> Without *any* other feeling than that of profound regrets,—I beg you
> to give this your immediate attention, as it is absolutely impossible for me
> to wait any longer. A delay will force me to publish the situation I would
> like to have kept secret.

She kept him waiting for a fortnight, and then sent his 2,000 dollars.
Mrs Thurber was a most determined lady. Despite her very embarrassing situation, and her evident wish to avoid making personal contact
with Dvořák at this critical time, she was well aware that to make
certain that she retained his services she must get him to sign a new
contract before he returned home. She must have felt that even in such
adverse circumstances she could still rely on his fundamental loyalty and
his genuine desire to serve the cause of American music. Realising he
did not wish to shorten his vacation in Bohemia in order to be back in

New York for the September examinations, she proposed engaging him for only six months in 1894–5 and eight months in the following year. For financial and other reasons she did not expect him to conduct any public concerts, and so offered him 8,000 dollars for the first year and 10,000 dollars for the second. Dvořák refused to agree to this proposition until she settled her debt to him, which she in turn described as 'rather unkind'. However, after a week he agreed to return by 1 November and signed the new two-year contract, and at the same time received from her a written promise that she would pay him the 7,500 dollars that she owed on or before 6 October. Four days later he and his family embarked on S.S. *Aller* for Europe.

It was a tremendous relief to Dvořák to get right away from his financial worries in America and the hurly-burly of life in a great city, and to be able to have a really restful time at Vysoká. Shortly after his arrival he visited the little church at Třebsko, a prominent landmark from his modest home in the country, in order to play the hymns at mass, just as he had at Spillville. Finding that the organ was old and ramshackle, he decided to give the church a new one in thanksgiving for his safe return, and the dedication took place on his birthday. He refused to be tempted to make the journey to London to conduct the first English performance of the Symphony *From the New World*, knowing that the Philharmonic Society would be disappointed. He continued the revision of *Dimitrij* that he had begun in New York, composed the *Humoresques*, and paid visits to his good friends Rus at Písek and Göbl at Sychrov.

His idyllic existence was disturbed in mid August by a note from Mrs Thurber enclosing an article from *The Illustrated American*,[10] quoting words attributed to him which provided powerful backing to an appeal for funds for the National Conservatory. This was a sharp reminder that in a few weeks his period of freedom would be at an end. It is clear from the reply he sent that he was not entirely confident that what was still owing to him would be forthcoming. But there was still time left for him to take part in a concert of his chamber music in Prague and to conduct the first performance there of the E minor Symphony, together with the Serenade for strings and, very appropriately, the Overture *My Home*. Mrs Thurber reassured the composer by cable on 5 September that she would fulfil the contract, and three days later she confirmed she would cable the balance of his salary on 6 October and was mailing the steamer tickets. It was therefore something of a shock to him when he received another cable on 9 October stating: 'Cabled 3750 dollars pay other half on arrival'. On the 12th he replied: 'Maybe canot come without receiving all cabled'. What was he to do? There was hardly any time left in which to make a decision.

According to the letter he wrote to Mrs Thurber in August, Dvořák envisaged the possibility that she might not be able to pay off the full 7,500 dollars, or even half that sum, but he insisted that in that case it was imperative for him to have the steamer tickets. In view of this it would have been unreasonable had he refused to return. He therefore departed with his wife and Otakar on 16 October. It is clear, however, that he was uneasy about the situation. He had previously told Dr Tragy that by going to America he hoped to be able to save enough to provide for his old age, but latterly he had deliberately avoided breathing a word about his financial anxieties. In his rather belated letter to Tragy, written at Hamburg on 17 October, asking for further leave from the Prague Conservatory, he limited his request to one year. He had signed a contract for two years, but knew in his heart that he might be forced to reduce the period of time.

The splendid performance put up by S.S. *Bismarck* in encountering stormy weather, but nevertheless steaming the 3,100 miles from Southampton to New York Harbour 'in 6 days, 10 hours and a few minutes' delighted Dvořák, and he kept a careful record of the distance they had travelled each day. A few days later he was also pleased to learn that the New York Philharmonic Society had made him an honorary member, and they were about to give yet another performance of the E minor Symphony. But Dvořák was far from happy in New York that winter. He missed his children very much, and complained that his duties at the Conservatory robbed him of time when he might be composing, and when he was free to compose it often happened that he was not in the mood to do so.[11] All the same he completed the Cello Concerto in B minor between 8 November 1894 and 9 February in the following year, which was a day less than he had spent on the D minor Symphony ten years earlier. He seemed satisfied with what he had written and he became excited whenever he played over the beautiful horn solo in the first movement.[12] At one of Walter Damrosch's New York Symphony Society concerts he was struck by the tremendous power of Rubinstein's *Ocean* Symphony, of which he had no idea when he played in this work many years before; and in the same concert the

---

11 Letter of 15 January 1895 from Dvořák to J. Boleška.
12 Letter of 10 December 1894 from Dvořák to Göbl.

incomparable Ysaye played one of the Bruch D minor violin concertos making a deep impression on Dvořák.[13] He was cheered too on hearing in mid-January that the Kneisel Quartet had just given their fiftieth performance of his F major Quartet.

A year earlier, after Dvořák had resumed normal relations with Simrock, Brahms was generous enough to take over the task of correcting the proofs of his friend's works then being published, realizing how inconvenient it would be to send them back and forth across the Atlantic. Dvořák was astonished by this, and remarked to Simrock: 'It seems incomprehensible to me that he has undertaken the unpleasant task of correcting these things. I can't imagine there can be any other such musician in the world who would do this.' He had not seen Brahms since December 1889, and wanted very much to visit him during the summer of 1894, to express his gratitude to him in person. The visit, however, did not take place. Eventually, just after Christmas, he made an effort to thank him in a letter, from which it may be seen how difficult it was for him to express in words how deeply he appreciated Brahms's self-sacrifice and unfailing devotion.[14]

Dvořák left New York for home on 16 April, several days before his six months had expired, missing the première of *The American Flag* on 4 May. Naturally he was glad to be home again, and he was particularly keen to see his very dear sister-in-law Josefina Kaunitzová again. For several years he had been concerned about her heart condition. When he saw her during the summer of 1894 her state of health was poor, and her letter to him of 26 November that year had given him further cause for anxiety. In consequence of this he had introduced a song she particularly admired, 'Leave me alone' from his Op. 82, into the central section of the Adagio of the Cello Concerto, on which he was just then engaged. Shortly after he returned home she died; and so, in order that his new work might serve as a memorial to her, he completely revised the coda to the finale, bringing in this song for the second time.

When writing an important work, Dvořák was usually obliged to rely on trial and error and redrafting, before he was satisfied with what he had written. He began sketching his great Cello Concerto in D minor before realizing that B minor would be more suitable. He ruminated for a considerable time over his D major horn melody in the first movement, and took a little while before he knew how to give it

---

13 Letter of 8 December 1894 from Dvořák to J. von Kàan.

14 This little known letter appears in full in my article 'Dvořák's relations with Brahms and Hanslick', *Musical Quarterly*, lvii (1971), p. 253. The original German text appears in *Hudební věda*, x (1973), pp. 222-3.

the perfect shape that it now has. He twice sketched the first section of the Adagio, and his second version in some respects differs from what he eventually wrote even more than the earlier draft. And in the finale he miscalculated seriously when he introduced his G major melody very early on, and had to make considerable readjustments later.[15] Yet when listening to the Concerto we are scarcely aware that it did not flow spontaneously from his pen. This noble work is notable for the richness of its invention and its imaginative and inspired colouring. To allow the solo cello to enter for the first time in the tonic major was bold, and the omission of the whole of the first subject and transition, in order to lead directly from the development to a full orchestra version of the horn theme, is a clear indication of Dvořák's genius. Josefina's song forms the basis of the G minor episode in the Adagio. During the revised coda there are wistful references to the first movement's main theme and to this song. There is little doubt that this work is the greatest of all cello concertos.

When he wrote to Göbl on 20 June he confessed that he was 'a lazy fellow', and intended 'to rejoice in heavenly nature' and 'be completely idle' that summer, but he made no mention of the fact that he had had a visit from Adele Margulies three days earlier. To be reminded by her of his undertaking to spend a fourth winter in New York was likely to upset his equanimity and interfere with his hope of genuine relaxation. Miss Margulies and he discussed the payment of 3,700 dollars which the Conservatory still owed him; and he seems to have made it clear that if he were to return it could only be for six months, and not the eight months stated in his second contract. Mrs Thurber informed him by cable in mid-July that she had secured tickets on the *Augusta Victoria*, which was due to leave Hamburg on 17 October, and she followed this with a letter on the 18th confirming the arrangements. We can be certain that Dvořák discussed his problem with Rus when he visited him at the beginning of August. After chewing over it very briefly, he and his wife went to Lužany to consult Josef Hlávka about it, and they came to the conclusion that for family reasons it was not possible for him to go back to America. After reporting their decision to Dr Tragy the composer wrote a letter of resignation to Mrs Thurber on 17 August, which he and his wife signed.

The main reason given for resignation was that the composer's mother-in-law was now too old to be able to look after the children,

---

15 *Vide* 'Dvořák's Cello Concerto in B minor: a masterpiece in the making', *The Music Review*, xl, no. 3 (Aug 1979).

327 East 17th Street, New York City, where the Dvořáks lived in the United States of America

Big Moon, the leader of the party of Indians who visited Spillville

Dvořák conducting at the World's Fair, Chicago

but there were other reasons besides. Dvořák's wife could not bear being separated from the children, they were worried about Anna's and Zinda's health, Otilka's education was an important factor, Mařenka was now old enough to go to school, and the two boys needed the influence of their parents. Dvořák was kind enough to avoid any reference to the still uncertain financial situation and the fact that Mrs Thurber had found it impossible to fulfil her promises. Instead he provided reasons that were genuine, convincing and cogent, and likely to appeal to her humane and compassionate nature. Knowing Dvořák as she did she would have understood the situation completely, and presumably accepted it with deep regret but with a good grace.

10 A New Lease of Life

From time to time Dvořák took a complete break from composition, giving himself a chance to build up his reserves for the next demands on his creative energy. At the beginning of September 1895 he told Göbl that his muse was completely at rest, but added that he had not been entirely idle. 'I often cogitate and reflect,' he said, 'and when alone I examine myself and others. That too is good.'[1] He had never before had so long a fallow period as that between February and November of that year, for he had done little more than write the first hundred bars of a new String Quartet in A flat major, revised the ending of the Cello Concerto, reduced the orchestral parts of this for piano and adapted *St Ludmila* for a stage performance. A break was essential at this time, but before he felt ready to embark on anything new he needed to resume contact with his fellow musicians, after being absent for so long, and to become fully aware of the pulse of artistic life in Prague. This he was able to achieve in two ways. He joined and became chairman of a group which met at Mahulík's inn, not far from the National Theatre, but invariably departed punctually at 9 o'clock so that he could retire early to bed. He also went regularly on Friday evenings with his wife to Josef Hlávka's soirées, at which he met the poets Zeyer and Vrchlický, the sculptor Myslbek, the statesman Dr Ladislav Rieger and other distinguished men.

When he began composing again he found that his musical thought flowed easily and he was very satisfied with what he wrote. He composed two string quartets, one after the other. First came the G major Quartet, op. 106, which occupied him for about a month until 9 December, and he followed this with the A flat Quartet, op. 105, on which he had made a start before leaving New York, and which took him even less time. He finished this on 30 December. The Bohemian Quartet gave the première of the G major Quartet in Prague on 9 October in the following year, and a month later, on 10 November, the Rosé Quartet presented the A flat Quartet in Vienna.[2]

1 Letter of 2 September 1895.

The G major Quartet has such a masterly first movement, brimming over with happiness and *joie de vivre*, followed by an intensely sorrowful Adagio through which runs a ray of hope, ranking among the composer's finest slow movements, that we are strongly inclined to accept the light-weight but enjoyable scherzo, and the not wholly satisfactory finale. The weakness of this occurs when themes from the first movement, at a reduced tempo, alternate with one of the finale's less distinguished ideas. The first movement's upward leaping and downward skittling theme is succeeded by another which is heard more fully when it settles down in the tonic key. A sudden shift to the unexpected key of B flat major brings with it the gracious subordinate theme in triplet rhythm. These three themes form the basis for one of Dvořák's most powerful developments. In the reprise the main theme appears enchantingly refurbished with a countermelody and a patterned foundation, and the second theme is held in reserve for the coda. A dual theme, or rather a single theme with two aspects, one major but including bittersweet harmony, and the other minor, is treated in the manner of free variations in the Adagio ma non troppo, in E flat major and minor. When tension reaches its peak in F sharp minor, Dvořák, following Smetana's example in the Largo sostenuto of his String Quartet 'From my life', presents a splendidly emphatic affirmation of his theme, in massive chords in the key of C major. But the transitory nature of this exaltation is plainly seen immediately in the composer's profound and heartfelt comment:

2 Information supplied to the author by J. Burghauser.

Although Dvořák completed the A flat String Quartet, his last chamber music composition, in just under three weeks, including the New York sketch of the first movement's exposition, it is by common consent considered to be one of his best. The first movement is full of interest, its second theme is highly original, and the first pair of themes which are completely absent from the reprise, are deployed most effectively in the coda. In the Lento there is some particularly dark chromatic writing in the middle section, and when the first theme, returns it is attractively decorated. The spirited finale ensures that the greatest excitement is reserved for the end. But the real glory of the work is its second movement, the scherzo. At the end of the Trio there is a hint of the Count's aria in *The Jacobin* (quoted on p.93). It is possible that the scalewise ascent and similar rhythm of the Trio theme may have reminded Dvořák of his opera. The scherzo itself is a particularly splendid furiant, founded on a theme that swaggers in a defiant manner, in perfect accord with the spirit of this dance:

A few days after finishing off the second of these quartets, and greatly elated by the fertility of his muse, the Czech composer launched out on a project that was very dear to his heart. For many years he had had a deep affection for the ballads of K. J. Erben, one of which in the form of a cantata had brought him tremendous acclaim in Birmingham some years before. He now took three more of the ballads, 'The Water Goblin', 'The Noon Witch' and 'The Golden Spinning Wheel', and in no more than two and a half weeks, between 6 and 22 January 1986, made complete sketches for three symphonic poems. There is an exceptionally intimate relationship between Erben's poems and the music, because Dvořák made settings of a number of his lines and then incorporated these themes into his works. With great enthusiasm he went ahead rapidly on the scoring of his new compositions, finishing *The Water Goblin* on 11 February, *The Noon Witch* on 27 February, and *The Golden Spinning Wheel*, the longest of the three, on 25 April.

Apart from satisfying his deep-seated desire to turn again to Erben's ballads as a source of inspiration for his compositions, this venture of Dvořák's into the alluring territory of the symphonic poem presented him with a unique opportunity to display to an even greater extent than before his exceptional gifts as a master of orchestral colour. Fortunately some Dvořák letters which discuss the content of these symphonic poems have recently come to light,[3] making it possible to supplement and also correct Šourek's descriptions of these works. The composer's scheme for *The Water Goblin* is as follows:

Allegro vivo (B minor): motif of the water goblin, flutes (bars 9–16).

Andante sostenuto, cue 4 (B major): the girl's theme, clarinets.

Cue 5 (B minor): the mother's theme, violins. She relates a dream, as a warning to her daughter not to go to the lake to wash her garments.

Cue 8 (B minor): the girl ignores the warning, violins and oboe.

Allegro vivo: a plank breaks; the girl falls into the water, and thus into the power of the water goblin, who exults diabolically over his triumph.

Andante mesto come prima, cue 13 (B minor): the misery and hopelessness of the girl's existence as the water goblin's wife in his underwater kingdom.

Un poco più lento e molto tranquillo, cue 16: she sings a lullaby to her child, flute and oboe.

Andante, cue 18: in a fury he tells her to stop singing. She tries to calm him. He rejects her plea to visit her mother, but finally he relents.

Lento assai, cue 23 (B major): she goes alone to her mother's cottage, cellos accompanied by trombones. A sad reunion. New version of the mother's theme, for clarinet, oboe and flute, followed by tam tam *pp*.

Allegro vivace, cue 24: A storm on the lake. Evening bells (bars 634–655). Cue 26: the water goblin knocks at the door, violas and cellos (bars 658–9 etc.), later full orchestra; increasing agitation within. The water goblin kills the child, *ff* diminished seventh chords (bars 748–752).

Andante sostenuto, cue 30: croaking of frogs, piccolo and flutes (bars 759ff.); the mother's and warning theme, bearing out that Friday was an unlucky day, cor anglais and bass clarinet. Cue 31: the mother's terrible distress, oboes, cellos and basses. The water goblin mysteriously disappears into the depths of the lake (bar 788 to end).

Another of these letters provides us with the composer's plan for the second symphonic poem, *The Noon Witch*:

3 *Vide* my article 'Dvořák's Unknown Letters on his Symphonic Poems', *Music & Letters*, lvi (1975), pp. 277–287. The German text appears in *Österreichisches Musikzeitschrift*, xxxi (1976), pp.645–658.

Allegretto (C major): the child plays quietly, clarinet (bar 5). He plays with a toy cockerel, oboe on B flat (bar 23).

Poco più animato, non tanto: the mother becomes angry, strings on A flat (bar 52).

Cue 2: the child cries, flutes, oboes and clarinets on E and F sharp. The mother, becoming quarrelsome, scolds the child, violins supported by strings (bar 86).

Poco meno mosso, cue 3: motif of the noon witch, whom the mother threatens to fetch, clarinets and bassoon.

The child calms down and the scene is re-enacted.

Andante sostenuto e molto tranquillo: the noon witch slowly opens the door and approaches the mother, muted strings, bass clarinet, followed by a new, menacing form of the witch motif, bassoons and bass clarinet.

Più animato, ma non troppo: the witch says: 'Give me your child', trumpet, with horns and trombones; the mother becomes desperate, strings (bar 274). The witch snatches at the mother, who shrinks back, clutching the child to her bosom.

Allegro, 3/8: a description of the witch, piccolo, flute and oboe; 2/8: the mother screams, woodwind (bar 344). The mother, almost dead from being chased, and scarcely breathing, collapses, strings (bar 402).

Meno mosso, allegretto, cue 14: ringing of bells at noon, violins (bar 438).

Andante, cue 15: the father prays, ignorant of what has happened, violins; he opens the door, _ff_ C major chord for strings (bar 463); the mother lies in a faint, oboe (bar 485). He attempts to revive her; she begins to breathe again, flutes (bar 477).

Più lento, cue 16: (modulation to A major): she regains consciousness, flutes; the father becomes agitated, violins and woodwind (bar 484).

Maestoso, cue 17: discovering that his child is dead, the father displays the greatest agitation, violins and violas. The witch vanishes, violins and violas (bar 498).

It is interesting to note that the child playing and the noon witch are both represented by different versions of the same musical thought. The same thing occurs in _The Wild Dove_ and the opera _Kate and the Devil;_ and in _The Golden Spinning Wheel_ the themes of the king, the step mother and the mysterious old man will be found to be closely related. Dvořák did not write a letter describing the details of this third symphonic poem. However, as also in the case of _The Water Goblin,_ he took the unusual step of evolving many of his themes by setting a number of Erben's lines to music, not of course expecting them to be sung. Hence there is an intimate relationship between the ballad and the musical basis of the symphonic poem. Also it helps considerably with identifying the incidents that occur in this fantastic tale.[4] Dvořák, who had thought about turning 'The Golden Spinning Wheel' into a cantata when he was in America, was enthusiastic about his new work, and produced an entrancing and surely the richest of his orchestral scores. The colouring, especially when the spinning wheel reveals the step-mother's guilty secret, is exquisite. The work as a whole is by no means as finely shaped as *The Noon Witch*, but it has many compensating features, not the least of which are its abundant invention and its simple and natural sincerity.

Bennewitz conducted a rehearsal of all three symphonic poems before an invited audience at Prague Conservatory on 3 June 1896, which gave Dvořák the opportunity to make a few modifications before Simrock published them that autumn. The first public performance took place in London. Richter presented *The Golden Spinning Wheel* on 26 October, and Henry J. Wood introduced the other two works at Promenade Concerts, *The Water Goblin* on 14 November and *The Noon Witch* a week later. Theodore Thomas gave the first American performance of *The Golden Spinning Wheel* at Chicago on 1 January 1897.

At Cincinnati, New York and Chicago, Thomas was quite as active in promoting Dvořák's music for the first time as August Manns was in giving first English performances at the Crystal Palace. In all he was responsible for eleven such performances in the United States,[5] and these included the 3rd *Slavonic Rhapsody*, the 6th and 7th Symphonies, the *Scherzo capriccioso*, the *Symphonic Variations*, and Dvořák's fourth symphonic poem, *The Wild Dove*, While giving credit, we must not overlook what Charles Hallé did, but not for introducing works for the first time to England, for he can only lay claim to that for the 1st *Slavonic Rhapsody*, the 10 *Legends*, the G minor Trio and the Piano Quartet in D major. He certainly rendered Dvořák a valuable service by including his works as frequently as he did in his programmes. To have given forty-two performances of his orchestral and choral music in Manchester alone during the fifteen years up to his death is impressive, particularly when the combined efforts of Richter, Gericke, Jahn and Dvořák himself during the same period were not able to present more than twenty-one similar performances in Vienna.

Having written his B minor Cello Concerto expressly for his friend Hanuš Wihan, who had asked Dvořák before he left for America the first time to write one for him, the composer naturally expected Wihan

4 The reader is referred to Burghauser's introduction to the Artia miniature score, or to Šourek's *The Orchestral Works of Antonín Dvořák*.

5 In *A Musical Autobiography* (Chicago 1905), Thomas incorrectly claimed to have given the first American performances of *The Spectre's Bride* and the *Hussite* Overture.

to give the first performance. He asked the cellist to finger and bow the
solo part, and while staying with Hlávka at Lužany in September 1895,
the two men tried the work through. Thinking to improve the solo
part, Wihan made a number of alterations and added cadenzas to the
first and last movements. In a fury, Dvořák told Simrock these changes
and in particular the two cadenzas were unauthorised, and contrary to
the spirit of his work. He was determined it should remain a fitting
memorial to Josefína Kaunitzová. He offered the Concerto and the *Te
Deum* to his publisher for 6,000 marks, but only on condition that the
cadenzas were omitted. Šourek was convinced that Dvořák prevented
Wihan from giving the première because he was so incensed with the
changes he proposed to make. But was he justified in coming to this
conclusion?

Berger wrote early in November 1895 to invite Dvořák to conduct
some of his works at a Philharmonic Society concert in London, to
which the composer very readily agreed, mentioning that he had a new
Cello Concerto. He said this could be played by Wihan, and he hoped
that it would be. In his next letter, written on Christmas Day, Dvořák
confirmed that Wihan had accepted the Society's terms and was willing
to play the concerto, although 19 March, a date that Berger had suggested, did not suit the cellist. April, on the other hand, would be convenient. Having decided that the new work would be included in the
programme, the correspondence that followed was concerned with the
other works by Dvořák which were to go with it. Quite out of the blue,
the Society informed the composer in February that they had fixed the
concert for 19 March and engaged the English cellist Leo Stern to play
Dvořák's concerto. The composer was stunned by this news, and on 14
February sent this curt note to Berger:

I am sorry to announce you that I cannot conduct the performance of the
celo conzerto. The reason is I have promised my friend Wihan—*he will
play it*. If you put the conzerto into the program, I could not come at
all, and will be glad to come another time.

Berger was horrified and greatly embarrassed. Dvořák's appearance
had been announced months before in all the papers, but he undertook
to remove the new concerto from the programme. He had unfortunately overlooked the fact that the composer had attempted to steer him
away from an unsuitable date, but his most serious mistake was to
engage Stern without seeking the composer's approval, even though he

could not have realized that he might be placing Dvořák in an impossible position.

Dvořák's letter to Berger of 1 March is now missing. However, it is virtually certain that he must have explained the situation to Wihan, and we can be reasonably confident that his cellist friend was considerate enough to release him from his promise. When Dvořák wrote again to Berger on 3 March, he had already agreed to conduct his concerto, even though it would not be played by Wihan, and he reported: 'M. Stern plays every day with me and I hope he will be all right. We leave Prague 14th of March . . .'[6]

Besides conducting the first performance of the Cello Concerto at the concert at the Queen's Hall on 19 March, Dvořák directed his G major Symphony and Catherine Fisk's performance of the new orchestral version of the first five *Biblical Songs*. Mackenzie took charge of Emil Sauer's performance of Beethoven's *Emperor* Concerto and the remaining items. By a mischance the concert clashed with the London Symphony Orchestra's Beethoven evening which Henschel conducted. Due to this the Philharmonic Society had been obliged to rely on numerous deputies, which led to disagreements over pitch during Sauer's performance. Dvořák declared himself satisfied with Stern's playing and the audience showed how enthusiastic they were about the new concerto.[7] Stern repeated the work in Prague on 11 April, and on 12 December played it under Manns's direction at the Crystal Palace. Carl Schroeder, the cellist in the Kneisel Quartet, presented it in Boston at a public rehearsal and a concert on 18 and 19 December. It was then performed by Carl Fuchs at Manchester on 7 January 1897, by Stern at Chicago on 29 and 30 January and at New York on 5 and 6 March, and on the following day Hugo Becker played it in Vienna under Richter's direction. Hausmann played it at the Crystal Palace in the following November, but it was not played by Wihan until 25 January 1899 at a concert conducted by Mengelberg at The Hague.

In the first months of 1896 Dvořák paid two visits to Vienna, each of which was memorable in its own way. He went there first for Richter's highly successful performance of the Symphony *From the New World* on 16 February, and shared the Director's box with Brahms. The Largo made so great an impression that he was obliged to rise

---

6 Letters referred to here are in the possession of the Royal Philharmonic Society (custody of the British Library) and Dvořák's heirs.

7 *The Athenaeum* and *Monthly Musical Record* deferred judgement on the concerto, because it appeared in the second half of an over-long programme.

three times to bow his acknowledgements to the audience. On the second occasion he went to the Austrian capital with the Bohemian Quartet, who were giving a performance of his String Sextet, and while there he conducted a performance of *The Spectre's Bride* on March 25th, sung by the Ljubljana Choral Society (Glasbena matica). He might possibly have gone with the quartet to visit Bruckner, who was seriously ill. Dvořák was very anxious to see Brahms again. When he did so Brahms tried hard to persuade him to move to Vienna and become a professor at the Conservatory, mainly for his own good, but also to counterbalance the influence of Bruckner. Suk quoted Brahms as saying: 'Look here, Dvořák. You have a lot of children, and I have practically no one [to support]. If you need anything, my fortune is at your disposal.' Dvořák was deeply moved and tears came to his wife's eyes, but it was quite impossible for him, a Czech, to contemplate leaving Bohemia. On that same day he was distressed to discover that his noble friend was an agnostic. On the way back to their hotel Dvořák was more silent than usual, and then said: 'Such a man, such a fine soul, yet he doesn't believe in anything, he doesn't believe in anything'.[8]

Later that year he asked Simrock to send him a copy of Brahms's *Four Serious Songs*, because he did not know them, yet everyone was saying how beautiful they were. When news reached him in the following March that his good friend's health was failing, he immediately went to Vienna, and was shocked to find Brahms was little more than a shadow of his former self. On hearing he had passed away on 3 April, he returned to Vienna to pay his last respects to the great German composer.

After completing *The Golden Spinning Wheel*, Dvořák allowed almost half a year to slip by without composing anything new; but towards the end of October 1896 he turned once more to Erben, and in less than a month he had added *The Wild Dove* to his set of symphonic poems.

With Dvořák's own outline of the content of this work before us, there is no difficulty at all in following the action. This is his description:

I.   Andante, Marcia funebre. Lamenting, the young woman follows the coffin of her deceased husband.

II. Allegro, later Andante. A jovial, handsome young man meets the beautiful widow; he comforts her, and persuades her to forget her grief and accept him as her husband.

8 J. Suk: 'Aus meiner Jugend'. *Der Merker*, ii (Vienna 1910). p. 147.

III. Molto vivace, later Allegro grazioso. She fulfills his desire for marriage; a gay wedding.
IV. Andante. From the branches of a fresh green oak, which overshadows the grave of her first husband, whom she had poisoned, the mournful cooing of the wild dove is heard. The melancholy sounds pierce to the heart of the criminal woman, who, tormented by pangs of conscience, becomes insane and drowns herself in the waves.
V. Andante, Tempo I. Epilogue.

In the first section the guilt (or curse) motif is first heard on a clarinet and trumpet (cue 2); and when towards the climax of the work the remarkable cooing of the self-righteous dove is heard, this motif reappears much more ominously on the bass clarinet. It is puzzling to know what kind of dove the pigeon-fancier composer had in mind, for although the cooing does bear some resemblance to that of a turtle dove, that bird, so beloved by poets, is unlikely to have acted like Erben's 'little dove'.

In May 1897 Dvořák and the Czech Philharmonic Orchestra went to Brno to present *The Noon Witch* and *The Golden Spinning Wheel*, together with the Symphony *From the New World*. As a result, Janáček became full of enthusiasm for the symphonic poems. They made such a deep impression on him that he wrote a series of articles on them in *Hlídka*, and persuaded Dvořák to entrust the first performance of *The Wild Dove* to him. He conducted the new work in Brno on 20 March 1898. On 10 October, just after the work was published, the second performance took place in London under the direction of Henry J. Wood.

Between 4 August and 25 October 1897, Dvořák produced yet another symphonic peom, *Heroic Song*, op. 111, but without turning to any literary source for his inspiration on this occasion. This latest work was written in the year before Strauss's *Ein Heldenleben*, and although there is no evidence to suggest that Dvořák's work is autobiographical, it is interesting to find that he anticipated Strauss's main idea of the artist as hero. Explaining that he was not thinking of some hero that the bards might have sung about, he said:

Naturally I was thinking more of a champion of the spirit, an artist, and I believe I depicted the hero accurately in the first theme. This theme is full of energy, resolution and power (Molto vivace) [Allegro con fuoco]. In the second theme (Adagio, quasi marcia) [Poco adagio, lacrimosa] in B flat minor, sorrow, lamentation, etc. are expressed for the first time in conflict with D flat major, which symbolizes hope and consolation. Fresh joy and hope for a happier future are introduced in the E major 2/4 section (Allegretto grazioso), and at the end great turbulence leads to ultimate victory for the spiritual and artistic ideal (*Sieg der Idee*).[9]

In the D flat major section there is more than a hint of King Vladislav's entrance in Smetana's *Dalibor*, and the key is identical. The gracious E major melody, which forms the central portion of the whole work, will be recognized as a derivative of the pregnant main theme:

Mahler gave the first performance in Vienna on 4 December 1898, Nedbal introduced it to Prague eight weeks later; and towards the end of 1899 when the work was published it was taken up by Henry J. Wood and Manns in London, by Nikisch in Berlin and Leipzig, and by Gericke at Boston.

With the rosy prospect of better times ahead, when, as seemed virtually certain, the republican McKinley would sweep the incumbent President Cleveland from office in the rapidly approaching American election, Mrs Thurber saw her chance of enticing Dvořák back to the United States. 'Under great direction,' she told him, 'great results must follow', and only he could achieve these.[10] She invited him to return a year later, in 1897, and in the meantime hoped to have the advantage of using his illustrious name. The Vienna *Tageblatt* suggested that Dvořák was accepting her offer, and so the *New York Herald* proclaimed delightedly, 'Dr Dvořák is Coming Back'.[11] The probability is that the composer had avoided giving Mrs Thurber a definite answer, but he may inadvertently have referred to the question of his possible return to New York within the hearing of someone who then gave this

9 For the complete letter, consult footnote 3.
10 Letter of 4 September 1896 from Mrs Thurber to Dvořák.
11 2 January 1897.

rumour circulation. When Mrs Thurber knew that the composer was unwilling to return for a whole winter, she tried to encourage him to come for several weeks in the spring of 1898, to supervise the annual examinations, judge the prize competitions and resume his classes for promising students. For this she offered him a salary of 2,667 dollars, to be paid four weeks before he left Europe, and at the same time she promised she would pay him 1,500 dollars which she had owed him ever since 1895.[12]

Miss Margulies, while spending her vacation in Austria, tried her utmost to get Dvořák to accept this offer, but he was not prepared to come to any decision until he had consulted Dr Tragy. Even after seeing Tragy he remained non-commital. Although he appeared to be willing to consider a brief visit, he was not disposed to sign any contract until this was drafted just as he wished it to be, and he stipulated that on no account must the possibility that he might accept be mentioned in the Press. He found Mrs Thurber's envoy's persistence extremely irritating, and told her bluntly that it would be fruitless for them to meet; but she insisted on discussing the matter personally with him at Budweis on 25 August. After this meeting Dvořák cabled to Mrs Thurber: 'Yes can use my name as director of National Conservatory', showing that he was only prepared to serve as her honorary director, without any duties or obligations whatsoever.[13]

Early in 1898 two attempts were made to persuade Dvořák to return to England. He welcomed the Philharmonic Society's invitation to conduct again at one of their concerts, and since on these occasions he always introduced a new work of his, he suggested one of the last two symphonic poems would be suitable, alongside other works which were already familiar. But when he realized that his Conservatory students needed extra tuition before they sat their examinations he went back on his word, much to the annoyance of the Society. He hoped to make amends in the following season, but since by then he had no work that would be a novelty in London, there was no justification for making the journey.[14] The second approach came from the Sheffield Music Festival and their musical director August Manns. They asked him to compose either a choral or an orchestral work which could be given its

12 Letter of 4 January 1897 from Mrs Thurber to Dvořák, enclosing draft contract.

13 English translations of the letters from Dvořák to Miss Margulies appear in P. Stefan's 'Why Dvořák would not Return to America', *Musical America*, lviii (25 February 1938), p. 34.

14 Letters of 21 January, 5 and 11 May 1898 and of 12 October 1899, from Dvořák to the Philharmonic Society (Royal Philharmonic Society—British Library).

première under his personal direction at their 1899 Festival.[15] Since this offer came just as the composer had set to work on a full scale opera, it was quite impossible for him to give a favourable response. He had in fact already paid his final visit to England.

In the last years of his life opera became an all-absorbing passion, fostered by the realization that he had hitherto been rather less successful in this field than in symphonic, choral and chamber music. His taste for music for the stage intensified during the interval between writing *The Wild Dove* and *Heroic Song*, while he was engaged on reshaping the third act of *The Jacobin*, using Marie Červinková's textural revision, and again after completing the fifth symphonic poem, while he was making improvements to the second act. These modifications, like those he had already made in *Dimitrij*, were influenced by the discussions he had had with Seidl on the subject of Wagner. In the summer of 1898 he told Richter he had a great longing to go to Bayreuth, but despite this strong urge he did nothing about it. He does not seem to have wanted to travel so far, and in any case he was making rapid progress on a new opera, *Kate and the Devil*, to a libretto by Josef Wenig based on a familar Czech fairy tale.

Starting on 9 May, he sketched and scored the first two acts in four and a half months, and only when he reached the third act and his commitments at the Conservatory reduced the available time did he become bogged down. At the same time he was involved in preparations for a delightful double celebration, his and Anna's silver wedding and the marriage of their daughter Otilka to Josef Suk, Dvořák's pupil and the man whose leg he once pulled for imagining the number of a locomotive was to be found on the tender. The vivid joy of that happy day, 17 November 1898, was scarcely dimmed when, to cap it all, Dvořák received news that the emperor was awarding him the gold medal for *Litteris et Artibus*, indeed an outstanding honour. In the following June the composer was given an audience by Franz Joseph to receive what he liked to call his 'big golden platter'.

The whole opera and its overture was finished by 27 February, and early in the following season, on 23 November 1899, it was mounted successfully at the National Theatre. *Kate and the Devil* was warmly received by the public and praised by the critics, it was given eight times before the year was out, and in 1900 it was performed fifteen times. Dvořák was well satisfied, and encouraged to strive for an even greater success next time.

15. Letter of 3 September 1898 from Manns to Dvořák (Heirs of Dvořák).

In *Kate and the Devil* we observe that Lucifer, by seeking out only the greatest sinners to be his victims, was an indirect benefactor of those being sinned against. The serfs had good reason to regard their princess as the very devil, but Jirka, a hard-done-by shepherd, sees a possibility of securing benefits for all, which at the same time could spare the princess from her fate. In general the characters are convincingly presented, although the charming aristocratic dance that precedes the last act and the princess's pentatonic theme are incongruous with her state of terror, so vividly expressed in her scene. As in *Der Freischütz* and Smetana's *Devil's Wall*, there is a distinctive zigzag motif representing devilry of various kinds (and for good measure it occurs even at the mention of the 'poor devil' who might find himself landed with Kate as a wife). Other themes, following the example of Smetana's *Wallenstein's Camp* and Dvořák's *Golden Spinning Wheel*, assume a great variety of forms to suggest different concepts and personal characteristics. Thus the bagpipe tune at the beginning of the opera serves to reflect Kate's garrulity, in addition to becoming the main element of the exuberant ballet in hell. Similarly the theme associated with the downtrodden peasants undergoes many modifications, but none more significant than that of Lucifer judging the princess's guilt:

The opera makes good entertainment, it is at times suitably dramatic, and is enriched from the composer's seemingly inexhaustible store of attractive musical ideas.

During the summer following his completion of *Kate and the Devil* Dvořák spent most of the time relaxing at Vysoká. When the winter came on he found time to go to Berlin for Nikisch's performance of *Heroic Song*, and six weeks later he went to Budapest to take part in a chamber concert of his own compositions on 19 December, and to conduct *Heroic Song*, the Cello Concerto, with Wihan as the soloist, and *Carnival* Overture on the next evening at a Philharmonic concert. But during all this time he wrote nothing new for lack of a suitable opera libretto. He again toyed with the idea of setting Karel Pippich's text on the legend 'The Death of Vlasta', but this failed to satisfy him. At the Czech Philharmonic concert on 4 April 1900, which was the last time of all that Dvořák appeared on the rostrum at home or abroad, he very appropriately departed from the tradition that he had established. Instead of restricting himself to his own compositions, he chose to perform works that he particularly admired written by other composers. His programme began with Brahms's *Tragic* Overture and Schubert's *Unfinished* Symphony, and in the second half he performed Beethoven's 8th Symphony and his own *Wild Dove*.

Rather by chance an opera libretto came into Dvořák's hands when he was about to write a *Festival Song* for Dr Tragy's 70th birthday celebrations. Jaroslav Kvapil, a thirty-one-year-old poet, had written one on a plot derived from Fouqué's 'Undine', Hans Anderson's 'Little Mermaid', Hauptmann's 'Sunken Bell' and other sources, and given it a distinctly Czech character. When he approached Nedbal, J. B. Foerster, Karel Kovařovic and Josef Suk, for a variety of reasons they all turned it down. He was far too reticent to think of letting so great a composer as Dvořák see it, but he told F. A. Šubert, the director of the National Theatre, about it, and he saw that it had potentialities. Šubert arranged for Dvořák to meet the young man in his office, and on his recommendation the composer read the libretto and discovered that it was exactly what he had been searching for. He was much happier about setting a tragic fairy tale than a tragic legend. He sketched the first act of *Rusalka* (The Water Nymph) between 21 April and 8 May 1900, and finished scoring this by 27 June. He dealt with the short prelude next, instead of leaving this to the last, and continued on the second and third acts, working on the sketch and score simultaneously. Act 2 was finished on 4 September and he reached the end of the opera by 27 November.

The settings for Kvapil's adaptation of Hans Anderson's 'Little Mermaid' with borrowings from Hauptmann's 'Sunken Bell' and other sources, appealed strongly to Dvořák. Within the framework of pool, stream and forest, he was able to conceive his supernatural characters in real terms, their aspirations and desires, their mutual understanding and love, and their disappointments and sorrows. And he was not seriously inhibited by his heroine's acceptance of the loss of speech, since she

Group of Czech musicians: (seated) Dvořák, Kàan, Fibich, (standing) Bendl,
J. B. Foerster and Kovařovic

(*above*) Dvořák in his coffin

(*right*) Bust of Dvořák by L. Šaloun

could still communicate with supernatural beings, and a love duet with the Prince was possible after she was transformed into a will-o'-the-wisp. The humans also, and especially the Prince and the two comic characters, are vividly portrayed. Dvořák employed a moderately comprehensive leitmotiv system, with themes for Rusalka, her father the Water Goblin, the Prince, and several others besides. Šourek has identified a somewhat Wagnerian motif as 'Rusalka's curse':

although it might be preferable to label it her fate motif. It is certainly doom-laden and is reserved for times of crisis; but curiously enough it is first heard before Rusalka appears and before she is even mentioned. The work is more symphonic than *Kate and the Devil*, but it includes several closed forms, the best known being Rusalka's beautiful 'Invocation to the Moon'. At times there is an intense sense of drama, and elsewhere there are sudden eruptions of spontaneous concern and anxiety by the entire spirit world over what is happening to Rusalka.

It was recognized at the National Theatre that this new stage work of Dvořák's, completed in his sixtieth year, was without a shadow of doubt a work of considerable significance, and that every effort should be made to ensure that its production was worthy in every way. A strong cast was chosen. Růžena Maturová, who had filled the part of the Princess in *Kate and the Devil*, was selected for the title rôle, and Bohumil Pták and Václav Kliment, the Marbuel and Jirka of the previous production, were given the parts of Vodník (the water sprite and father of Rusalka) and the Prince. Robert Polák, who had so recently sung the part of Lucifer, was entrusted with the production, and Karel Kovařovic, the newly appointed chief conductor of the theatre, was responsible for the music. Sixteen months after *Kate and the Devil* was launched, the musical public awaited in eager anticipation the première of a new major work by their greatest living Czech composer, and when on 31 March 1901 *Rusalka* was mounted they were more than satisfied.

They immediately accepted the new opera as a treasured possession and it quickly became one of the best loved manifestations of the Czech musical art. The critics praised it in glowing terms, referring in particular to its brilliant colouring, its rich melodiousness and radiant lyricism. But there was one dissenting voice. Zdeněk Nejedlý, who deeply deplored the shocking way that Smetana's unique and priceless contribution to Czech music was constantly misunderstood, reviled and ignored, and not a little envious of Dvořák's remarkable success at home and abroad, decided that a powerful attack on Dvořák might well assist him in his resolve to elevate Smetana to his rightful place of honour. So he opened his long and virulent campaign with a broadside in the provincial paper *Pelolové rozhledy*,[16] aimed at Dvořák's inability to create a work that was genuinely dramatic. He and his friends succeeded in dividing music lovers into two camps, of which there are still signs today. But by the time Helfert deserted the cause and acknowledged that Bohemia was greatly indebted to both Smetana and Dvořák, Nejedlý's zeal was beginning to wane.

During the first year *Rusalka* was performed sixteen times, and by 6 June 1907 it had been staged no fewer than fifty times. After a long struggle Dvořák had at last composed an opera which became an essential part of the Czech repertory, a work for the stage which was regarded with love and affection by his fellow countrymen, and which was to hold a permanent and honoured place in the national heritage.

On the morning after the première of *Rusalka* Dvořák arrived at the theatre in the best of humours. On seeing Kvapil he said: 'Hurry, hurry—a new libretto!' When the poet explained that he had not got one, the composer replied: 'Then write one quickly while I am in the mood! One with a fine role for Maturová.'

16 25 May 1901, p. 205, quoted in Šourek: *Život a dílo Antonína Dvořáka*, iv, 2nd edn., pp. 150–151 (footnote).

11 The Last Years

When the Austrian emperor discovered how deeply the Czechs and Moravians resented the decree of 16 October 1899, banning the use of the Czech language in the administration of local government and the courts of law, he felt it was advisable to make some gesture which would help to placate his subjects. Due to this he decided to make some of the most eminent Czechs members of the Herrenhaus, the Austrian House of Peers. Dvořák, the doyen of Czech musicians, and Jaroslav Vrchlický, the leading poet, were honoured in this way. They were received by the president, Prince Windischgraz, and took the oath (in Czech, as was customary) on 14 May 1901. As they left the Chamber Dvořák called out to the waiting journalists: 'We carved them up!' [literally 'slit them open'.] What the composer appreciated most about this sole appearance of his in the Upper Chamber, was the plentiful supply of fine pencils they had provided for him, and which he knew would be extremely useful to him when he was composing.

At this time plans were being laid in various parts of Bohemia, and especially in the capital itself, to celebrate the composer's sixtieth birthday. When September arrived concerts were given and operas were performed, special editions of journals appeared, speeches were made and there was a presentation, and also vocal scores of the last two operas were being prepared for eventual publication. One of the organisers' chief concerns was to make the celebration a really festive occasion. A number of prominent people made contributions to the five issues of the musical paper *Dalibor* that commemorated the jubilee, one of which was a poem written by the gifted young dramatic soprano Emma Destinnová. The National Theatre mounted six of the composer's operas, spread over a period of seven weeks, and followed these with the first stage performance of *St Ludmila*.[1] Two months

---

1 The *Slavonic Dances*, provided with choreography, were included in the first of the programmes, on 8 September. Šourek, and also J. Němeček, who relied on him in his *Opera Národní divadla v období Karla Kovařovice* (1968), were incorrect in thinking there was a cycle of nine commemorative performances at the theatre. Dvořák received no special publicity when Šamberk's play *J. K. Tyl* was presented with his incidental music. Dvořák was featured in seven productions, and after the first the description 'cycle' was dropped. Information from J. Burghauser.

after the time of the actual jubilee the Umělecká beseda launched a festive week of the composer's works with a performance of the *Slavonic Dances*. They followed this with a presentation of *Rusalka*, a chamber concert, the Requiem Mass, an orchestral programme which included the 9th Symphony, and wound up with a gala performance of *St Ludmila*. On the first evening the Prague Hlahol Choral Society, bearing torches aloft, marched to the composer's flat where they serenaded him; and on the penultimate evening a banquet was held in Dvořák's honour, at which the Philharmonic Orchestra provided the music.

Dvořák, who disliked public adulation, wondered what all the fuss was about, and frequently was heard to say. 'Is all this really necessary?' He was present at all the Umělecká beseda functions, but was in Vienna when the National Theatre initiated their series of performances with *The Stubborn Lovers* and he did not trouble to turn up for either *The Cunning Peasant* or even *Dimitrij*. He summed up his attitude to and distrust of public opinion in this manner:

> Well, it's difficult to believe anything. They like something today and jeer at it tomorrow. I've already had a taste of that. And it's particularly hard for the Czech musician. Only now are they giving Smetana a real chance, long after his death. So not even the greatest success causes me to become conceited. I work with integrity and do best in that way. This conviction gives me the greatest satisfaction. If I have created something for posterity, then my devotion to music and work of many years will have fulfilled its most splendid purpose. However, I distrust popularity.[2]

The mood in Vienna appears to have been conducive towards a modest tribute to the master on his jubilee, and so Hellmesberger was able to include *The Golden Spinning Wheel* in the Vienna Philharmonic concert on 3 November. This was followed up by two programmes in mid December devoted almost entirely to Dvořák's music, the first being a recital by the Bohemian String Quartet, and the second a concert by the Czech Philharmonic Orchestra, directed by Nedbal, in which Karel Hoffmann played the Violin Concerto and the orchestra performed the 9th Symphony and other works.

In the previous spring Dvořák became aware that Mahler was very keen to perform *Rusalka* at the Vienna Court Opera. This was a most interesting development, yet at the same time one that needed to be

---

2 Emil Koberg quoted Dvořák as having said this, in his article 'Persönlische Erinnerungen an Meister Dvorzak' which appeared in *Neue Freie Presse* after the composer's death.

handled with caution. Dvořák was not satisfied at being offered five per cent of the takings on the nights his opera was performed, but nothing at all from the season tickets; so he was relieved to hear from Mahler's letter of 4 December, that the administration was prepared to bow to his request for a similar payment on the receipts from the subscribers. Soon after this Dvořák went to Vienna to discuss the cast and the contract with Mahler, and everything seemed to point to a production in the following March, until the bass singer, Vilém Heš, fell ill. Dvořák signed the contract in the first half of May, confidently hoping that *Rusalka* would be mounted in the autumn, but something that it is not easy to be sure about went wrong. In the light of his past experience, it is certainly possible that Dvořák may have been a little apprehensive about the outcome of the production, though it is certain that he was deeply disappointed that the opera could not be performed at that time. There is no doubt at all that Mahler was most enthusiastic about Dvořák's score, barring his reservations about the gamekeeper and scullion; but due to anti-semitic pressures he was not entirely master of his own house, although trouble from that quarter did not come to a head until much later. Whatever the reason may be, *Rusalka* was not performed in Vienna until after Dvořák's death.[3]

When Bennewitz retired from the Directorship of Prague Conservatory in the summer of 1901, Dvořák was chosen to succeed him, or at least to take over his title. It was common knowledge that Dvořák was not an administrator. This responsible work was therefore placed in the hands of Karel Knittl, so that Dvořák could continue teaching composition as before. It is wholly characteristic of the great man's modesty, that whenever he felt the need to take a break and spend a few days at Vysoká, he asked his deputy to grant him permission.

Ever since the successful launch of *Rusalka* in March 1901, Dvořák had been on the lookout for a suitable subject for his next big work. He rather fancied writing an oratorio. 'Nazareth' and 'Golgotha' were possibilities, but he came to the conclusion that the second of these would prove to be too daunting a task. Vrchlický offered him a text based on the life of St Adalbert, but he felt obliged to reject this because it lacked female characters. It seemed better for him to return once again to opera. He turned down Pippich's text 'The Death of Vlasta', but when routing around the archives of the National Theatre he came across something much more attractive. This was Hostinský's libretto

---

3 At the time it was being said that the opera's dramatic features were too strongly outweighed by its lyricism, but this explanation may have been offered at least in part to distract attention from any political or racial motivation.

for Rozkošný's most successful opera *Cinderella* (Popelka), produced for the first time as long ago as 1885. But it was impossible to use this without Rozkošný's consent, and he may have thought it would be wiser not to ask for this favour.

The months slipped by and still Dvořák could not find a libretto that satisfied him.[4] At last, however, after examining Vrchlický's adaptation of the story of Armida and Rinaldo, he came to the conclusion that this provided him with the scope that he needed, and with a few modifications it would be suitable.[5] He realized that by choosing this subject there was a better chance that his opera would find favour abroad than if he had selected a purely Czech theme. He foresaw too that he could provide a splendid part for Růžena Maturová, and perhaps he may also have felt he was under some obligation to the great poet whose oratorio libretto he had so recently rejected. Vrchlický's 'Armida' libretto differs strikingly from Tasso's original version of the tale and from those used by Lully, Handel, Gluck and many others, for he very successfully grafted on to it the conclusion of the Tancred and Clorinda episode for his dénouement.

At the beginning of March 1902 Dvořák decided on some of the themes for his new opera, and then between 11 March and 23 May he prepared the continuous sketch of the first two acts, scoring these from 2 June to 17 August. He then worked on the sketches and full score simultaneously, completing the third act between 8 October and 20 January 1903, and the fourth act between 14 February and 29 June. There was no great hurry to write the overture, so he took a break and then composed it between 17 and 23 August. He was engaged on *Armida* for a little longer than he had taken over *Dimitrij*, but in that earlier case his progress had been slowed down by the need to work on other things at the same time. While sketching the first act of *Armida* he told Dr Rezek how lucky he was to be able to write an opera without paying any attention to what others wanted him to compose.

This celebrated subject, centering on the conflicting claims of love and duty, opened up many possibilities for the composer. After setting the scene well with the Muezzin's call to prayer, there follow various features that are characteristic of grand opera: choruses of crusaders, songs and dances of sirens and nymphs in Armida's magic gardens, an abduction of the hero and heroine in Ismen's fiery chariot drawn by

4 On 11 February 1902 he told Dr Kozánek: 'For more than fourteen months I have done *no work* and been unable *to make up my mind*, and I don't know how long this state of affairs will continue'. He had written only one song and some recitatives for *St Ludmila* since finishing off *Rusalka*.

5 Vrchlický had written this libretto more than a dozen years earlier for Kovařovic, who is thought to have abandoned his project while sketching the second act.

dragons, and other spectacular dramatic happenings, a trio for Armida, Rinaldo and his rival Ismen, love duets, and a death scene after Armida has been mortally wounded unwittingly in combat with her lover. The cunning magician Ismen emerges unmistakably as a powerful dramatic figure, who has the dominating role in Act 3. Armida is almost the only female character, though one is hardly aware of this, because whether she is on or off the stage, her presence is invariably felt. The changes of mood that Rinaldo goes through, first lackadaisical, then the passionate lover, and finally the courageous warrior, are reflected vividly in his music, and his monologue at the beginning of the last act is particularly fine. Armida's hauntingly beautiful 'I hurried after a slender gazelle', which she sings when in a trance, and the striking form that Ismen's theme takes when he threatens to destroy Armida's palace if she will not yield to him, are shown here:

Dvořák used an even greater number of leitmotivs in this work than in *Rusalka*, and there are several instances of the motifs being combined with one another in Act 4.

The new work was as strongly influenced by Wagner as any he had written previously. This would almost certainly have been the case, even if there had been no similarities in the plots of *Armida*, *Tannhäuser* and *Parsifal*. Wagner still meant a great deal to Dvořák and he still had a strong wish to go to Bayreuth, but as he explained to Richter, it was so difficult for him to get there.[6] As he got older he was far less prepared to travel than before. He made a point of attending the first performance in the Czech capital of Charpentier's *Louise* and was deeply impressed by it. A month later he welcomed the chance of meeting Grieg when he arrived in Prague, and his daughter Magda sang at the Norwegian composer's concert. A few months later there was a flurry of excitement in the family when Dvořák's daughter Anna married Dr Josef Sobotka. This happy occasion was followed by three sad events, the deaths of Dvořák's dear friend Antonín Rus, his eighty-year-old mother-in-law, and then of the conductor who had done more than any other man to make his music known in Prague, Adolf Čech.

Even before he had completed *Armida*, Dvořák was thinking ahead about the next opera he would write. He became interested in a libretto 'Horymír' by Rudolf Stárek,[7] partly because it was set in a mining district. He told the Vysoká miners that a mine, complete with its machinery, would have to be created on the stage for one of its acts. Directly after finishing the overture for *Armida* he began to sound out some of the new subject's possibilities by making sketches for several suitable themes. He cogitated over it for a long time, for he preferred it to two other librettos that he had by him, but he realised that it would need to be modified in some ways. He wrote to the author at the end of February 1904, suggesting they should meet to discuss possible altera-tions, but nothing was arranged and they failed to meet.

Preparations for the National Theatre production of *Armida* began in November 1903, with Karel Kovařovic, Adolf Čech's successor, taking charge of the rehearsals. At the beginning of January, with the première only two months away, Kovařovic announced that he was exhausted due to overwork, and that it was essential for him to take a complete rest for eight weeks. He arranged for František Picka to take

---

6 Letter of 11 February 1902, in reply to Richter's letter of 24 January. These were the last two letters they wrote to each other.

7 Dr Rudolf Stárek was a leading authority on coloured fabrics, and directed a mill at Lang-Enzensdorf, near Vienna. He provided librettos for several minor composers.

his place, although Dvořák would undoubtedly have very much preferred Moric Anger to take over the conducting. It was obvious enough that Kovařovic, who was a gifted composer, disliked the prospect of being the architect for a successful outcome of Dvořák's newest work, especially since this opera was written on the very same libretto that he himself had attempted to set nine years earlier, but had failed to complete.

On the day of the dress rehearsal, 1 March, Bohumil Pták, who was chosen for the part of Rinaldo, was suffering from a throat infection and failed to appear. Picka's conducting was insensitive and inefficient, and he was incapable of imposing his will on the performers. Janáček, who was present, reported that he had never before seen Dvořák so irritated. The first performance had to be postponed. The next attempt to hold a dress rehearsal was equally unsatisfactory. Kovařovic, now back in harness after his absence, openly reproved Picka in front of those sitting in the auditorium for his inability to keep the singers and orchestra together, and for allowing mistakes to pass uncorrected. When Dvořák complained several times that the offstage sirens were scarcely audible, Kovařovic tartly responded that he was entirely satisfied by what he heard. Until tempers had had a chance to cool, a performance was out of the question.

Vrchlický had introduced a fantastic and astonishing sequence of events into his third act, which are not found in Tasso. Briefly, Armida's palace and gardens are destroyed by the jealous ruler of Syria, Ismen, involving his magic powers; they are restored again due to the intense love for each other of Rinaldo and Armida, and then, when Rinaldo has been enticed away, they are again laid waste by Ismen. This was probably the poet's most serious error of judgement, but since it was accepted by Dvořák, he must bear some of the responsibility. Emanuel Chvála, the leading Czech critic, blamed neither of these men for these incredible events when the first performance took place on 25 March, but instead directed his fire at Robert Polák, the producer, for the ridiculous and clumsy way he had thought to present the opera's magic scenes.[8] Thanks to Picka's incompetent direction and Kovařovic's attitude to the production,[9] there was little chance that the richness and beauty of the composer's score would be fully revealed. *Armida* was given seven performances and then shelved for twenty-one years. There is no excuse for the shameful neglect of this fine work today.[10]

8 *Národní politika*, 27 March 1904.

9 In later years Kovařovic regretted having been unfair to Dvořák.

10 *Armida* was presented in a shortened version at Bremen in 1961, and Prague Radio have given it in a more complete version. During the last 50 years it has not had a fair chance on the stage.

At the première an acute pain in his side forced Dvořák to leave early. He believed he had lumbago, and was furious afterwards when Jan Malát, the composer, frightened him by suggesting it was kidney trouble. He was reassured by his doctor, Professor Hnátek, who told him all would be well if he took a few days rest. Shortly before Easter he felt much better, and so set off for Vinohrady station to see the locomotives and chat with the railway engineer. But he lingered there too long and caught a chill. After this Dvořák's state of health fluctuated, sometimes showing considerable improvement and occasionally giving real cause for anxiety. Hnátek was sent for at 3 am one night. He suspected that the composer was suffering from kidney disease and cerebral arteriosclerosis, and he obtained confirmation for this from Professor Janovský, whom he called in for a second opinion. Dvořák was particularly sorry not to be able to witness the arrival of spring at Vysoká, and it seemed uncertain whether he would recover in time to conduct *The Spectre's Bride* in May at Kroměříž with Magda singing the soprano solos.

His doctor was so pleased with his improvement on 30 April, that he gave him permission to get up for lunch on May Day, a festival which the composer's family celebrated. Dvořák was assisted to dress next day, and he then walked round the room before seating himself at the head of the table. He consumed his soup with relish, but immediately afterwards he grew pale, said he felt dizzy, and slumped back in his chair unable to speak. He was helped to bed and Hnátek was summoned immediately, but by the time he arrived the composer was dead.

Dvořák's sudden death,[11] which came as a shock to many, was mourned throughout the land. At the funeral and the memorial service which followed it, representatives of the country's political, administrative, religious and cultural life paid homage to this genius who rose from humble beginnings to bring such honour to Bohemia both far and wide. The coffin lay in state at St Salvator's church until 5 May, the day of the funeral. From there the cortège, led by the Prague Hlahol Choral Society and representatives of choral societies throughout the country, wound its way slowly to the National Theatre where the opening section of Dvořák's Requiem Mass was sung. It continued on its way to the Vyšehrad cemetery where graves of the nation's greatest men are found. Here, close by the tomb of the great statesman Palacký, the

---

11 For a pathologist's considered view of the causes of Dvořák's illness and death, the reader is referred to Appendix I in this book.

Hlahol Choir sang again and Karel Knittl, Dvořák's deputy at the Conservatory, pronounced the funeral oration before the great man was finally laid to rest. The memorial service took place two days later at the Týn church, where they sang the Requiem Mass of Mozart, the composer who reminded Dvořák of sunshine, and whom he thought of when he saw a Raphael madonna in London.

12 Dvořák as a Teacher

If we are to see the way that Dvořák conducted his composition classes in a proper perspective, it is advisable to bear in mind the kind of tuition that he himself experienced. Little is known about the teaching he received from Hancke at Česká Kamenice. At Zlonice, however, we are told what subjects he studied under Liehmann, and, when playing from a figured bass, whenever he made a mistake he received a blow from his master. At the Prague Organ School he was required to learn the basic skills that are essential for every organist, which apart from being able to play the organ well and having a good knowledge of liturgical music, meant studying harmony, counterpoint, fugue and canon, and being able to play fluently from a figured bass, and to be able to transpose at sight. He composed preludes and fugues, but never received the systematic training and experience of composing in larger forms, as Smetana had when he studied for three years under Josef Proksch. It will be noticed that Dvořák had no professional instruction in the two subjects which he was to teach later, advanced composition and orchestration, in both of which he was entirely self-taught.

When Dvořák resigned from the orchestra of the Provisional Theatre, it was necessary for a while for him to accept private pupils for several years to make ends meet. The situation was transformed by his international successes, so that for a decade he was free of this chore and could devote his entire energies to composition. He was reluctant to tie himself down to a teaching post, and had to be pressed three times before he finally agreed in October 1890 to become a professor at the Prague Conservatory at the beginning of the following year. The impression seems to be that he did not regret having taken this decisive step. It may well have been a good deal more decisive as regards his future than he could have imagined at the time. If he had not accepted this pedagogic position, would Mrs Thurber have been so keen to invite him to become the Director of her National Conservatory of Music of America? It would have been a gamble which might have led to disaster if she had made an equally generous offer to a musician without any experience of teaching composition at a high level and who had not shown previously that he had any particular interest in work of this kind. She required not only a big name to add lustre to her institution, but also a man capable of realizing her dream of founding a national school of composition in the United States.

It was essential for Dvořák to make a careful personal selection of the students he was willing to accept in his classes, both in Prague and in New York; they had to have an adequate mastery of counterpoint, the determination to work hard, and sufficient natural ability to give a reasonable guarantee that they would be likely to succeed in the musical profession. He made considerable demands on those he accepted, both as regards quantity and quality of work, and, according to Harry Rowe Shelley, expected his American students to produce a piece of composition at each of their three weekly classes.[1] They were well aware that if they brought unsatisfactory work, or showed themselves to be incompetent in their class work, they would be thrown out of the class without hope of reprieve. Janák and Praus, two of Karel Stecker's best pupils who became members of Dvořák's first class in Prague, failed to stay the course,[2] and in America the class diminished considerably for similar reasons.

Dvořák was tough and severe with all his students, however talented, and the mild and gentle Josef Suk, and the rebel Vítězslav Novák, 'that dishevelled philosopher with his cravat askew', were by no means exempt from doses of harsh criticism. Dvořák's spontaneous comments, his irritability, anger and sarcasm, which poured out when he encountered work which did not please him, frequently cut his students to the quick, but they acknowledged that however unpalatable the criticism, it was offered for the ultimate benefit of the individual concerned. Dvořák had no intention of allowing those that he taught to foster illusions about their competence. It was of course possible that an irate comment might be misinterpreted, or even regretted by Dvořák himself. On one occasion he exclaimed: 'You are a big ass', when handing back some work. He then noticed that the unfortunate youth, having picked up his hat and coat, was quietly leaving the classroom. Dashing after him, he brought him back with the words: 'You are not a big ass'. When the class was over, Dvořák went up to the student and whispered almost inaudibly: 'But you are a little one'.[3]

The classes started very punctually at 8 o'clock in the morning and

1 H. R. Shelley: 'Dvořák as I Knew Him', *The Etude*, xxxi (August 1913), pp. 541–542.

2 V. Novák: *O sobě a o jiných* (Prague, 1946), p. 36.

3 A. Pellegrini: 'Persönliche Erinnerungen . . .' *Prager Presse*, 1 May 1929.

continued for three hours. During the first hour or perhaps hour and a half, Dvořák, seated at the piano and with a ring of students standing around him, played through in turn each of the compositions brought for his inspection, pointing out where the faults and weaknesses lay. He never offered any solution, always believing that it was up to the student to find out how it could be improved. The whole class followed the score, and drank in everything he said. This was followed by a break of some five to ten minutes, during which Dvořák dropped his customary severity, and for a while would chat informally with his pupils. The remaining time was spent on class work. A student would be sent to the blackboard and given some exercise in composition or orchestration, or he would be told to perform various tasks at the keyboard. In either case everything he did was punctuated with the professor's criticism in front of the whole class. Dvořák's demands were far-reaching, and with practically no time for reflection, the student was kept on his toes. It was usually very difficult to know which of a number of solutions to a problem or which answer to a question was the one that Dvořák expected to hear. This school work was without question the most exacting that the students experienced. It was far from easy to satisfy their much revered but irascible teacher.

Not long after beginning his teaching at Prague Conservatory, Dvořák tried the experiment of getting the whole class collectively to compose a complete sinfonietta on the blackboard. Thanks no doubt to the unequal ability of the individual students, the outcome seems to have been rather disappointing, judging by the fact that the experiment was not repeated. Very much later one of the pupils, taking as a challenge Dvořák's assertion, that not a single member of the class was capable of composing a trio such as Haydn might have written, produced a trio movement of his own that was written in a style as near as he could manage to that of Haydn himself. Expecting to receive praise for what he had done, he was crestfallen at being told that it was nothing, just pure Haydn. Dvořák always expected originality in work submitted to him, and invariably drew attention to themes and passages reminiscent of well known compositions. At another time Josef Michl, after days of hard slogging, produced the first twenty bars of a piece modelled on the beginning of the *Tannhäuser* Overture and presented it to Dvořák, who expressed his warm approval, together with the comment that it included some hints of Berlioz. But he pointed out that it needed to be rounded off with a couple more bars. However, when Michl pointed out that it was the opening Lento of a Wagner-type overture, the maestro protested vehemently. In that case he said the Lento would need to be followed by other sections, and he foresaw that that would inevitably lead to catastrophe. Wagner, he explained, was so great a genius, that he was capable of doing things that were beyond the reach of other composers.[4] This experience of Michl's provides an important clue to one of Dvořák's frequent cryptic and laconic remarks. When Novák, rather audaciously, enquired why Dvořák did not compose operas like Wagner, since he was such a great admirer of his music, he received the reply: 'That's just what I don't like about him'.[5]

There was always a great deal that the students could learn from the example of Beethoven, and not least of all from his development sections. Shelley informs us that when composing a symphony, while having tuition from the Czech maestro, he worked and reworked the fifty-bar development section of the first movement over and over again, submitting it to his teacher three times a week extending over a period of forty weeks. He estimated that he must have written some five thousand bars before Dvořák made the long-awaited comment: 'Jetz haben Sie recht, mein Lieber'. Beethoven inspired Dvořák with a tremendous feeling of awe. When he played his music to the students he found it difficult to put into words what he thought about it, and quite often he allowed the music to speak for itself. But when he came to the 13th and 14th bars of the Adagio of the *Hammerklavier* Sonata:

raising his voice, he said: 'That is something! *That is profundity*! *That is an abyss*!!'[6]

Since Dvořák was subject to moods, it was not possible to anticipate how he would react to whatever piece of music he was scrutinizing. As his pupils noticed, there were times when he contradicted his earlier statements. In early May 1903, a time when he was always longing to be at Vysoká, the members of the class found it particularly difficult to

4 J. Michl: 'Rok u Dvořáka', *Hudební revue*, vi (1913), esp. pp. 172–4.

5 Novák, *op. cit.*, p. 36.

6 Michl: 'Z Dvořákovy školy', *Hudební revue*, iv (1911), pp. 490–493.

satisfy their master. When Pellegrini submitted a sonata for piano and violin in A minor, Dvořák objected to the very first page, which he said was too simple in style and needed a countermelody or perhaps some imitation to improve it. After revising the beginning in the manner Dvořák had suggested, Pellegrini was greatly upset at being asked why he had written such a bombastic opening, when something simple would be so much more effective. All this was very perplexing, until Dvořák made it clear that he would be prepared to accept something in A minor in the autumn, but not in the spring, when E flat major would be so much better.[7]

Michl described in detail the exceptionally thorough manner in which Dvořák discussed the possibilities when improvising, and the brilliant way he could demonstrate how it might be done, without undue repetition of rhythmic fragments (which he likened to a stretched-out noodle), and giving the whole a sense of purpose, leading up to a climax and a suitable conclusion.[8] His classes were greatly impressed with his fluency in playing from an orchestral score. He was also able to recall from memory numerous extracts from works of the great masters, whenever he needed one to illustrate some point he wished to make. To a large extent he relied upon his instinct when declaring that a student's work was good or bad, and if asked to give a reason, he was unable to provide one. Dvořák trusted his instinct implicitly and would not budge from the conviction that he was right. Sometimes there was no need at all for him to express what he thought in words, for the expression of his face would convey all that was needed. And since he believed in getting a student to fathom for himself what the fault was in his work, and how it might be overcome, he adopted the following tactic. He would play through the entire composition perhaps three times and then return it to the student without making any comment. He would first play it just as it was written. Next he repeated it slightly differently. Finally he would play it through making gigantic changes. This was quite sufficient to cause the student to make a supreme effort to transform his composition into something infinitely more satisfactory.[9]

Dvořák was essentially a practical musician, one who had little regard for 'musical theory', and is reported to have made disparaging remarks about fugue. He was quite obviously completely at home over

7 Pellegrini, *op. cit.*
8 Michl: 'Rok u Dvořáka', pp. 176–177.
9 'Rok u Dvořáka', p. 175.

Statue of Dvořák by Karel Kuneš at Karlovy Vary

Dvořák Museum, Prague

the handling of an orchestra, and consequently he had much valuable advice to offer in his orchestration classes. As a violinist and viola player he recognised the necessity of imparting detailed information about string technique to his pianist and organist pupils who were wholly ignorant of these instruments. However, presumably irritated by the frequent references of critics to his fine orchestration, Dvořák placed no particular value on this skill of his. As he remarked to Harry Patterson Hopkins, any conductor could score as well as he could.[10]

The composer was seen in rather different circumstances by Hopkins, an American who studied privately with him both in Prague and at Vysoká, where he became a member of the Dvořák household. The lessons were informal, and Dvořák, drinking coffee and smoking a long black cigar, was far more relaxed, and particularly so at Vysoká. It became immediately apparent when he returned to Prague after the summer vacation that there were various things that worried him and made him irritable. If, as often happened, there were callers from the National Theatre, he would make his escape with Hopkins by the back entrance, so as to avoid being involved in any controversy. At Vysoká it was apparently normal for Hopkins's lessons to be accompanied by grinning faces peeking out from behind furniture, a towsled head appearing wearing Dvořák's silk hat, for one or two drum beats of the hat box to come from a cupboard, or for a wet wad of paper to whizz past the composer's head, through all of which Dvořák continued with discussion of the special circumstances in which the low notes of the clarinet would be most effective, or the very different nature of music intended for the horn and the trumpet, seemingly oblivious of what was going on. It was quite another matter at mealtimes: Dvořák would then become extremely irritable and angered by what he regarded as misdemeanours of his children.

If there was a thunderstorm, Dvořák immediately became nervous. He would break off the lesson, see that all the shutters were closed, light the lamps, and in an endeavour to blot out the crashes of thunder would play as loudly as he could on the piano. He also had a deep-rooted fear of thieves and fire. Whenever he left the house, whether it was to go on long tramps deep into the forest with Hopkins, or short strolls with his family, he invariably took the manuscript score or sketch on which he was working, rolled up in a shawl-strap, and would never allow this to pass into anyone else's hands.[11]

---

10 Hopkins: 'How Dvořák Taught Composition', *The Etude*, xlix (1931), pp. 97–98.

11 Hopkins: *op. cit.*; also his 'Student Days with Dvořák', *The Etude* xxx (1912), pp. 327–8.

As a largely self-taught composer with a natural inclination towards empiricism, a disregard and distrust of rigid rules, who at the same time was intensely sensitive and responsive to music, it was almost inevitable that Dvořák as a teacher would be unorthodox. He was not a suitable teacher for some of his pupils. As Michl has pointed out, some failed to understand him when he was enigmatic and answered questions obliquely, whilst those who understood his unusual way of expressing himself found him both interesting and stimulating. And he went on to claim that Dvořák's reprimands were beneficial because they 'instigated thought, refined taste and compelled self criticism'. Pellegrini admitted that he was not a born teacher, but was aware that by setting high standards, he gave those who studied with him a valuable target to aim at.

Oskar Nedbal, who was very conscious of the bond which Dvořák created with his pupils, spoke of his teacher in this way: 'It is difficult to express how we honoured and loved Dvořák as a teacher and paternal friend. On the one hand he was perhaps almost a comrade, and on the other perhaps our God. These two extremes may describe our relationship best.'[12]

---

12 Nedbal: 'Drobné vzpomínky na Dvořáka', *Hudební revue,* iv (1911), pp. 481–4. For extracts from Dvořák's *New York Herald* interview on his teaching see Appendix 3.

Appendix I

Dvorak's Final Illness

There is evidence that in the early months of 1904 Dvořák complained occasionally of pains in his side, and an incident in the Café Imperial between Dvořák and Malát is quoted in this connection. In late February and early March 1904 the composer was seriously concerned about a forthcoming production of his opera *Armida*. The musical direction and production were less than adequate and Janáček noted that the composer was irritated during one of the final rehearsals.

On 25 March Dvořák complained of a pain in his side and left the theatre early; on the following day his doctor (Professor Jan Hnátek) advised rest for a few days. By 30 March Dvořák was sufficiently recovered to go train spotting; after this excursion he caught a chill and was confined to bed on 31 March. It was known to members of the family that he had consumed beer 'over the measure' about this time and suffered increased discomfort as a result. His doctor attended him on 3 and 4 April, and at 3 am on 5 April was summoned again because the patient was feeling worse. From letters of Otakar Dvořák (cited Šourek, *A. D. zivot a dílo* iv, 2nd edn., 254; Fric, *A. D. a Kroměříz*, 85) and Hovorka (Šourek, 254; Fric, 85–6), it is known that the 'first disease' was a cystitis and that the composer had difficulty in micturition. The patient was confined to bed but was well enough to get up on 17 April. On the following day he was not so well and was thought to have contracted influenza. He returned to bed on 18 April and it is probable that he remained there until 30 April, when Hnátek suggested that he might dress and join the family for a celebration May Day luncheon. Family reminiscences quoted by Šourek (p. 254) speak clearly of him getting up 'after rather a long time' and described him as 'considerably weakened by long lying in bed'.

On 1 May Dvořák dressed with the help of his wife and son Otakar and 'made a small walk round the room' (Šourek, 254) before sitting down at table and consuming his soup with relish. Immediately thereafter he remarked 'I am feeling rather dizzy. I shall be glad to lie down' (special issue of *Dalibor*, 2 May 1904). He grew pale at once and then

immediately became flushed and sank back into his chair. He attempted
to speak again but was unable to do so. Those present got him to bed
with difficulty; by then he was unconscious and paralysed. By the time
the doctor arrived the composer was dead.

An autopsy was not carried out on Dvořák and the precise nature of
his final illness remains unknown. There are, however, some features
which are indicative of a possible diagnosis.

The diagnosis of cerebral arteriosclerosis reached by Hnátek and
Janovský early in April 1904 may have referred to the composer's
marked irritability earlier in the year or, possibly, to his known
hesitation in dealing with the problems of crowded streets and busy
traffic. These shortcomings may be attributed to temperament or mood.
There is no record of symptomatology directly referable to circum-
scribed lesions of the central nervous system.

There seems no doubt that by early 1904 Dvořák was suffering from
urinary obstruction and that this was relieved from time to time by
catheterization. In the circumstances, cystitis and possibly an ascending
pyelonephritis may have supervened with some degree of uraemia.
The febrile episodes of 31 March–1 April and of 18 April are possibly
referable to exacerbations of urinary infection rather than to chills or
influenza. The composer's appetite at his luncheon, however, does not
suggest that any biochemical disturbance was, as yet, of severe degree.

As a young man Dvořák had been rejected for military service on
medical grounds on three occasions, but the nature of his disability
cannot be ascertained from military archives because existing recruiting
records date only from 1912. It has been suggested, however, that
varicose veins may have been the cause of his rejection. This disability
is known to have had an hereditary component and Dvořák's children
especially Otilka, were affected by it.

There does not seem to be any doubt that Dvořák was confined to
bed for the best part of a month before his death, and that he got up on
1 May, the day of his death, specially for a family luncheon party. For a
man in his seventh decade with some degree of vascular degeneration, a
month in bed without careful physiotherapy would now be recognized
as likely to give rise to peripheral thrombosis. The sequence of events at
the luncheon table on 1 May is fairly detailed. Immediately after consuming his soup Dvořák collapsed, and shortly thereafter was dead.
His final words are indicative of cerebral anoxia and the rapidity with
which death supervened is strongly suggestive of a major vascular
catastrophe. The composer did not complain of acute pain, which
might have accompanied sudden vascular impairment of heart or brain,

and which certainly would have attended a rupture or aneurysm. The intermittent attacks of pain in the side in the early months of 1904 could be interpreted as small pulmonary infarcts following impaction of emboli in the distal pulmonary arteries. The last month of his life, when the composer was confined to bed, was conducive to the development or extension of peripheral thrombosis. The presence of pelvic congestion associated with some degree of cystitis, could again have been a factor in the further extension of such thrombosis in the pelvic veins. The 'small walk' before luncheon on his last day may have provided the immediate cause of detachment of an embolus large enough to occlude a major pulmonary artery.

DR JOHN STEPHENS
University of Edinburgh

Appendix 2

Chronicle of Events

1841
8 September   Born at Nelahozeves, near Kralupy nad Vltavou.

1847
Autumn   Enters the village primary school.

1853
Summer   Leaves school. Begins assisting his father in the butcher's trade.

1854
?   Goes to Zlonice to gain a wider experience of the butcher's trade. Antonín Liehmann assists him in his musical studies.

1856
Autumn   Goes to the school at Česká Kamenice to learn German.

1857
31 July   Obtains school leaving certificate.
Autumn   Becomes a student at the Organ School, Prague.
Begins playing viola in the St Cecilia Society concerts.

1859
30 June   Graduates from the Organ School.
September   Joins the Karel Komzák Band.

1861
6 June–?   Composes String Quintet in A minor, op. 1.

1862
March   Composes String Quartet in A major, op. 2.
18 November   Provisional Theatre, Prague, inauguration. Becomes viola player in the orchestra; conductor: J. N. Maýr.

1863
8 February   Plays in a concert of Wagner's music, the composer conducting.

1865

?   Begins giving piano lessons to Josefina Čermáková.

14 February–   Composes *The Bells of Zlonice* (Symphony No. 1), *Cypresses*
9 October   Song Cycle and B flat Symphony (No. 2).

1866

September   Smetana becomes chief conductor of the Provisional
Theatre.

1870

26 May–   Secretly composes the opera *Alfred* (three acts).
19 October

1871

April–   Composes *King and Charcoal Burner*, original version (three-
20 December   act opera).
July   Resigns from Provisional Theatre orchestra after nine years
as principal viola.

1872

May [?]–   Composes the cantata *The Heirs of the White Mountain*.
3 June

1873

January   Engaged to teach piano in the Neff family.
9 March   *The Heirs of the White Mountain* performed in Prague,
Dvořák's first success.

April–4 July   Composes Symphony in E flat, op. 10 (No. 3).
September   *King and Charcoal Burner* (I) rejected by the theatre management.
17 November   Marries Anna Čermáková.
December[?]   Begins sketching D minor Symphony, op. 13 (No. 4).

1874

15 February   Begins duties as organist of St Adalbert's church.
26 March   D minor Symphony completed.
29 March   Symphony in E flat performed at Philharmonic concert,
conducted by Smetana.

4 April   Otakar (I), son, born.
April [?]–   *King and Charcoal Burner* entirely recomposed. Overture
12 August   written in late autumn.
? September–   *The Stubborn Lovers* (one-act opera) composed.
24 December

20 October   Smetana now totally deaf, forcing him to resign from his
conducting post.

24 November	*King and Charcoal Burner* (II) performed (Čech).

1875

February	Dvořák wins the Austrian State Prize for the first time.
15 June– 23 July	F major Symphony, op. 76 (op. 24) (No. 5) composed
9 August– 22 December	*Vanda* (five-act opera) composed.
19 September	Josefa, daughter, born.
21 September	Josefa dies.

1876

4–20 January	Piano Trio in G minor, op. 26, composed.
19 February– 7 May	*Stabat Mater* sketched.
17 April	*Vanda* performed (Čech).
17–21 May	*Moravian Duets*, op. 29, composed.
26 June–13 July	*Moravian Duets*, op. 32, composed.
August [?]– 14 September	Piano Concerto, op. 33, composed.
18 September	Růžena, daughter, born.

1877

February– July	*The Cunning Peasant* (two-act opera) composed.
15 February	Resigns his organ post at St Adalbert's.
22 April	Janáček performs the Serenade in E, op. 22, at Brno.
6 August– 28 September	Symphonic Variations, op. 78 (op. 28) composed.
13 August	Růžena dies.
8 September	Otakar (I) dies, leaving the Dvořáks childless.
2 October [?]– 13 November	*Stabat Mater* full score completed.
30 November	Hanslick informs Dvořák that Brahms wants to arrange publication of *Moravian Duets* in Germany.
2 December	Symphonic Variations performed (Procházka).
7–18 December	String Quartet in D minor, op. 34, composed.

1878

4–18 January	Serenade in D minor for wind instruments, op. 44. composed.
27 January	*The Cunning Peasant* performed (Čech).

13 February– 17 March	*Slavonic Rhapsody* in D, op. 45, no. 1, composed.
18 March– 7 May	*Slavonic Dances*, op. 46 (Set I) for piano duet composed. Orchestrated April–22 August.
24 March	Piano Concerto performed by Slavkovský in Prague (Čech).
14–27 May	String Sextet in A, op. 48, composed.
6 June	Otilie, daughter, born.
20 August– 3 December	*Slavonic Rhapsodies* in G minor and A flat, op. 45, nos. 2 and 3, composed.
15 November	*Moravian Duets* and *Slavonic Dances* reviewed by Ehlert in the *Nationalzeitung*, Berlin.
17 November	*Slavonic Rhapsodies*, nos 1 and 2, performed in Prague, the composer conducting.
25 December	Begins composing String Quartet in E flat, op. 51.

1879

January	Selected dances from *Slavonic Dances*, orchestral version, performed at Hamburg and Nice.
15 February	Three *Slavonic Dances* performed by Manns at the Crystal Palace, London.
25 March	F major Symphony performed in Prague (Čech).
28 March	String Quartet in E flat completed.
29 June	Piano Trio in G minor performed at Turnov (Lachner, Neruda, Dvořák).
5 July	Begins composing the Violin Concerto, op. 53.
29 July	String Sextet and E flat String Quartet privately performed by Joachim in Berlin.
3 September	*Slavonic Rhapsody* no 2 performed at Dresden (Gottlöber).
24 September	First performance of *Slavonic Rhapsody* no. 3 given by Taubert in Berlin.
7 November	Two *Slavonic Dances* performed at Boston, Mass.
9 November	First public performance of String Sextet, by Joachim in Berlin.
16 November	Richter directs *Slavonic Rhapsody* no. 3 in Vienna.
23 November	Hanslick's first critical notice on Dvořák in the *Neue Freie Presse*.
28 November	Serenade in D minor performed at Wiesbaden.
17 December	E flat String Quartet performed in Prague.

1880

7 January	E flat String Quartet performed in Hamburg by Bargheer.
13 January	Anna, daughter, born.

18 January[?]–	*Gipsy Melodies* composed.
23 [?] February	
4 February	Theodore Thomas performs *Slavonic Rhapsody* no. 3 at Cincinnati.
21 February	Hamerik performs *Slavonic Rhapsody* no. 1 at Baltimore.
24 April	G minor Piano Trio played at Hamburg (Procházka).
21 May	Hallé plays the G minor Trio in London.
25 May	Violin Concerto completed. Revised in 1882.
27 August–	Symphony in D major, op. 60 (No. 6), composed.
15 October	
23 December	*Stabat Mater* performed in Prague (Čech).

1881

25 March	D major Symphony performed in Prague (Čech).
8 May–	The sketch for *Dimitrij* (four-act opera) completed.
? October	
11 June	Prague National Theatre opens.
17 August	Magda, daughter, born.
2 October	*The Stubborn Lovers* performed in Prague (Čech).
? October–	String Quartet in C major, op. 61, composed.
10 November	
11 December	Begins working on the full score of *Dimitrij*.

1882

14 February	D major Symphony performed at Leipzig (P. Klengel).
27 February	D minor String Quartet performed in Prague.
2 April	*Stabat Mater* performed by Janáček at Brno.
5 April	*Stabat Mater* performed by Bellovits at Budapest.
23 September	Full score of *Dimitrij* completed.
8 October	*Dimitrij* performed at New Czech Theatre (Anger).
24 October	*The Cunning Peasant* performed at Dresden (von Schuch).
2 November	C major String Quartet performed by Joachim in Berlin.
8 December	Dvořák elected an honorary member of the Umělecká beseda.
5 December	Anna Dvořáková, the composer's mother, dies.

1883

3 January	*The Cunning Peasant* performed at Hamburg.
? January–	Piano Trio in F minor, op. 65, composed.
? May [?]	
7 March	Antonín, son, born.
4 April–2 May	*Scherzo capriccioso*, op. 66, composed.

16 May	*Scherzo capriccioso* performed in Prague (Čech).
3 August	Invitation to London from the Philharmonic Society.
? August– 9 September	*Hussite* Overture, op. 67, composed.
13 October	Piano Concerto played by Beringer at the Crystal Palace (Manns).
14 October	Violin Concerto performed by Ondříček in Prague (Anger).
27 October	F minor Piano Trio performed at Mladá Boleslav (Lachner, Neruda, Dvořák).
18 November	*Hussite* Overture performed in Prague (Anger).
2 December	Violin Concerto played by Ondříček in Vienna (Richter).

1884

13 March	Dvořák conducts his *Stabat Mater* at the Royal Albert Hall, London.
20 March	Conducts his *Hussite* Overture, Symphony in D major and *Slavonic Rhapsody* no. 2 at the Philharmonic Society concert, London. F minor Trio performed by Hellmesberger in Vienna.
22 March	Dvořák conducts the *Scherzo capriccioso* and *Nocturne* for strings, op. 40, at the Crystal Palace, London.
3 April	Thomas performs the *Stabat Mater* in New York.
12 May	Smetana dies.
26 May– 27 November	Composes *The Spectre's Bride* for Birmingham.
3 July	Accepts the offer of honorary membership of the Philharmonic Society, London.
11 September	Dvořák conducts his *Stabat Mater* and D major Symphony at Worcester.
25 October	*Hussite* Overture performed by Van der Stucken in New York.
8 November	*Scherzo capriccioso* performed by Thomas at Brooklyn. Dvořák conducts his *Hussite* Overture and Piano Concerto.
21 November	(Grosser-Rilke) at the Philharmonic Society concert in Berlin.
13 December	Begins composing Symphony in D minor, op. 70 (No. 7), for London.

1885

9 February	Otakar (II), son, born.
17 March	Completes Symphony in D minor, op. 70.
28 March	Conducts *The Spectre's Bride* at Pilsen.

22 April	Dvořák conducts the first performance of the D minor Symphony, op. 70, at the Philharmonic Society concert, London.
6 May	Conducts his Piano Concerto (Franz Rummel) at the Philharmonic Society concert, London.
13 May	Conducts *The Heirs of the White Mountain* in London.
27 August	Dvořák conducts *The Spectre's Bride* at Birmingham.
17 September	Begins composing *St Ludmila* for Leeds.
18 November	*The Spectre's Bride* performed at Providence, Rhode Island.
19 November	*The Cunning Peasant*, performed in Vienna, is a fiasco.

1886

9 January	D minor Symphony, op. 70, performed in New York (Thomas).
30 May	Completes *St Ludmila*.
? June– 9 July	Composes *Slavonic Dances*, op. 72 (Set II) for piano duet. Orchestrated November 1886–5 Jan 1887.
15 October	Dvořák conducts the first performance of *St Ludmila* at Leeds.
21 October	Conducts his Symphony in D major at Birmingham.
29 October	Conducts *St Ludmila* at St James's Hall, London.
1 November	Hans von Bülow conducts the *Hussite* Overture at Hamburg.
6 November	Dvořák conducts *St Ludmila* at the Crystal Palace, London.

1887

7–14 January	Composes the Terzetto, op. 74.
6 March	After long neglect the *Symphonic Variations* is conducted by Dvořák in Prague.
26 March– 17 June	Composes the Mass in D major, op. 86.
16 May	Richter conducts the *Symphonic Variations* in London.
18 August– 3 October	Composes the Piano Quintet in A major, op. 81.
10 November	Begins sketching the opera *The Jacobin*.

1888

6 January	First performance of Piano Quintet in A in Prague.
14–16 February	Firm friendship formed between Dvořák and Tchaikovsky.
11 March	First performance of Symphony in B flat, op. 4 (composed 1865) in Prague.
28 March	Dvořák conducts the *Stabat Mater* in Budapest.

4 April	Aloisie (Zinda), daughter, born.
7 April	Manns conducts the first performance of the revised F major Symphony, op. 76, at the Crystal Palace, London.
9 May	*St Ludmila* performed at Troy, NY (van Olinda).
11 May	A major Piano Quintet performed in London (Hallé).
19 July	*Symphonic Variations* performed by Thomas at Chicago.
18 November	Completes *The Jacobin*.
November (?December)	Tchaikovsky invites Dvořák to Moscow.

1889

12 February	First performance of *The Jacobin* in Prague (Čech).
27 February	E major String Quartet, op. 80, played by Kneisel Quartet at Boston, Mass. Probable first performance.
13 March	Dvořák conducts his Symphony in F major, *Nocturne* for strings and *Slavonic Rhapsody* No. 2 at Dresden.
4 April	Programme of Dvořák's chamber music at Manchester. (Bauerkeller).
16 April–6 June	Composes *Poetic Tone Pictures*, op. 85.
? June	Awarded the Austrian Order of the Iron Crown.
10 July–19 August	Composes Piano Quartet in E flat, op. 87.
26 August–8 November	Composes Symphony in G major, op. 88 (No. 8).
27 and 28 October	Von Bülow performs the Symphony in D minor, op. 70, in Berlin.
9 December	Received in audience by Emperor Franz Josef.

1890

1 Jan–31 Oct	Composes the Requiem Mass, op. 89, for Birmingham.
2 February	Dvořák conducts the first performance of the G major Symphony in Prague.
27 February	149th Psalm performed at Boston, Mass. (Osgood). Earliest known performance of the revised work.
11 March	Dvořák conducts the F major Symphony, Adagio from the Serenade in D minor, *Scherzo capricicoso*, *Slavonic Rhapsody* No. 1 and *Symphonic Variations* in Moscow.
22 March	Conducts his Symphony in D major and *Scherzo capriccioso* in St Petersburg.
24 April	Dvořák conducts his Symphony in G at a Philharmonic Society concert in London.

11 October	Dvořák's relations with Simrock reach breaking point.
7 November	Dvořák conducts his *Hussite* Overture and Symphony in G at Frankfurt-am-Main.
? November	Begins composing the *Dumky* Trio, op. 90.
23 November	Piano Quartet in E flat performed in Prague.

1891

? January	Commences his duties as professor of composition at Prague Conservatory.
12 February	Completes the *Dumky* Trio.
17 March	Receives the PhD degree, *honoris causa*, of Charles University, Prague.
31 March–8 July	Composes *In Nature's Realm* Overture, op. 91.
11 April	Gives the first performance of the *Dumky* Trio (with Lachner and Wihan) in Prague.
5 June	Offered the directorship of the National Conservatory of Music of America, New York.
15 June	Conducts his Symphony in G and *Stabat Mater* at Cambridge.
16 June	Receives the MusD degree, *honoris causa*, of Cambridge University.
28 July–12 September	Composes *Carnival* Overture, op. 92.
9 October	Conducts the first performance of the Requiem Mass at Birmingham.
? November	Begins composing *Othello* Overture, op. 93.
23 [?] December	Signs a two-year contract with the National Conservatory of Music of America.

1892

3 Jan.–29 May	Concert tour of Bohemia and Moravia.
18 January	Completes *Othello* Overture.
24–25 February	Public rehearsal and performance of the Requiem Mass in New York (R. H. Warren).
27 February	Nikisch performs the Symphony in G at Boston.
28 April	Dvořák conducts the first performance of his *Triple Overture* (opp. 91, 92, 93) in Prague.
2 June	*Dimitrij* performs at the International Exhibition, Vienna.
25 June–28 July	Composes the *Te Deum*, op. 103, for his unaugural concert in New York.

3 August	Begins composing *The American Flag*, op. 102.
27 September	Dvořák arrives in New York.
21 October	Dvořák conducts the *Triple Overture* and the first performance of the *Te Deum* in New York.
29 and 30 November	Dvořák conducts the public rehearsal and performance of his Requiem Mass in Boston.
17 December	Dvořák conducts his Symphony in D major at a Philharmonic Society concert in New York.

1893

8 January	Completes *The American Flag*.
10 January– 24 May	Composes Symphony in E minor *From the New World*, op. 95 (No. 9).
6 April	Dvořák conducts the *Hussite* Overture in New York.
21 May	Interview with the *New York Herald:* 'Real Value of Negro Melodies'.
28 May	*New York Herald* publishes a letter from Dvořák.
5 June	Dvořák and his family arrive at Spillville, Iowa.
8–23 June	Composes String Quartet in F *The American*, op. 96.
26 June– 1 August	Composes String Quintet in E flat *The American*, op. 97.
28 June	Resumes relations with Simrock.
12 August	Conducts his Symphony in G, *Slavonic Dances* op. 72, nos 6, 2 and 3, and *My Home* Overture at the World Columbian Exposition, Chicago.
13 August	Interview with the *Chicago Tribune:* 'For National Music'.
2–3 September	Dvořák at Omaha.
4–5 September	Dvořák at St Paul, Minnesota.
6 November	Tchaikovsky dies.
19 November– 3 December	Composes Sonatina in G for violin and piano, op. 100, for his children.
15 and 16 December	Public rehearsal and first performance of Symphony *From the New World*, conducted by Seidl at Philharmonic Society concert in New York.

1894

1 January	First performance of String Quartet in F, given by Kneisel Quartet at Boston.

12 January	First performance of String Quintet in E flat, given by the Kneisel Quartet and Zach in New York.
12 February	Hans von Bülow dies.
5–26 March	Composes the *Biblical Songs*, op. 99.
19 March	Henschel performs *Carnival* Overture in Glasgow.
24 March	Manns performs *Othello* Overture at the Crystal Palace, London.
28 March	František Dvořák, the composer's father, dies.
28 April	Dvořák signs a contract undertaking to remain at his New York post for two more years.
	Manns performs *In Nature's Realm* Overture at the Crystal Palace.
30 May	Dvořák arrives back in Prague.
21 June	Mackenzie performs Symphony *From the New World* in London.
July	Dvořák's article 'Schubert' appears in the *Century Illustrated Monthly Magazine*.
20 July	Labitzký performs Symphony *From the New World* at Karlovy Vary (Carlsbad).
7–21 August	Composes the *Humoresques*, op. 101.
13 October	Dvořák conducts a farewell concert in Prague (Symphony *From the New World*, *My Home* Overture, Serenade in E major).
26 October	Arrives in New York.
8 November	Begins composing the Cello Concerto in B minor, op. 104.
1895	
January	Dvořák's article 'Music in America' appears in *Harper's New Monthly Magazine*.
? January	Kneisel Quartet give their fiftieth performance of the String Quartet in F.
31 January	String Quartet in F performed in Prague (Prague String Quartet).
9 February	Completes the Cello Concerto in B minor.
16 February	Dvořák given honorary membership of *Gesellschaft der Musikfreunde*, Vienna.
26 March– 30 December	Composes String Quartet in A flat, op. 105.
27 April	Dvořák arrives in Prague.

4 May	First performance of *The American Flag* in New York (Dossert).
27 May	Josefina Kaunitzová, Dvořák's sister-in-law, dies.
17 August	Dvořák resigns his directorship of the National Conservatory of Music of America.
1 November	Resumes his duties as professor of composition at Prague Conservatory.
11 November–9 December	Composes String Quartet in G, op. 106.

1896

4 January	Dvořák conducts the first performance of *Biblical Songs*, nos 1–5 (orchestral version) in Prague.
6 January–11 February	Composes *The Water Goblin*, op. 107.
11 January–27 February	Composes *The Noon Witch*, op. 108.
15 January–25 April	Composes *The Golden Spinning Wheel*, op. 109.
19 March	Dvořák conducts the first performance of the Cello Concerto in B minor (L. Stern), together with *Biblical Songs*, 1–5, and Symphony in G at a Philharmonic Society concert, London.
25 March	Dvořák conducts *The Spectre's Bride* in Vienna.
11 April	Conducts his Cello Concerto (Stern) in Prague.
9 October	First performance of String Quartet in G by the Bohemian String Quartet in Prague.
22 October–18 November	Composes *The Wild Dove*, op. 110.
26 October	First performance of *The Golden Spinning Wheel*, by Richter in London.
10 November	First performance [?] of String Quartet in A flat by the Rosé Quartet in Vienna.
14 November	First performance of *The Water Goblin*, by Henry J. Wood in London.
21 November	First performance of *The Noon Witch*, by H. J. Wood in London.
24 November	Nedbal performs the Symphony in D minor in Prague.

1897

1 January	*The Golden Spinning Wheel* performed by Thomas in Chicago.

7 March	Cello Concerto performed in Vienna (Becker/Richter).
? March	Visits Brahms during his final illness.
3 April	Brahms dies.
6 April	Dvořák attends Brahms's funeral.
? May– 25 August	Attempts made to persuade Dvořák to return to the post in New York.
4 August– 25 October	Composes *Heroic Song*, op. 111.
? November	Becomes a member of the jury for the Austrian State Prize for the Arts.
14 November	*St Ludmila* performed in Vienna by *Gesellschaft der Musikfreunde* (R. von Perger).

1898

13 February	Mengelberg conducts a concert of Dvořák's works in Amsterdam: *In Nature's Realm* Overture; Violin Concerto; Symphony *From the New World*.
20 March	First performance of *The Wild Dove*, conducted by Janáček at Brno.
5 May	Begins composing *Kate and the Devil*.
17 November	Wedding of Otilka and Josef Suk. Celebration of the Dvořák's silver wedding.
25 November	Honoured with the gold medal for 'Litteris et Artibus' by Emperor Franz Joseph of Austria.
4 December	First performance of *Heroic Song*, by Mahler in Vienna.

1899

7 February	Klenovsty performs Symphony *From the New World* at Tiflis.
27 February	Completes *Kate and the Devil*.
10 October	*The Wild Dove* performed by H. J. Wood in London.
20 October	*The Wild Dove* performed by Thomas at Chicago.
23 November	*Kate and the Devil* given first performance in Prague (Čech).
19 December	Concert of Dvořák's chamber music in Budapest, the composer playing piano.
20 December	Budapest Philharmonic Society concert of Dvořák's works conducted by the composer: *Heroic Song: Cello Concerto* (Wihan); *Carnival* Overture.

1900

4 April	Dvořák's last conducting engagement: the Brahms *Tragic* Overture, Schubert's *Unfinished Symphony*, Beethoven's 8th Symphony and *The Wild Dove* at a Czech Philharmonic concert in Prague.

21 April– 27 November	Composes *Rusalka*.
27 April	Toscanini performs Symphony *From the New World* at La Scala, Milan.
23 and 24 July	Nedbal performs Symphony *From the New World* at the *Exposition mondiale*, Paris.
1 September	Nedbal performs Symphony *From the New World* at Pavlovsk, near St Petersburg.

1901

31 March	First performance of *Rusalka* in Prague (Kovařovic).
14 [?] April	Dvořák elected a member of the Austrian House of Peers.
15 April	*The Wild Dove* performed in Prague by the Berlin Philharmonic Orchestra directed by Nikisch.
6 July	Dvořák appointed director of the Prague Conservatory.
8 September– 30 October	Celebration of the composer's 60th birthday with a cycle of his operas and other works at the National Theatre, Prague.
6–11 November	Concerts and celebrations in the composer's honour in Prague.
17 December	Nedbal conducts the Czech Philharmonic Orchestra in Vienna in a programme of Dvořák's works: *Carnival* Overture; Violin Concerto; Symphony *From the New World*.

1902

11 March	Begins composing *Armida*.

1903

25 March	Meets Grieg in Prague.
23 August	Completes *Armida*.
22 October	Antonín Rus dies.
27 December	Adolf Čech dies.
	Kate and the Devil performed at Pilsen.

1904

1 and [?] March	Unsatisfactory rehearsals of *Armida*.
25 March	First performance of *Armida* at National Theatre, Prague (F. Picka). Dvořák obliged to leave early, due to illness.
18 April	Deterioration in the composer's condition.
1 May	Dvořák dies.
5 May	The composer is laid to rest at the Vyšehrad cemetery.

Appendix 3

Interviews with American Newspapers

REAL VALUE OF NEGRO MELODIES
(*New York Herald* 21 May 1893)

I am now satisfied that the future music of this country must be founded upon what are called the negro melodies. This must be the real foundation of any serious and original school of composition to be developed in the United States. When I first came here last year I was impressed with this idea and it has developed into a settled conviction. These beautiful and varied themes are the product of the soil. They are American. I would like to trace out the traditional authorship of the negro melodies, for it would throw a great deal of light upon the question I am most deeply interested in at present.

These are the folk songs of America and your composers must turn to them. All of the great musicians have borrowed from the songs of the common people. Beethoven's most charming scherzo is based upon what might now be considered a skilfully handled negro melody. I myself have gone to the simple, half forgotten tunes of the Bohemian peasants for hints in my most serious work. Only in this way can a musician express the true sentiment of his people. He gets into touch with the common humanity of his country.

POSSIBILITIES OF NEGRO MELODY

In the negro melodies of America I discover all that is needed for a great and noble school of music. They are pathetic, tender, passionate, melancholy, solemn, religious, bold, merry, gay or what you will. It is music that suits itself to any mood or any purpose. There is nothing in the whole range of composition that cannot be supplied with themes from this source. The American musician understands these tunes and they move sentiment in him. They appeal to his imagination because of their associations.

When I was in England one of the ablest musical critics in London complained to me that there was no distinctively English school of music, nothing that appealed particularly to the British mind and heart. I replied to him that the composers of England had turned their backs upon the fine melodies of Ireland and Scotland instead of making them the essence of an English school. It is a great pity that English musicians have not profited out of this rich store. Somehow the old Irish and Scotch ballads have not seized upon or appealed to them.

I hope it will not be so in this country, and I intend to do all in my power to call attention to the splendid treasure of melody which you have.

Among my pupils in the National Conservatory of Music I have discovered strong talents. There is one young man upon whom I am building strong expectations. His compositions are based upon negro melodies, and I have encouraged him in this direction. The other members of the composition class seem to think that it is not in good taste to get ideas from the old plantation songs, but they are wrong, and I have tried to impress upon their minds the fact that the greatest composers have not considered it beneath their dignity to go to the humble folk songs for motifs.

I did not come to America to interpret Beethoven or Wagner for the public. That is not my work and I would not waste any time on it. I came to discover what young Americans had in them and to help them to express it. When the negro minstrels are here again I intend to take my young composers with me and have them comment on the melodies.

ANTONÍN DVOŘÁK ON NEGRO MELODIES
(Letter, *New York Herald* 28 May 1893)

To the Editor of the Herald:

I was deeply interested in the article in last Sunday's Herald, for the writer struck a note that should be sounded throughout America. It is my opinion that I find a sure foundation in the Negro melodies for a new national school of music, and my observations have already convinced me that the young musicians of this country need only intelligent direction, serious application and a reasonable amount of public support and applause to create a new musical school in America. This is not a sudden discovery on my part. The light has gradually dawned on me.

The new American school of music must strike its roots deeply into its own soil. There is no longer any reason why young Americans who have talent should go to Europe for their education. It is a waste of money and puts off the coming day when the Western world will be in music, as in many other things, independent of other lands. In the National Conservatory of Music, founded and presided over by Mrs Jeannette M. Thurber, is provided as good a school as can be found elsewhere. The masters are competent in the highest sense and the spirit of the institution is absolutely catholic. A fresh proof of the breadth of purpose involved in this conservatory is the fact that it has been opened without limit or reservation to the Negro race.

I find good talent here, and I am convinced that when the youth of the country realizes that it is better now to stay at home than to go abroad we shall discover genius, for many who have talent but cannot undertake a foreign residence will be encouraged to pursue their studies here. It is to the poor that I turn for musical greatness. The poor work hard; they study seriously. Rich people are apt to apply themselves lightly to music, and to abandon the painful toil to which every strong musician must submit without complaint and without rest. Poverty is no barrier to one endowed by nature with musical talent. It is a spur. It keeps the mind loyal to the end. It stimulates the student to great efforts.

If in my own career I have achieved a measure of success and reward it is to some extent due to the fact that I was the son of poor parents and was reared in an atmosphere of struggle and endeavour. Broadly speaking the Bohemians are a nation of peasants. My first musical education I got from my schoolmaster, a man of good ability and much earnestness. He taught me to play the violin. Afterward I travelled with him and we made our living together.[1] Then I spent two years at the organ school in Prague. From that time on I had to study for myself. It is impossible for me to speak without emotion of the strains and sorrows that came upon me in the long and bitter years that followed. Looking back at that time, I can hardly understand how I endured the privations and labour of my youth.

Could I have had in my earlier days the advantages, freely offered in such a school as the National Conservatory of Music, I might have been spared many of my hardest trials and have accomplished much more. Not that I was unable to produce music, but that I had not technique enough to express all that was in me. I had ideas but I could not utter them perfectly.

There is a great opportunity for musicians in America and it will

---

1 This statement is misleading. Dvořák cannot have earned very much by playing with Liehmann in the region around Zlonice.

increase when grand opera sung in English is more firmly established, with public or private assistance. At the present time this country needs also the materials for orchestral work. The dearth of good native performers on reeds and brass instruments is marked. Every one wants to sing or play the piano, violin or violoncello. Nobody seems to realize the importance of good cornetists, trombonists, clarinetists, oboists, flutists, trumpeters and the like. In Bohemia applicants for admission to the Conservatory are assigned to instruments according to the necessities of the time. Of course nearly every young musician wants to play the violin, but to encourage that tendency would be to undermine the orchestral system and leave composers without the means of properly presenting their works.

I do not agree with those who say that the air here is not good for vocalists. The American voice has a character of its own. It is quite different from the European voice, just as the English voice is different from the German and Italian. Singers like Lloyd and M'Guckin have an entirely different vocal quality from that of German singers and members of the Latin race. The American voice is unlike anything else, quite unlike the English voice. I do not speak of method or style, but of the natural quality, the timbre of the voice. I have noticed this difference ever since I have been in New York. The American voice is good; it pleases me very much.

Those who think that music is not latent in the American will discover their error before long. I only complain that the American musician is not serious enough in applying himself to the work he must do before he is qualified to enter upon a public career. I have always to remind my most promising pupils of the necessity of work. Work! work! work! to the very end.

The country is full of melody, original, sympathetic and varying in mood, colour and character to suit every phase of composition. It is a rich field. America can have great and noble music of her own, growing out of the very soil and partaking of its nature—the natural voice of a free and vigorous race.

This proves to me that there is such a thing as nationality in music in the sense that it may take on the character of its locality. It now rests with the young musicians of this country and with the patrons of music to say how soon the American school of music is to be developed. A good beginning has been made in New York. Honour to those who will help to increase and broaden the work.

ANTONÍN DVOŘÁK
New York. 25 May 1893

FOR NATIONAL MUSIC
(*Chicago Tribune* 13 August 1893)

Every nation has its music. There is Italian, German, French, Bohemian, Russian; why not American music? The truth of this music depends upon its characteristics, its colour. I do not mean to take these melodies, plantation, Creole or Southern, and work them out as themes; that is not my plan. But I study certain melodies until I become thoroughly imbued with their characteristics and am enabled to make a musical picture in keeping with and partaking of those characteristics. The symphony is the least desirable of vehicles for the display of this work, in that the form will allow only of a suggestion of the colour of that nationalism to be given. Liberty in this line is never allowable. Opera is by far the best mode of expression for the undertaking, allowing as it does of freedom of treatment. My plan of work in this line is simple, but the attainment is subtle and difficult because of the minute and conscientious study demanded and the necessity to grasp the essence and vitality of the subject. I have just completed a quintet for stringed instruments, written lately at Spielville [sic], Ia. The quintet will be played in New York during the winter. In this work I think there will be found the American colour with which I have endeavoured to infuse it. My new symphony is also on the same lines—namely: an endeavour to portray characteristics, such as are distinctly American. At present I have studying with me in New York seven pupils; next year I shall have a much larger number. I take only those far advanced in composition; that is, understanding thorough bass, form, and instrumentation. The most promising and gifted of these pupils is a young Westerner, [Maurice Arnold] Strathotte by name, a native of St Louis. A suite of 'Creole Dances' written by him, and which contain material that he has treated in a style that accords with my ideas, will be given in New York during the winter. Gottschalk also recognized and worked upon this plan.

DVOŘÁK ON HIS NEW WORK
(*New York Herald* 15 December 1893)

Since I have been in this country I have been deeply interested in the national music of the Negroes and the Indians. The character, the very nature of a race is contained in its national music. For that reason my attention was at once turned in the direction of these native melodies. I found that the music of the two races bore a remarkable similarity to the music of Scotland. In both there is a peculiar scale, caused by the absence of the fourth and seventh, or leading tone. In both the minor scale has the seventh invariably a minor seventh, the fourth is included and the sixth omitted.

Now the Scotch scale, if I may so call it, has been used to impart a certain color to musical composition. I need only instance Mendelssohn's 'Hebrides' Overture. The device is a common one. In fact the scale in question is only a certain form of the ancient ecclesiastical modes. These modes have been employed time and time again. For example Félicien David in his symphonic ode 'Le Desert', Verdi in 'Aida'. I have myself used one of them in my D minor Symphony.

Now, I found that the music of the Negroes and of the Indians was practically identical. I therefore carefully studied a certain number of Indian melodies which a friend gave me, and became thoroughly imbued with their characteristics—with their spirit, in fact.

It is this spirit which I have tried to reproduce in my new Symphony. I have not actually used any of the melodies. I have simply written original themes embodying the peculiarities of the Indian music, and, using these themes as subjects, have developed them with all the resources of modern rhythms, harmony, counterpoint and orchestral color.

The Symphony is in E minor. It is written upon the classical models and is in four movements. It opens with a short introduction, an Adagio of about thirty bars in length. This leads directly into the Allegro, which embodies the principles which I have already worked out in my Slavonic Dances; that is, to preserve, to translate into music, the spirit of a race as distinct in its national melodies or folk songs.

The second movement is an Adagio [sic]. But it is different to the classic works in this form. It is in reality a study or sketch for a longer work, either a cantata or opera which I purpose writing, and which will be based upon Longfellow's 'Hiawatha'. I have long had the idea of someday utilizing that poem. I first became acquainted with it about thirty years ago through the medium of a Bohemian translation. It appealed very strongly to my imagination at the time, and the impression has only been strengthened by my residence here.

The Scherzo of the Symphony was suggested by the scene at the feast in 'Hiawatha' where the Indians dance, and is also an essay which I made in the direction of imparting the local color of Indian character to music.

The last movement is an Allegro con feroce [sic]. All the previous themes reappear and are treated in a variety of ways. The instruments are only those of what we call the 'Beethoven orchestra', consisting of strings, four horns, three trombones, two trumpets, two flutes, two oboes, two clarinets, two bassoons and tympani. There is no harp and I did not find it necessary to add any novel instrument in order to get the effect I wanted.

I have indeed been busy since I came to this country. I have finished a couple of compositions in chamber music, which will be played by the Kneisel String Quartet, of Boston, next January, in Music Hall. They are both written upon the same lines as this Symphony and both breathe the same Indian spirit. One is a String Quartet in F major, and the other a Quintet in E flat for two violins, two violas and violoncello.

HOW DR DVOŘÁK GIVES A LESSON
(Part of an unsigned article *New York Herald* 14 January 1884)

If you write well by accident once, you will be just as likely to write badly ten times. Have a reason for everything you do. Examine your reason from every point of view. Make up your mind as to the merit of a musical theme, its treatment or its accompaniment, only after careful thorough consideration. Then, having come to a decided opinion on the matter, set to work and write it out. You may find many things to change upon further reflection, you may modify the work in many ways, but if your reasoning has been thorough you will find that the foundation, the kernel, of your work remains just the same. I have no patience with the people who write down the first thing that comes into their head, who accompany it with the harmonies that happen to suggest themselves at the moment, who then score it for any instrument, or combination of instruments, that catches their fancy without any regard to effect! There would not be so much nonsense written if people thought more.

You must not imitate. Model your style upon all that is best, all that is noble and elevated in the literature of music, but remain yourself. Do not become the copyist of anyone, for you will invariably copy your model's defects, while his merits will be so subtle that they will escape you.

Mozart! Ah, Mozart is the greatest of them all. Beethoven is grand. His works are always sublime in conception and sublime in working out. But it is awe that he inspires, while Mozart touches my heart. His melodies are so lovable, are so inspired and so inspiring, that only to hear them is the greatest enjoyment that exists in the world for me. Schubert also has somewhat of Mozart's qualities so far as impressing me is concerned.

Appendix 4

Catalogue of Compositions

The following information is given immediately after the title of each work, or, in the case of vocal works, after the name of the author or source of the text: (i) Burghauser Catalogue number, or numbers, preceded by the letter 'B'; (ii) date of composition, and of revision, if any; (iii) the first publisher, with date of publication; (iv) the volume of the Critical Edition in which the work appears, or will appear. The following abbreviations are used:

BB	Bote & Bock, Berlin	N	Novello, Ewer & Co.,
BH	Breitkopf & Härtel, Leipzig		London (Sevenoaks)
	(Wiesbaden)	O	Orbis, Prague
Cr	Cranz, Leipzig (Wiesbaden)	S	N. Simrock, Berlin (Leipzig)
FAU	F. A. Urbánek, Prague	Sch	Schlesinger, Berlin
H	F. Hofmeister, Leipzig	SN	Státní nakladatelství KLHU,
	(Wiesbaden)		Prague
Ha	J. Hainauer, Breslau (Berlin)	St	E. Starý, Prague
HM	Hudební matice, Prague	SV	Collected Critical Edition
JV	J. R. Vilímek, Prague		of Dvořák's Works, Prague
K	F. Kistner, Leipzig	UE	Universal Edition, Vienna
MU	M. Urbánek, Prague	W	E. Wetzler, Prague

I OPERAS AND INCIDENTAL MUSIC

Op.
— *Alfred*, heroic opera in three acts, text in German by K. T. Körner. B. 16; 1870; unpublished (except overture, *q.v.*); SV,i,1.
— *King and Charcoal Burner* (*Král a uhlíř*), comic opera in three acts, version I, libretto by B. J. Lobeský. B.21; 1871; unpublished; SV,i,2.
14 *King and Charcoal Burner* (*Král a uhlíř*), comic opera in three acts, version II. B.42, 115, 151; 1874, revised 1887 (revisions to libretto by V. J. Novotný); HM (vocal score) 1915; SV,i,3.

Op.

17 *The Stubborn Lovers* (*Tvrdé palice*), comic opera in one act, libretto by J. Štolba. B.46; 1874; S (vocal score) 1882; SV,i,4.

25 *Vanda*, tragic opera in five acts, libretto by V. B. Šumavský. B.55; 1875, revised 1879 and 1883; unpublished, except for 'Wanda Mazurka', arr. for piano solo: Cr 1912, and overture (q.v.); SV,i,5.

37 *The Cunning Peasant* (*Šelma sedlák*), comic opera in two acts, libretto by J. O. Veselý. B.67; 1877; S 1882; SV,i,6.

62 *Josef Kajetán Tyl*, overture and incidental music to the play by F. F. Šamberk. B.125; 1881–2; St (piano duet version) 1882, S (overture 'My Home', 'Mein Heim') 1882; SV,i,9.

64 *Dimitrij*, historical opera in four acts, libretto by M. Červinková-Riegrová. B.127, 186; 1881–2, revised 1885 and 1894–5; St (vocal score) 1886, HM (vocal score, first version revised by Kovařovic) 1912); SV,i,7 and 8.

84 *The Jacobin* (*Jakobín*), opera in three acts, libretto by M. Červinková-Riegrová. B.159, 200; 1887–8, revised 1897; HM (vocal score, first version revised by Kovařovic) 1911, HM (vocal score, Dvořák's second version) 1941 [?], SV (full score) 1966; SV,i,10.

112 *Kate and the Devil* (*Čert a Káča*), comic opera in three acts, libretto by A. Wenig. B.201; 1898–9; MU (vocal score) 1908, SV (full score) 1972; SV,i,11.

114 *Rusalka*, lyric fairy tale in three acts, libretto by J. Kvapil. B.203; 1900; MU (vocal score) 1905, SV (full score) 1960; SV,i,12.

115 *Armida*, opera in four acts, libretto by J. Vrchlický. B.206; 1902–03; Heirs of Dvořák (vocal score) 1941; SV,i,13.

II CANTATA, MASS AND ORATORIO

Op.

— Mass in B flat major. B.2; 1857/59 [?]. Lost.

30 Hymnus: *The Heirs of the White Mountain* (*Dědicové bílé hory*), poem by V. Hálek, mixed chorus and orchestra. B.27, 102, 134; 1872, revised 1880 and 1884; N 1885; SV,ii,5.

58 *Stabat Mater*, SATB soli, chorus and orchestra. B.71; 1876, 1877; S 1881; SV,ii,1.

79 149th Psalm, text from Bible of Kralice, male voice chorus and orchestra, revised version for mixed chorus and orchestra. B.91, 154; 1879, revised 1887; S 1888; SV,ii,6.

Op.

69 *The Spectre's Bride* (*Svatební košile*), on a ballad by K. J. Erben, STB soli, chorus and orchestra. B.135; 1884; N 1885; SV,ii,2.

71 *St Ludmila*, libretto by J. Vrchlický, SATB soli, chorus and orchestra, B.144, 205; 1885–6, 1901 (recitatives to text by Vrchlický and V. J. Novotný); *Hlas národa* (Bořivoj's aria) 23 April 1886, N (complete) 1887; SV,ii,3.

86 Mass in D major, SATB soli (or semi-chorus), chorus and organ; later version with orchestra. B.153, 175; 1887, revised 1892, N 1893; SV,ii,7 and 8.

89 Requiem Mass, SATB soli, chorus and orchestra. B.165; 1890; N 1891; SV,ii,4.

103 *Te Deum*, soprano and bass soli, chorus and orchestra. B.176; 1892; S 1896; SV,ii,6.

102 *The American Flag* (Americký prapor), poem by J. R. Drake, ATB soli, chorus and orchestra. B.177; 1892–3; Schirmer (vocal score) 1895; SV,ii,5.

113 *Ode*, or *Festival Song* (*Slavnostní zpěv*), poem by J. Vrchlický, mixed chorus and orchestra. B.202; 1900; MU (vocal score with piano duet accompaniment) 1902, SV (full score) 1972; SV,ii,5.

III ORCHESTRAL WORKS

A *Symphonies and Concertos*

Op.

— Symphony no. 1 in C minor, *The Bells of Zlonice* ('Zlonické zvony'). B.9. 1865; SV 1961; SV,iii,1.

— Cello Concerto in A major, cello with piano accompaniment. B.10; 1865; full score orchestrated by J. Burghauser: Supraphon 1977; Günter Raphael's shortened and recomposed version: BH 1929; SV,iv,2.

4 Symphony no. 2 in B flat major. B.12; 1865; SV 1959; SV,iii,2.

10 Symphony no. 3 in E flat major. B.34; 1873; S 1911; SV,iii,3.

13 Symphony no. 4 in D minor. B.41; 1874; S 1912; SV,iii,4.

76 (24) Symphony no. 5 in F major. B.54; 1875, revised 1887; S 1888 ('No. 3'); SV,iii,5.

33 Piano Concerto in G minor. B.63; 1876, revised 1883 [?]; Ha 1883; SV,iii,10.

53 Violin Concerto in A minor. B.96, 108; 1879, 1880, revised 1882; S 1883; SV,iii,11.

60 Symphony no. 6 in D major. B.112; 1880; S 1882 ('No. 1'); SV,iii,6.

Op.

70 Symphony no. 7 in D minor. B.141; 1884–85; S 1885 ('No. 2');
     SV,iii,7.

88 Symphony no. 8 in G major. B.163; 1889; N 1892 ('No. 4');
     SV,iii,8.

95 Symphony no. 9 in E minor, *From the New World* (Z nového
     světa). B.178; 1893; S 1894 ('No. 5'); SV,iii,9.

104 Cello Concerto in B minor. B.191; 1894–5 (revised 1895);
      S 1896; SV,iii,12.

B *Overtures and Symphonic Poems*

Op.

—   Tragic Overture (Dramatic Overture), overture to the opera
     Alfred. B.16a; 1870; S 1912; SV,i,1.

—   Concert Overture in F major. Overture for the 1st version of
     King and Charcoal Burner. B.21a; 1871; unpublished; SV,i,2.

—   *Romeo and Juliet* Overture. B.35; 1873; lost.

25 *Vanda* Overture, overture to the opera. B.97; 1879; Cr 1885;
     SV,iii,24.

(62) *My Home* Overture (*Domov můj*), overture to J. K. Tyl. B.125a;
       1882; S 1882; SV,i,9.

67 *Hussite* Overture (*Husitská*), dramatic overture. B.132; 1883;
     S 1884; SV,iii,13.

91 *In Nature's Realm* Overture (V přírodě). B.168; 1891; S 1894;
     SV,iii,13.

92 *Carnival* Overture (*Karneval*). B.169; 1891; S 1894; SV,iii,13.

93 *Othello* Overture. B.174; 1891–2; S 1894; SV,iii,13. The three
     overtures, opp. 91–3, together form the *Triple Overture*, and were
     originally called *Nature, Life and Love*.

107 *The Water Goblin* (*Vodník*), symphonic poem. B.195; 1896;
      S 1896; SV,iii,14.

108 *The Noon Witch* (*Polednice*), symphonic poem. B.196, 1896;
      S 1896; SV,iii, 14.

109 *The Golden Spinning Wheel* (*Zlatý kolovrat*), symphonic poem.
      B.197; 1896; S 1896; SV,iii,14.

110 *The Wild Dove* (*Holoubek*), symphonic poem. B.198; 1896;
      S 1899; SV,iii,15.
         (Opp. 107–110 are based on ballads by K. J. Erben.)

111 *Heroic Song* (*Píseň bohatýrská*), symphonic poem. B.199; 1897;
      S 1899; SV,iii,15.

c *Serenades, Suites and Dances*

Op.

— *The Woman Harpist* (Harfenice), polka. B.4; 1860 [?]; lost.

— Polka and Galop. B.5 and 6; 1861/62?; lost. (For orchestra?)

22 Serenade in E major, for strings. B52, 1875; arr. for piano duet: St 1877, score: BB 1879; SV.iii,16.

28 Two Minuets B.58; 1876[?]; version for orchestra lost.

44 Serenade in D minor for wind instruments (2 ob, 2 cl, 2 fag, contra fag, 3 hn, vc, db). B.77; 1878; S 1879; SV,iii,16.

46 *Slavonic Dances*, series I. B.83; 1878; S 1878; SV,iii,19: 1 C major; 2 E minor; 3 A flat major; 4 F major; 5 A major; 6 D major; 7 C minor; 8 G minor.

54 *Festival March* (*Slavnostní pochod*), for the silver wedding of Franz Joseph and Elisabeth of Austria. B.88; 1879; St 1879; SV,iii,24.

39 *Czech Suite* in D major. B.93; 1879; Sch 1881; SV,iii,17.

— *Prague Waltzes* (*Pražské valčíky*), D major. B.99, 1879; SV 1961 (Dvořák's arrangement for piano solo: FAU 1880); SV,iii,24.

— Polonaise in E flat major. B.100; 1879; SV 1961 (piano duet version, arranged by J. Zubatý and revised by Dvořák: FAU 1883); SV,iii,24.

54/1,4 Two Waltzes for string orchestra. B. 105; 1880; S 1911; SV,iv,6. See Waltzes, op. 54, for piano.

53A/1 Polka 'For Prague Students' ('Pražským akademikům'), in B flat major. B.114; 1880; SV 1961 (arranged for piano solo, by Dvořák[?]: St 1882, in 'Taneční album, op.53', with Two Minuets, op. 28, and Scottish Dances, op. 41); SV,iii,24.

53A/2 Galop in E major. B.119; 1881[?]; version for orchestra lost, arrangement for piano solo by ?: St 1882, in 'Taneční album, op. 53' (see Polka 'For Prague Students' above).

72 *Slavonic Dances*, series II. B.147; 1886–87; S 1887; SV,iii,20: 1 (9) B major; 2 (10) E minor; 3 (11) F major; 4 (12) D flat major; 5 (13) B flat minor; 6 (14) B flat major; 7 (15) C major; 8 (16) A flat major.

98B Suite in A major. B.190; 1895–96; S 1911; SV,iii,17.

d *Miscellaneous Works*

Op.

— Intermezzi (Meziaktní skladby). B.15; 1867; unpublished; SV,iii,24.

— Three Nocturnes (No. 2: 'May Night', 'Májová noc'). B.31; 1872; unpublished; SV,vii. MS. incomplete.

Op.

14   Symphonic Poem (Rhapsody in A minor). B.44; 1874; S 1912;
     SV,iii,18.

40   Nocturne in B major, for string orchestra. B.47; 1875[?], revised
     1882/83?; BB 1883; SV, iii,24. Originally part of the String
     Quartet in E minor (1870?), and later of the String Quintet in G
     (1875).

78 (28) *Symphonic Variations*, on a theme from the male voice chorus 'I
     am a fiddler' ('Já jsem huslař') (1877). B.70; 1877; S 1888;
     SV,iii,22.

45   *Slavonic Rhapsodies:* No. 1, D major; No. 2, G minor; No. 3,
     A flat major. B.86; 1878; S 1879; SV,iii, 18.

59   *Legends*, B122; 1881; S 1882; SV,iii, 21:
     1 Allegretto non troppo, quasi andantino, D mi; 2 Molto
     moderato, G ma; 3 Allegro giusto, G mi; 4 Molto maestoso, C
     ma; 5 Allegro giusto, A flat ma; 6 Allegro con moto, C sharp mi;
     7 Allegretto grazioso, A ma; 8 Un poco allegretto, F ma;
     9 Andante con moto, D ma; 10 Andante, B flat mi.

66   *Scherzo capriccioso*. B.131; 1883; BB 1884; SV,iii,22.

—   Fanfares, for the festive opening of the Regional Exhibition in
     Prague, 15 May 1891. B.167; 1891; unpublished; SV,vii.

E *Small Works for Solo Instrument and Orchestra*

Op.

11   Romance in F minor, violin and orch. B.39; 1873/77[?]; S 1879;
     SV,iii,23. Transcription of the Andante con moto of the String
     Quartet in F minor, op. 9 (1873).

—   Capriccio (Concertstück), violin and orch. B.81; 1878; orchestral
     version lost.

49   Mazurek, violin and orch. B.90; 1879; S 1879; SV,iii,23.

94   Rondo in G minor, cello and orch. B.181; 1893; S 1894; SV,iii,
     23.

68/5 *Silent Woods (Klid)*, cello and orch. B.182; 1893; S 1894; SV,iii,23.
     See: IV, Chamber Music, D.

IV CHAMBER MUSIC

A *Strings only*

Op.

1   String Quintet in A minor (2 vn, 2 va, vc). B.7; 1861, revised
     1887? HM 1943; SV,iv,8.

Op.

2 String Quartet in A major. B.8; 1862, revised 1887; HM 1948; SV,iv,5.

— String Quartet in B flat major. B.17; 1869/70? SV 1962; SV,iv,5.

— String Quartet in D major. B.18; 1869/70?; SV 1964; SV,iv,5.

— String Quartet in E minor. B.19; 1870?; SV 1968; SV,iv,5.

9 String Quartet in F minor. B.37; 1873; original version unpublished — MS missing, BH (version edited by G. Raphael) 1929; SV,iv,5. N.B. Dvořák rewrote the second movement for violin and piano; Romance in F minor, op. 11.

12 String Quartet in A minor. B.40; 1873; SV 1979; SV,iv,5. Left unfinished, but completed by J. Burghauser.

(12) Andante appassionato, for str. quartet. B.40A (originally part of op. 12.

16 String Quartet in A minor. B.45; 1874; St (parts only) 1875, BB (score) 1894[NB]; SV,iv,6.

77(18) String Quintet in G major (2 vn, va, vc, db). B.49; 1875, revised 1888; S 1888; SV,iv,8.

80(27) String Quartet in E major. B.57; 1876, revised 1888; S 1888; SV,iv,6.

34 String Quartet in D minor. B.75; 1877, revised 1879; Sch 1880; SV,iv,6.

48 Sextet in A major (2 vn, 2 va, 2 vc). B.80; 1878; S 1879; SV,iv,8.

51 String Quartet in E flat major. B.92; 1878–9; S 1879; SV,iv,6.

54/1,4 Two Waltzes (2 vn, va, vc, db ad lib). B.105; 1880; S 1911; SV,iv,6. Transcribed from Waltzes, op. 54, for piano.

— Quartet movement in F major (1st movement of a projected string quartet). B.120; 1881; O 1951; SV,iv,6.

61 String Quartet in C major. B.121; 1881; S 1882; SV,iv,7.

74 Terzetto in C major (2 vn, va). B.148; 1887; S 1887; SV,iv,4.

75a Miniatures (Drobnosti) (2 vn, va). B.149; 1887; HM 1945; SV,iv,4. The original form of the *Romantic Pieces* for violin and piano, op. 75.

— *Cypresses* (2 vn, va, vc). B.152; 1887; HM (nos 1–9 and no. 11, parts, edited J. Suk) 1921, SV (complete) 1957; SV,iv,7. Revisions and transcriptions of nos 6, 3, 2, 8, 12, 7, 9, 14, 4, 16, 17 and 18 of the *Cypresses* song cycle of 1865.

— Gavotte for three violins (unaccompanied). B.164; 1890; JV 1890; SV,iv,4.

96 String Quartet in F major, *The American*. B.179; 1893; S 1894; SV,iv,7.

Op.

97   String Quintet in E flat major, *The American* (2 vn, 2 va, vc).
     B.180; 1893; S 1894; SV,iv,8.

106 String Quartet in G major. B.192, 1895; S 1896; SV,iv,7.

105 String Quartet in A flat major. B.193; 1895; S 1896; SV,iv,7.

                                              B *Pianoforte and Strings*

Op.

—   Sonata in F minor, for cello and piano. B.20; 1870–71; piano part
     destroyed and cello part missing.

(13/1) Piano Trio. B.25; 1871/72?; lost.

(13/2) Piano Trio. B.26; 1871/72?; lost.

5   Piano Quintet in A major. B.28; 1872; SV 1959; SV,iv,11.

—   Sonata in A minor, for violin and piano. B.33; 1873; lost.

21   Piano Trio in B flat major. B.51; 1875; Sch 1880; SV,iv,9.

23   Piano Quartet in D major. B.53; 1875; Sch 1880; SV,iv,10.

26   Piano Trio in G minor. B.56; 1876; BB 1879; SV,iv,9.

47   Bagatelles (Maličkosti), for 2 violins, cello and harmonium. B.79,
     1878; S 1880; SV,iv,10.

57   Sonata in F major, for violin and piano. B.106; 1880; S 1880;
     SV,iv,1.

65   Piano Trio in F minor. B.130; 1883; S 1883; SV,iv,9.

81   Piano Quintet in A major. B.155; 1887; S 1888; SV,iv,11.

87   Piano Quartet in E flat major. B.162; 1889; S 1890; SV,iv,10.

90   *Dumky* Trio, piano trio. B.166; 1890–91; S 1894; SV,iv,9.

100 Sonatina in G major, for violin and piano. B.183; 1893; S 1894;
     SV,iv,1.

                                       C *Works including Wind Instruments*

Op.

—   Clarinet Quintet in B flat minor. B.14; 1865/69?; lost.

—   Octet (Serenade), for 2 violins, viola, double bass, clarinet,
     bassoon, horn and piano. B.36; 1873; lost.

                                          D *Miscellaneous Compositions*

Op.

11   Romance in F minor, violin and piano. B.38; 1873/77?; S (arr.
     J. Zubatý) 1879; SV,iv,1. Transcription of the Andante con moto
     quasi allegretto from the String Quartet in F minor, op. 9 (1873).

Op.
40 Nocturne in B major, violin and piano. B.48; 1875/83?; BB 1883; SV,iv,1. Transcription of the Nocturne for string orchestra (1875).

— Capriccio (Concertstück), for violin and piano (or orchestra); also called 'Rondo, op. 24'. B.81; 1878; BH (arr. G. Raphael 1929; SV,iv,1.

49 Mazurek, for violin and piano. B.89; 1879; S 1879; SV,iv,1.

— Polonaise in A major, for cello and piano. B.94; 1879; UE 1925; SV,iv,3.

15/1 Ballad in D minor, for violin and piano. B.139; 1884; *Magazine of Music* (London) 1884, FAU 1885; SV,iv,1.

75 *Romantic Pieces*, for violin and piano. B.150; 1887; S 1887; SV,iv,1.

— Gavotte for three violins (unaccompanied). B.164; 1890; JV 1890; SV,iv,4.

46/2 *Slavonic Dance* in E minor, for violin and piano. B.170; 1891; unpublished; SV,iv,1. Transcription from op. 46 for piano duet.

94 Rondo in G minor, for cello and piano. B.171; 1891; S.1894; SV,iv,3.

46/8 *Slavonic Dance* in G minor, for cello and piano. B.172; 1891; unpublished; SV,iv,3. Transcription from op. 46 for piano duet.

68/5 *Silent Woods* (*Klid*), for cello and piano. B. 173; 1891; S 1894; SV,iv,3. Transcription from *From the Bohemian Forest* for piano duet (1883–84).

V KEYBOARD WORKS

A *Pianoforte Solo*

Op.
— *Forget-me-not Polka* (*Polka pomněnka*), C major. B.1; 1855/56?; unpublished; SV,vii. Trio by A. Liehmann.

— Polka in E major. B.3; 1860; unpublished; SV,v,1. Dubious?

— Potpourri on the opera *King and Charcoal Burner* (version I of the opera). B.22; 1871/73?; St 1873; SV,vii.

— Potpourri on the opera *King and Charcoal Burner* (version II of the opera). B.43; 1874/75(?); W 1875; SV,vii.

28 Two Minuets. B.58; 1876[?]; St 1879; SV,v,1:
    1 A flat major; 2 F major.

35 Dumka, D minor. B.64; 1876; BB 1879; SV,v,1.

36 Theme and Variations, A flat major. B.65; 1876; BB 1879; SV,v,1.

Op.

41   Scottish Dances, D minor. B. 74; 1877; St 1879; SV,v,1.

42   Furiants. B.85; 1878; BB 1879; SV,v,1:
1 D major; 2 F major.

8   *Silhouettes*. B.98; 1879; H 1880; SV,v,1.
1 Allegro feroce, C sharp minor; 2 Andantino, D flat major;
3 Allegretto, D flat major; 4 Vivace, F sharp minor; 5 Presto, F
sharp minor; 6 Poco sostenuto, B flat major; 7 Allegro, B minor;
8 Allegretto, B minor; 9 Allegro, B major; 10 Allegretto grazioso,
E minor; 11 Allegro moderato, A major; 12 Allegro feroce, C
sharp minor. Early drafts for some of these pieces were made in
c. 1870–2.

54   Waltzes. B.101; 1879–80; S 1880; SV,v,2:
1 A major; 2 A minor; 3 E major; 4 D flat major; 5 G minor,
6 F major; 7 D minor; 8 E flat major.

56   *Eclogues*. B.103; 1880; HM 1921; SV,v,2:
1 Allegro non tanto (quasi polka), F major; 2 Quasi allegretto,
D major; 3 Moderato, G major; 4 Allegretto, E major.

—   Album Leaves (Lístky do památníku). B.109; 1880; 2–4: HM
1921, 1 unpublished; SV,v,2:
1 G major (incomplete); 2 Allegro con moto, F sharp minor;
3 Allegro molto, F major; 4 Allegretto, G major.

52   Piano Pieces. B.110; 1880; 1–4: H 1881, 5: HM 1921, 6 unpublished; SV,v,2:
1 Impromptu, G minor; 2 Intermezzo, E flat major; 3. Gigue, B
flat major; 4 Eclogue, G minor; 5 Allegro molto, G minor;
6 Tempo di marcia, E flat major.

56   Mazurkas. B.111; 1880; BB 1880; SV,v,2:
1 A flat major; 2 C major; 3 B flat major; 4 D minor; 5 F major;
6 B minor;

—   Moderato, A major. B.116; 1881; HM 1921; SV,v,2.

—   'Question' ('Otázka'). B.128a; 1882; unpublished; SV,v,2.

—   Impromptu, D minor. B.129; 1883; *Humoristické listy* (JV) 1883,
S 1916; SV,v,3.

12/1 Dumka. B.136; 1884; FAU 1885; SV,v,3.

12/2 Furiant. B.137; 1884; *Magazine of Music* 1884, FAU 1885; SV,v,3.

—   Humoresque, F sharp major. B.138; FAU 1884; SV,v,3.

—   *Two Little Pearls* (*Dvě perličky*). B.156; 1887; FAU 1888; SV,v,3.
1 In a ring (Do kola); 2 Grandpa dances with Grandma (Dědeček
tančí s babičkou).

Op.

— Album leaf (Lístek do památníku), E flat major. B.158; 1888; unpublished; SV,v,2.

85 *Poetic Tone Pictures (Poetické nálady)*. B.161; 1889; S 1889; SV,v,3:
1 Nocturnal route (Noční cestou); 2 Toying (Žertem); 3 At the Old Castle (Na starém hradě); 4 Spring Song (Jarní); 5 Peasant's Ballad (Selská balada); 6 Reverie (Vzpomínání); 7 Furiant; 8 Goblins' Dance (Rej skřítků); 9 Serenade; 10 Bacchanal (Bakchanale); 11 Tittle-tattle (Na táčkách); 12 By the tumulus (U mohyly); 13 On the Holy Mountain (Na svaté hoře).

— Theme for Variations, D minor. B.303; 1891[?]; FAU 1894; SV,vii.

98 Suite in A major. B.184; 1894; S 1894; SV,v,4.

101 Humoresques. B.187; 1894; S 1894; SV,v,4:
1 Vivace, E flat minor; 2 Poco andante, B major; 3 Poco andante e molto cantabile, A flat major; 4 Poco andante, F major; 5 Vivace A minor; 6 Poco allegretto, B major; 7 Poco lento e grazioso, G flat major; 8 Poco andante, B flat minor.

— Two Piano Pieces. B. 188; 1894; S 1911; SV,v,4:
1 Lullaby (Ukolébavka), G major; 2 Capriccio, G minor.

B *Pianoforte Duets*

Op.

46 *Slavonic Dances*, series I. B.78; 1878; S 1878; SV,v,5.:
1 C major; 2 E minor; 3 A flat major; 4 F major; 5 A major; 6 D major; 7 C minor; 8 G minor.
In the case of nos 3 and 6, the numbering given here corresponds with that of the orchestral version, and not with Simrock's piano duet numbering, where 3 = 6 and 6 = 3.

59 *Legends*. B.117; 1880–1; S 1881; SV,v,6:
1 Allegretto non troppo, quasi andantino, D minor; 2 Molto moderato, G major; 3 Allegro giusto, G minor; 4 Molto maestoso, C major; 5 Allegro giusto, A flat major; 6 Allegro con moto, C sharp minor; 7 Allegretto grazioso, A major; 8 Un poco allegretto, F major; 9 Andante con moto, D major; 10 Andante, B flat minor.

68 *From the Bohemian Forest (Ze Šumavy)*. B. 133; 1883–4: S 1884; SV,v,6.
1 At Spinning Time (Na přástkách); 2 By the Black Lake (U černého jezera); 3 Witches' Sabbath (Noc Filipojakubská);

Op.

4 On the Watch (Na čekání); 5 Silent Woods (Klid); 6 In Stormy Times (Z bouřlivých dob).

72 *Slavonic Dances*, series II. B.145; 1886; S 1886; SV,v,5:

1 (9) B major; 2 (10) E minor; 3 (11) F major; 4 (12) D flat major; 5 (13) B flat minor; 6 (14) B flat major; 7 (15) C major; 8 (16) A flat major.

c Organ

Op.

— Preludes and Fugues. B.302; 1859; Prelude in D ma and Fugue in D ma: SN 1954; SV,vii. Student compositions.

1 Prelude in D major; 2 Prelude in G major; 3 Prelude in A minor; 4 Prelude in B flat major; 5 Prelude in D major on a given theme; Fughetta, D major; Fugue in D major; Fugue in G minor.

VI SONGS AND DUETS

A *Songs with Piano Accompaniment*

Op.

— *Cypresses* (*Cypřiše*), poems by G. Pfleger-Moravský. B.11; 1865; no. 11: *Dvořákova čítanka*, SN 1929, the remainder unpublished unless revised, or arranged for string quartet (see Six Songs, op. 2, Love Songs, op 83, and *Cypresses* for string quartet); SV,vii.

  1 Sing fervent songs at nightfall (Vy vroucí písně spějte)

  2 When thy sweet glances on me fall (V té sladke moci oci tvych)

  3 Death reigns in many a human breast (V tach mnohém srdci mrtvo jest)

  4 Thou only, dear one, but for thee (Ó duše drahá jedinká)

  5 Oh, what a perfect golden dream (Ó byl to krásný zlatý sen)

  6 I know that on my love to thee (Já vím, že sladké naději)

  7 O charming golden rose (Ó zlatá růže, spanilá)

  8 Never will love lead us to that glad goal (Ó, naší lásce nekvete)

  9 I wander oft past yonder house (Kol domu se ted' potácím)

  10 Tormented oft by doubt am I (Mne často týrá pochyba)

  11 Downcast am I, so often with despair (Mé srdce často v bolesti)

  12 Here gaze I at that dear letter (Zde hledím na ten drahý list)

  13 Ev'rything's still in valley and mountain (Na horách tichoa, v údolí ticho)

Op.

14 In deepest forest glade I stand (Zde v lese u potoka)

15 Painful emotions pierce my soul (Mou celou duší zádumně)

16 There stands an ancient rock (Tam stojí stará skála)

17 Nature lies peaceful in slumber and dreaming (Nad krajem vévodí lehký spánek)

18 You are asking why my songs are raging (Ty se ptáš proč moje zpěvy bouří)

— Two Baritone Songs, poems by A. Heyduk. B. 13; 1865; unpublished; SV,vii:

1 If, dear lass (Kdybys, milé děvče); 2 If only there were a song I could sing eternally (A kdybys písní stvořena)

— *Krásnohorská Songs*, poems by E. Krásnohorská. B.23; 1871; nos 1 and 3: Sch 1880 (in 'Vier Lieder', op. 9), complete: SV 1959; SV,vi,1:

1 'The Reason' ('Proto'); 2 'Obstacles' ('Překážky'); 3 'Meditation' ('Přemítání'); 4 'Lime Trees' ('Lípy'); 5 'Remembrance' ('Vzpomínání'). No. 5 is incomplete.

5 'The Orphan' ('Sirotek'), ballad by K. J. Erben. B.24; 1871; FAU 1883; SV,vi,1.

— 'Rosmarine' ('Rozmarýna'), poem by K. J. Erben. B.24a; 1871 [?]; SV 1962; SV, vi,1.

6 *Four Songs on Serbian Folk Poems*, transl. by S. Kapper. B.29; 1872[?]; S 1879; SV,vi,1:

1 'The Maiden and the Grass' ('Panenka a tráva'); 2 'Warning' ('Připamatování'); 3 'Flowery Omens' ('Výklad znamení'); 4 'No Escape' ('Lásce neujdeš').

7 *Songs from the Dvůr Králové Manuscript*. B.30; 1872; No. 3: Dalibor 1873 (No. 10), nos 5, 4, 1, and 3 (revised): S 1879, complete: N 1887 ('Sixteen Songs'): SV,vi,1:

1 'The Cuckoo' ('Zezhulice'); 2 'The Forsaken Maid' ('Opuščená') 3 'The Lark' ('Skřivánek'); 4 'The Rose' ('Róže'); 5 'The Strawberries' ('Jahody').

3;9/ *Evening Songs* (*Večerní písně*), poems by V. Hálek. B.61; 1876;
3:31 Op. 3: H 1881, Op. 9: Sch 1880, Op. 31: FAU 1883, No. 12 unpublished; SV,vi,1.

Op. 3:

1 The stars that twinkle in the sky (Ty hvězdičky tam na nebi)

2 I dreamed last night that you were dead (Mně zdálo se žes umřela)

Op.

> 3 I am that knight of fairytale (Já jsem ten rytíř z pohádky)
>
> 4 When God was in a happy mood (Když bůh byl nejvíc rozkochán)
>
> Op. 9:
>
> 5 The soughing of the trees has ceased (Umlklo stromů šumění)
>
> 6 The spring came flying from afar (Přilítlo jaro z daleka)
>
> Op. 31:
>
> 7 When I was gazing at the skies (Když jsem se díval do nebe)
>
> 8 You little tiny singing birds (Vy malí drobní ptáčkové)
>
> 9 Just like a lime tree I reach out (Jsem jako lípa košatá)
>
> 10 All you with burdens hard to bear (Vy všichni, kdo jste stísněni)
>
> 11 That little bird sings with rapture (Ten ptáček, ten se nazpívá)
>
> Op. —:
>
> 12 Thus as the moon in heaven's dome (Tak jak ten měsíc v nebes báň)

50 *Three Modern Greek Poems* (*Tři novořecké básně*), transl. by V. B. Nebeský. B.84; 1878; Ha 1883; SV,vi,1:

> 1 'Koljas' (Klepht Song); 2 'Nereids' (Ballad); 3 'Parga's Lament' (Heroic Song) ('Žalozpěv Pargy').

55 *Gypsy Melodies* (*Cigánské melodie*), poems by A Heyduk. B.104; 1880, S 1880; SV,vi,1;

> 1 My song of love rings through the dusk (Má píseň zas mi láskou zní)
>
> 2 Hey! Ring out my triangle (Aj! Kterak trojhranec můj přerozkošně zvoní)
>
> 3 All round about the woods are still (A les je tichý kolem kol)
>
> 4 Songs my mother taught me (Když mne stará matka zpívat učívala)
>
> 5 Tune thy strings, O gypsy (Struna naladěna, hochu toč se v kole)
>
> 6 Wide the sleeves and trousers (Široké rukávy, a široké gatě)
>
> 7 Give a hawk a fine cage (or 'Cloudy heights of Tatra') (Dejte klec jestřábu ze zlata ryzého)

2 Six Songs, poems by G. Pfleger-Moravský. Revisions of *Cypresses* (1865), nos 1, 5, 9, 8, 13 and 11. B.123–4; 1881/1882[?]; Nos 1, 2, 6 and 5: St 1882 ('Vier Lieder'), complete: SV 1959; SV,vi,2:

> 1 Sing fervent songs at nightfall (Vy vroucí písně, spějte)
>
> 2 Oh! what a perfect golden dream (Ó byl to krásný zlatý sen)
>
> 3 I wander oft past yonder house (Kol domu se ted' potácím)

Op.

4 Never will love lead us to that glad goal (Ó, naši lásce nekvete)

5 Ev'rything's still in valley and mountain (Na horách ticho, a v uddi ticho)

6 Downcast am I, so often with despair (Mé srdce často v bolesti)

— 'The Wild Duck', folk poem. B.140; 1884; lost.

— Two Songs, on folk poems. B.142; 1885; HM 1921; SV,vi,2. Settings of German translations of Czech verses.

1 Sleep, my baby, sleep (Schlef, mein Kind)

2 When I see you, my sweetheart (Sch ich dich)

73 *In Folk Tone* (*V národním tonu*), folk poems (1, 2 and 4: Slovak; 3: Czech). B.146; 1886; S 1887; SV,vi,2.

1 Good night, my darling (Dobru noc, má milá)

2 When a maiden was a-mowing (Žalo dievča, žalo, trávu)

3 Nothing can change for me (Ach, není tu, co by mě těšilo)

4 I have a faithful mare (Ej, mám já koňa faku)

82 Four Songs, poems by O. Malybrok-Stieler. B.157; 1887–8; S 1889; SV,vi,2. Settings of German text.

1 'Leave me alone' ('Lasst mich allein')

2 'Over her Embroidery' ('Die Stickerin')

3 'Springtime' ('Frühling')

4 'By the Brook' ('Am Bache')

83 *Love Songs* (*Písně milostné*), poems by G. Pfleger-Moravský. Revisions of *Cypresses* (1865), nos 8, 3, 9, 6, 17, 14, 2 and 4. B.160; 1888; S 1889; SV,vi,2:

1 Never will love lead us to that glad goal (Ó, naší lásce nekvete)

2 Death reigns in many a human breast (V tak mnohém srdci mrtvo jest)

3 I wander oft past yonder house (Kol domu se ted' potácím)

4 I know that on my love to thee (Já vím, že v sladké naději)

5 Nature lies peaceful in slumber and dreaming (Nad krajem vévodí lehký spánek)

6 In deepest forest glade I stand (Zde v lese u potoka)

7 When thy sweet glances on me fall (V té sladké moci očí tvých)

8 Thou only dear one, but for thee (Ó duše drahá, jedinká)

Nos 1 and 3 are new versions of nos 4 and 3 of the Six Songs of 1881/82.

99 *Biblical Songs* (*Biblické písně*), text from the Bible of Kralice, Book of Psalms. B.185; 1894; S 1895; SV,vi,2:

Op.

1 Clouds and darkness are round about him (Oblak a mrákota jest vůkol Něho). Ps.97, 2–6.

2 Thou art my hiding place and my shield (Skrýše má a paveza má Ty jsi). Ps. 119, 114–115, 117, 120.

3 Give ear to my prayer, O God (Slyš, o Bože, slyš modlitba mou). Ps.55, 1–2, 4–8.

4 The Lord is my shepherd (Hospodin jest můj pastýř). Ps.23, 1–4.

5 I will sing a new song unto thee, O God (Bože! Bože! Píseň novou). Ps.144, 9; Ps.145, 2–3, 5–6.

6 Hear my cry, O God (Slyš, o Bože, volání mé). Ps.61, 1, 3–4; Ps.63, 1, 4.

7 By the rivers of Babylon (Při řekách Babylonských). Ps.137, 1–5.

8 Turn Thou unto me, and have mercy upon me (Popatříž na mne a smiluj se nade mnou). Ps.25, 16–18, 20.

9 I will lift up mine eyes unto the mountains (Pozdvihuji očí svých k horám). Ps.121, 1–4.

10 O sing unto the Lord a new song (Zpívejte Hospodinu píseň novou). Ps.98, 1, 4, 7–8; Ps.96, 12.

— 'Lullaby' ('Ukolébavka'), poem by F. L. Jelínek. B.194; 1895; *Květy mládeže*, ii, 1896 (no. 9); SV,vi,4.

— Song from *The Smith of Lešetín*, poem by Svatopluk Čech. B.204; 1901; S 1911; SV,vi,2.

B *Vocal Duets with Piano Accompaniment*

Op.

20 *Moravian Duets* (*Moravské dvojzpěvy*), for soprano (contralto) and tenor, Moravian folk poems. B.50; 1875; S.1879; SV,vi,3:
1 'Destined' ('Proměny'); 2 'The Parting' ('Rozloučení'); 3 The Silken Band' (Chudoba'); 4 'The Last Wish' (Vuře šuhaj, vuře...).

32 *Moravian Duets*, for soprano and contralto, Moravian folk poems. B.60 and 62; 1876; nos 1–5: St 1876 (as Op. 29), nos 6–13: St1 876 (Op. 32), 'The Soldier's Farewell': *Hudební revue*, November 1913, complete: SV 1955; SV,vi,3:
1 'From thee now I must go' (A já ti uplynu)
2 'Fly, sweet songster' (Velet', vtáčku)
3 'The Slighted Heart' (Dyby byla kosa nabróšená)
4 'Parting without sorrow' (V dobrým sme se sešli)
5 'The Pledge of Love' (Slavíkovský polečko malý)
6 'Forsaken' ('Holub na javoře')

Op.

   7 'Sad of Heart' ('Voda a pláč')
   8 'The Modest Maid' ('Skromná')
   9 'The Ring' ('Prsten')
 10 'Omens' ('Zelenaj se, zelenaj')
 11 'The Maid imprisoned' ('Zajatá')
 12 'Comfort' ('Neveta')
 13 'The Wild Rose' ('Šípek')
 — 'The Soldier's Farewell' ('Život vojenský').

38 *Moravian Duets*, for soprano and contralto, Moravian folk poems. B.69; 1877; S 1879; SV,vi,3.
   1 'Hoping in Vain' ('Možnost'); 2 'Greeting from Afar' ('Jablko'); 3 'The Crown' ('Věneček'); 4 'Sorrow' ('Hoře').

— 'There on our roof' (Na tej našej střeše), for soprano and contralto, Moravian folk poem. B.118; 1881; St 1882 (in the Umělecká beseda album commemorating the wedding of crown prince Rudolf and archduchess Stefanie); SV,vi,3.

c *Songs and Duets with Organ Accompaniment*

Op.

19B *Ave Maria*, for contralto (or baritone). B.68; 1877; St 1883; SV,vi,1.

— *Hymnus ad laudes in festo Sanctae Trinitatis*, for voice and organ. B.82; 1878; *Cyrill* 1911 (revd. J. Suk); SV,vi,1.

19B *Ave Maris Stella*, for voice and organ. B.95; 1879; St 1883; SV,vi,1.

19A *O sanctissima dulcis Virgo Maria*, duet for contralto and baritone. B.95a; 1879; St 1883; SV,vi,3.

19A *O sanctissima dulcis Virgo Maria*, duet for soprano and contralto. B.163a; 1890; unpublished.

d *Songs with Orchestral Accompaniment*

Op.

(50) *Three Modern Greek Poems* (see section A above). B.84a; 1878; missing, except for oboe part.

   3 *Evening Songs*, nos 2 and 3 (see section A above). B.128; 1882; unpublished; SV,ii,5.

 99 *Biblical Songs*, nos 1–5 (see section A above). B.189; 1895; transposed for high voice by V. Zemánek: S 1929, original version: SV 1960; SV,ii,6.

Op.

Nos 6–10, orchestrated by Zęmánek, were also published by Simrock in 1929.

E *Unaccompanied Duet*

Op.

— Child's Song (Dětská píseň), for two voices, poem by Š. Bačkora. B.113; 1880; *Hudební výchova*, iv 1956; SV,vi,3.
I cannot give Thee anything (Nemohu nic dáti vázaného Tobě).

VII MINOR CHORAL COMPOSITIONS
A *Female Voices*

Op.

32 *Moravian Duets* (*Moravský dvojzpěvy*), Moravian folk poems, four-part unaccompanied. B.107; 1880; unpublished; SV,vi,4.
1 'Forsaken' ('Holub na javoře'); 2 'Omens' (Zelenaj se, zelenaj); 3 'The Wild Rose' ('Šípek'); 4 'Fly, sweet songster' (Velet', vtáčku); 5 'The Slighted Heart' (Dyby byla kosa nabróšená).
Rearranged from nos 6, 10, 13, 2 and 3 of the duets op. 32 of 1876.

B *Male Voices*

Op.

— Choral Songs for Male Voices, nos 1 and 2: Moravian folk poems, no. 3: poem by A. Heyduk, four-part unaccompanied. B.66; 1877; HM 1921; SV,vi,4:
1 'The Ferryman' ('Převozníček'); 2 'The Beloved as Poisoner' ('Milenka travička'); 3 'The Fiddler' ('Já jsem huslař přeubohý').

41 *Bouquet of Czech Folk-Songs* (*Kytice z českych národních písní*), Czech and Moravian folk poems, four-part unaccompanied. B.72; 1877; nos 1–3: HM 1921, no. 4: privately issued, n.d; SV,vi,4.
1 'The Betrayed Shepherd' ('Zavedený ovčák'); 2 'The Sweetheart's resolve' ('Umysl milenčin'); 3 'The Guelder Rose' ('Kalina'); 4 'The Czech Diogenes' ('Český Diogenes').

— *The Song of a Czech* (*Píseň čecha*), poem by G. J. Vacek-Kamenický, four-part unaccompanied, unfinished. B.73; 1877[?]; HM 1921; SV,vi,4.

43 *From a Bouquet of Slavonic Folk-Songs* (*Z kytice národních písní slovanských*), nos 1 and 3: Slovak folk poems, no. 2: Moravian folk poem, four-part with piano accompaniment. B.76; 1887–78; unpublished in original form; version with accompaniment arranged for piano duet by J. Zubatý: K 1898; SV,vi,4.

Op.

1 'Sorrow' ('Žal');

2 'Miraculous Water' ('Divná voda');

3 'The Girl in the Woods' ('Děvče v háji').

27 Five partsongs for Male Voices (Pět sborů pro mužské hlasy), Lithuanian folk poems, translated by F. L. Čelakovský, four-part unaccompanied. B.87; 1878; FAU 1890, English edition: J.W. Chester 1923; SV,vi,4.

1 'Village Gossip' ('Pomluva'); 2 'Dwellers by the Sea' ('Pomořané'); 3 'Promise of Love' ('Přípověd' lásky'); 4 'The Lost Lamb' ('Ztracená ovečka'); 5 'The Sparrow's Party' ('Hostina').

c *Mixed Voices*

Op.

29 Four Partsongs for Mixed Choir (Čtyři sbory pro smíšené hlasy), nos 1 and 2: poems by A. Heyduk, nos 3 and 4: Moravian folk poems, four-part unaccompanied. B.59; 1876; St 1879; SV,vi,4.

1 'Evening's Blessings' ('Místo klekání'); 2 'Lullaby' ('Ukolébavka'); 3 'I don't say it' ('Nepovím'); 4 'The Forsaken One' ('Opuštěný').

63 *In Nature's Realm* (*V přírodě*), poems by V Hálek, four- to six-part unaccompanied. B.126; 1882; Cr 1882; SV,vi,6.

1 Music descended to my soul (Napadly písně v duši mou);

2 Bells ring at dusk (Večerní les rozvázal zvonky);

3 The rye field (Žitné pole);

4 The silver birch (Vyběhla bříza běličká);

5 With dance and song (Dnes do skoku a do písničky!).

28 *Hymn of the Czech Peasants* (*Hymna českého rolnictva*), poem by K. Pippich, four- to five-part with orchestral accompaniment. B.143; 1885; SV 1972, version with piano duet accompaniment by J. Zubatý: FAU 1885; SV,ii,5.

VIII ARRANGEMENTS

Two Irish Songs (Dvě irské písně), translation of no. 1 and verses of no. 2 may be by J. Srb-Debrnov, four-part male voice choir unaccompanied. B.601; 1878; unpublished; SV,vii.

1 Oh my Connor his cheeks are like the rose ('Dear Connor') (Můj Konnor má tváře jak červená růže)

Op.

2 Ho! adorn yourself with flowers (Nuž, zdobte se kvítím at' zaplane zář).

No. 2 derives from the folk-song 'Contented am I' ('Noch bonin shin doe'), which, after being given a new text in the mid 18th century, was known as 'The Battle Eve of the Brigade'.[1]

Hungarian Dances, nos 17–21, by Brahms, orchestrated by Dvořák. B.602; 1880; S 1881; SV,vii.

Russian Songs (*Ruské písně*), vocal duets with piano accompaniment, arrangements of folk-songs from M. Bernard's *Pyesni ruskogo naroda*. B.603; 1883[?]; O 1951; SV,vii.

1 Povylétla holubice pode strání (Vïletala golubina)
2 Čím jsem já tě rozhněvala (Chem tebya ya ogorchila?)
3 Mladá, pěkná krasavice (Belolitsa, kruglolitsa)
4 Cožpak, můj holoubku (Akh, chto zh tï golubchik)
5 Zkvétal, zkvétal v máji květ (Tsveli, tsveli tsvetiki)
6 Jako mhou se tmí (Akh, kak pal tuman)
7 Ach, vy říčky šumivé (Akh, rechenki, rechenki)
8 Mladice ty krásná (Molodka, molodaya)
9 Po matušce, mocné Volze (Vniz po matushke po Volge)
10 Na políčku bříza tam stála (Vo pole beryoza stoyala)
11 Vyjdu já si podle říčky (Vïydu ya na rechenku)
12 Na tom našem náměstí (Kak u nas na ulitse)
13 Já si zasil bez orání (Ya noseyal konopelku)
14 Oj, ty luční kačko malá (Akh, utushka lygovaya)
15 V poli zrají višně (Gey, u poli vishnya)
16 Oj, ktáče havran černý (Oy, kryache chernenkiy voron)

'Ah, that love . . .' ('Ha, ta láska'), song by Josef Lev, orchestrated by Dvořák. B.604; 1880/1884[?]; unpublished; SV,vii.

Old Folks at Home, by Stephen Foster, arranged for soprano and bass soli, chorus and orchestra by Dvořák. B.605; 1893/1894[?]; unpublished; SV,vii.

Vysoká Polka, anon, arranged for piano by Dvořák. B.606; 1902; unpublished; SV,vii.

---

1 Further information on these two songs will be found in my *Antonín Dvořák: Musician and Craftsman* (1966), p. 318.

Bibliography

I BOOKS

Aborn, M. R. *The Influence on American Musical Culture of Dvořák's Sojourn in America* (Ann Arbor 1966) University Microfilms Inc. (65–10, 798)

Altmann, W. 'Antonín Dvořák im Verkehr mit Fritz Simrock', *N. Simrock Jahrbuch*, ii (Berlin 1929), 84–151. Rev. edn. of article in *Die Musik*, xl (1910–11)

Bartoš, J. *Antonín Dvořák* (Prague 1913)

Belza, I. *Antonin Dvorzhak* (Moscow 1949) Transl: Bulgarian (Sofia 1955), Rumanian (Bucharest 1956)

Berkovec, J. *Antonín Dvořák* (Prague 1969)

Boese, H. Zwei Urmusikanten: Smetana—Dvořák (Vienna 1955)

Bráfová, L. *Rieger, Smetana, Dvořák* (Prague 1913)

Burghauser, J. *Orchestrace Dvořákových Slovanských tanců* (The orchestration of D's Slavonic Dances) (Prague 1959)

——. *Antonín Dvořák Thematic Catalogue, Bibliography, Survey of Life and Work*, in Czech, German and English (Prague 1960)

——. Critical editions of librettos of *Král a uhlíř* (Prague 1956) and *Dimitrij* (Prague 1963)

——. *Antonín Dvořák* (Prague 1966); German and English translations (1967)

—— (ed). Facsimile of Symphony in E minor 'From the New World', with commentary (Prague 1966)

Clapham, J. *Antonín Dvořák :Musician and Craftsman* (London 1966)

Fischl, V. (ed). *Antonín Dvořák: his Achievement* (London 1943)

Fric, O. *Antonín Dvořák a Kroměříž* (Kroměříž 1946). Includes letters

Ginsburg, L. (ed). *Antonin Dvorzhak: sbornik statyei* (Moscow 1967)

Hadow, W. H. 'Antonín Dvořák', *Studies in Modern Music*, 2nd Series (London 1895), 171–225

Harrison, J. 'Antonín Dvořák (1841–1904)', *The Symphony*, i (ed. R. Simpson) (Harmondsworth 1966), 354–378

Herzog, E. *Antonín Dvořák v obrazech* (A.D. in Pictures) (Prague 1966)

Hetschko, A. *Antonín Dvořák* (Leipzig 1965)

Hoffmeister, K. *Antonín Dvořák* (Prague 1924); English translation (London 1928)

Honolka, K. *Antonín Dvořák in Selbstzeugnissen und Bilddokumenten* (Reinbek 1974)

Hořejš, A. *Antonín Dvořák: the Composer's Life and Work in Pictures*, with simultaneous editions in German, French, Hungarian and Polish (Prague 1955)

Karel, R. 'Jak jsem se učil na konservatoři' (How I was taught at the Conservatory), *Sborník na pamět 125. let Konservatoře hudby v Praze* (Prague 1936), 312–316

Kull, H. *Dvořáks Kammermusik* (Bern 1948)

Květ, J. M. *Mládí Antonína Dvořáka* (The Youth of A.D.) (Prague 1943)

Layton, R. *Dvořák Symphonies and Concertos* (London 1978)

Leitner, K. *Antonín Dvořák jak učil* (How Dvořák taught) (New York 1943)

Newmarch, R. *The Music of Czechoslovakia* (London 1942), esp. pp. 125–175

Robertson, A. *Dvořák* (London 1945; revd. edn. 1964); German translation (Zurich 1947)

Sakka, K. *Dvořák* (Tokyo 1963)

Sirp, H. *Anton Dvořák* (Potsdam 1939)

Smetana, R. *Antonín Dvořák. O místo a význam skladatelského díla v českém hudebním vývoji* (A.D.: The place and meaning of D's compositions in the development of Czech music) (Prague 1956)

Šourek, O. *Dvořák's Werke: ein vollständiges Verzeichnis* (Berlin 1917)

——. *Zivot a dílo Antonína Dvořáka* (The Life and Work of A.D.), i–iv (Prague 1916–1933; 3rd revd. edn: i 1955, ii 1956; 2nd revd, edn: 1957, iv 1958)

——. *Antonín Dvořák* (Prague 1929; 4th edn. 1947). English translation: *Antonín Dvořák: his Life and Work* (Prague 1952) German translation (1953), and translations into several other languages

——. *Dvořákovy symfonie* (Prague 1922), 3rd edn. (1948)

—— *Dvořákovy skladby orchestralní*, i–ii (Prague 1944–46). Abridged translations of these items together: *Antonín Dvořák Werkanalysen I, Orchesterwerke* (Prague 1954); *The Orchestral Works of Antonín Dvořák* (Prague 1956)

——. *Dvořákovy skladby komorní* (Prague 1943; 2nd edn. 1949). Abridged translations: *Antonín Dvořák Werkanalysen II. Kammermusik* (Prague 1954); *The Chamber Music of Antonín Dvořák* (Prague 1956)

——. *Dvořák ve vzpomínkách a dopisech* (Prague 1938); 9th edn. 1951);

Translations: *Dvořák: Letters and Reminiscences* (Prague 1954); German translation (1955); Russian translation (Moscow 1964)

——. *Antonín Dvořák přátelům doma* (A.D. to his friends at home) (Prague 1941). 395 letters

——. *Antonín Dvořák a Hans Richter* (Prague 1942). Letters and commentary

Šourek, O. and Stefan, P. *Dvořák: Leben und Werk* (Vienna 1935). English translation published as: Stefan, P. *Anton Dvořák* (New York 1941)

Špelda, A. *Dr Antonín Dvořák a Plzeň* (Pilsen 1941). Includes letters and programmes

Sychra, A. *Estetika Dvořákovy symfonické tvorby* (The aesthetics of D's symphonic work) (Prague 1959). Translation: *Antonín Dvořák: zur Ästhetik seines sinfonischen Schaffens* (Leipzig 1973)

Tomek, F. *Dr Ant. Dvořák a olomoucký 'Žerotín'* (A.D. and the Olomouc choral society) (Olomouc 1929)

Tovey, D. F. *Essays in Musical Analysis*, ii (Symphonies 6, 7, 5 and 9, Symphonic Variations, Scherzo capriccioso), 89–110, 139–142, 147–151; iii (Cello Concerto), 148–152; iv (1st and 3rd Slavonic Rhapsodies) 137–139)

Yegorova, V. *Simfonii Dvorzhaka* (D's Symphonies) (Moscow 1979)

Zubatý, J. *Ant. Dvořák: ein biographische Skizze* (Leipzig 1886)

Antonín Dvořák sborník statí o jeho díle a životě (Umělecká beseda memorial volume of articles on D's life and work) (Prague 1912). Includes B. Kalenský: 'Antonín Dvořák, jeho mládí, příhody a vývoj k usamostatnění' (A.D., his youth, events and development to independence) 3–112, and studies of the music by Krejčí, Chvála, Knittl, Boleška, Hoffmeister, Hostinský, Stecker, Borecký, Vendler and Zamrzla

II PERIODICALS

Abraham, G. 'Verbal Inspiration in Dvořák's Instrumental Music', *Studia Musicologica Academiae Scientiarum Hungaricae*, ii (Budapest 1969), 27–34

Bennett, J. 'The Music of Anton Dvořák', *Musical Times*, xxii (1881), 165–169, 236–239

——. 'Anton Dvořák', *Musical Times*, xxv (1884), 189–192

Beveridge, D. 'Sophisticated Primitivism: the Significance of Pentatonicism in Dvořák's American Quartet', *Current Musicology*, no. 24 (1977), 25–36

Clapham, J. 'Dvořák's First Cello Concerto'. *Music & Letters*, xxxvii (1956), 350–355

——. 'Dvořák and the Philharmonic Society', *Music & Letters*, xxxix (1958), 123–134

——. 'The Evolution of Dvořák's Symphony "From the New World"', *Musical Quarterly*, xliv (1958), 167–183

——. 'The Operas of Antonín Dvořák', *Proceedings of the Royal Musical Association*, lxxxiv (1958), 55–69

——. 'Dvořák at Cambridge', *Monthly Musical Record*, lxxxix (1959), 135–142

——. 'Blick in die Werkstatt eines Komponisten: die beiden Fassungen von Dvořák's Klaviertrio f-moll', *Musica*, xiii (1959), 629–634

——. 'Dvořák's Symphony in D minor—the Creative Process', *Music & Letters*, xlii (1961), 103–116

——. 'The National Origins of Dvořák's Art', *Proceedings of the Royal Musical Association*, lxxxix (1963), 75–88

——. 'Dvořák's Visit to Russia', *Musical Quarterly*, li (1965), 493–506

——. 'Dvořák and the American Indian', *Musical Times*, cvii (1966), 863–867

——. 'Dvořák's Musical Directorship in New York', *Music & Letters*, xlviii (1967), 40–51

——. 'Dvořák's Relations with Brahms and Hanslick', *Musical Quarterly*, lvii (1971), 241–254; Czech translation, with letters in the original German text: *Hudební věda*, x (1973), 213–224

——. Dvořák's Unknown Letters on his Symphonic Poems', *Music & Letters*, lvi (1975), 277–287; German translation, with letters in the original German text: *Osterreichische Musikzeitschrift*, xxxi (1976), 645–658

——. 'Dvořák's Aufstieg zum Komponisten'. *Musikforschung*, xxx (1977), 47–55

——. 'Dvořák's Musical Directorship in New York: a postscript', *Music & Letters*, lix (1978), 19–27

——. 'Indian Influence in Dvořák's American Chamber Music', *Colloquium Musica Cameralis Brno 1971* (Brno 1977), 147–156, 525

——. 'Dvořák's First Contacts with England', *Musical Times*, cxix (1978), 758–761

——. 'Dvořák's Cello Concerto in B minor: a Masterpiece in the Making', *Music Review*, xl/3 (1979)

Colles, H. C. 'Antonín Dvořák. 1 Opera at Home; 2 Song and Symphony in England; 3 In the New World', *Musical Times*, lxxxii (1941), 130–133, 173–176, 209–211

Downes, O. 'A Dvořák Reminiscence: Man and Musician recalled in Memories of American Pupil', *New York Times*, 12 August 1934

Dvořák, A. 'Franz Schubert', in collab. with H. T. Finck, *Century Illustrated Monthly Magazine*, xlviii (New York 1894), 341–346. Reprinted in Clapham, J. *Antonín Dvořák: Musician and Craftsman*

——. 'Music in America', in collab. with E. Emerson, *Harper's New Monthly Magazine*, xc (New York 1895), 428–434. Abridged reprint in Morgenstern: *Composers on Music* (New York 1956)

Ehlert, L. 'Anton Dvořák', *Westermanns Illustrierte Deutsche Monatshefte*, xlviii (Brunswick 1880), 232–238

Evans, R. 'Dvořák at Spillville', *The Palimpsest*, xi (Iowa City 1930), 113–118

Hopkins, H. P. 'Student Days with Dvořák', *The Etude*, xxx (Philadelphia 1912), 327–328

——. 'How Dvořák Taught Composition', *The Etude*, xlix (Philadelphia 1931), 97–98

Janáček, L. 'České proudy hudební' (Czech musical currents), *Hlídka*, ii (xiv) (Brno 1897), 285–292, 454–459, 594–600, and *Hlídka*, iii (xv) (1898) 227–282. On Dvořák's symphonic poems

Jarka, V. H. 'Příspěvek k vídeňské korespondenci Antonína Dvořáka' (A contribution to D's Viennese correspondence), *Hudební revue*, vii (1914), 376–392. Correspondence with Mandyczewski

Kinscella, H. G. 'Dvořák and Spillville forty years after', *Musical America*, liii (25 May 1933), 4, 49. Reprinted in *Music on the Air* (New York 1934), 199–206

Krehbiel, H. E. 'Antonín Dvořák', *Century Illustrated Monthly Magazine*, xliv (New York 1892), 657–660

——. 1 'Dr Dvořák's American Symphony' (Symphony in E minor 'From the New World'); 2 'Dvořák's American Compositions in Boston' (String Quartet in F major); 3 'Dvořák's American Compositions' (String Quintet in E flat major), *New-York Daily Tribune* (15 Dec 1893, 1 Jan 1894, 7 Jan 1894). Musical examples

——. 'Antonín Dvořák', *The Looker-On*, iii (New York 1896), 261–271

Kuna, M. 'Antonín Dvořák a Rusko' (A.D. and Russia), *Hudební rozhledy*, xxx (1977), 386–392

——. and Pospíšil, M. 'Dvořák's "Dimitrij"', *Musical Times*, cxx (1979), 23–25

Michl, J. 'První přednáška u Antonína Dvořáka' (The first class with A.D.), *Hudební revue*, iv (1911), 461–465

——. 'Z Dvořákovy školy' (From D's school'), *Hudební revue*, iv (1911), 490–493

——. 'Rok u Dvořáka' (A year with Dvořák), *Hudební revue*, vi (1913), 169–180

——. 'Z Dvořákova vyprávění' (From what D related), *Hudební revue*, vii (1914), 400–404, 440–446

——. 'Vzpomínky na Antonína Dvořáka' (Recollections of A.D.), *Hudební revue*, x (1917), 293–302

Newmarch, R. 'The Letters of Dvořák to Hans Richter', *Musical Times*, lxxiii (1932), 605–609, 698–701, 795–797

'Pry, Paul', 'Enthusiasts Interviewed. "Pann" Antonín Dvořák', *Sunday Times* (10 May 1885)

Pellegrini, A. 'Zum 10. Todestag von A. Dvořák', *Neue Musikzeitung*, xxxv (Stuttgart 1914), 45ff

——. 'Persönliche Erinnerungen an Unterrichtsstunden bei Dvořák', *Prager Presse* (Prague 1 May 1929)

Sawyer, F. J. 'The tendencies of modern harmony as exemplified in the music of Dvořák and Grieg', *Proceedings of the [Royal] Musical Association*, xxii (1896), 53–88

Shelley, H. R. 'Dvořák as I knew him'. *The Etude*, xxxi (Philadelphia 1913), 541–542

——. 'Personal Recollections of a Great Master. Dvořák as I knew him', *The Etude*, xxxvii (Philadelphia 1919), 694

Šourek, O. 'Neznámé dopisy Dvořákovy', *Národní divadlo moravsko-slezské* (Moravská Ostrava 5 Apr 1940), 7–12. Letters from Margulies

——. 'Z neznámých dopisů Antonína Dvořáka nakladateli Simrockovi' (From the unknown letters of A.D. to the publisher Simrock), *Smetana*, xxxvii (Prague 1944), 119–123, 131–135

Stefan, P. 'Why Dvořák would not return to America', *Musical America*, lviii (New York 25 Feb 1938), 34. Lacks five of the Margulies letters included in Šourek's 1940 article listed above

Suk, J. 'Aus meiner Jugend. Wiener Brahms-Erinnerungen', *Der Merker*, ii (Vienna 1910). Czech translation: 'Několik vzpomínek', *Národní a Stavovské divadlo*, vi (Prague 3 June 1929); reprinted: *Národní divadlo*, xviii no. 13 (Prague 1941)

Taylor, S. 'Dvořák', *Cambridge Review*, xii (11 June 1891)

Thurber, J. M. 'Personal Recollections of a great Master. Dvořák as I knew him', *The Etude*. xxxvii (Philadelphia 1919), 693–694

Vojačková-Wetche, L. 'Anton Dvořák in the Class Room', *The Etude*, xxxvii (Philadelphia 1919), 135–136

'From Butcher to Baton', *Pall Mall Gazette* (13 Oct 1886). Interview with Dvořák

General Index

Index of Compositions